Books and Travel

MIX
Paper from
responsible sources
FSC
www.fsc.org   **FSC® C014540**

TOURISM AND CULTURAL CHANGE

Series Editors: Professor Mike Robinson, *Institute of Archaeology and Antiquity, University of Birmingham, UK* and Dr Alison Phipps, *University of Glasgow, Scotland, UK*

Understanding tourism's relationships with culture(s) and vice versa, is of ever-increasing significance in a globalising world. This series will critically examine the dynamic inter-relationships between tourism and culture(s). Theoretical explorations, research-informed analyses, and detailed historical reviews from a variety of disciplinary perspectives are invited to consider such relationships.

Full details of all the books in this series and of all our other publications can be found on http://www.channelviewpublications.com, or by writing to Channel View Publications, St Nicholas House, 31–34 High Street, Bristol, BS1 2AW, UK.

Books and Travel

Inspiration, Quests and Transformation

Jennifer Laing and Warwick Frost

CHANNEL VIEW PUBLICATIONS
Bristol • Buffalo • Toronto

Library of Congress Cataloging in Publication Data
Laing, Jennifer.
Books and Travel: Inspiration, Quests and Transformation/Jennifer Laing and Warwick Frost.
Tourism and Cultural Change: 31
Includes bibliographical references and index.
1. Travel in literature. 2. Tourism—Research. I. Frost, Warwick. II. Title.
PN56.T7L35 2012
809'.9332–dc23 2012022005

British Library Cataloguing in Publication Data
A catalogue entry for this book is available from the British Library.

ISBN-13: 978-1-84541-348-4 (hbk)
ISBN-13: 978-1-84541-347-7 (pbk)

Channel View Publications
UK: St Nicholas House, 31–34 High Street, Bristol, BS1 2AW, UK.
USA: UTP, 2250 Military Road, Tonawanda, NY 14150, USA.
Canada: UTP, 5201 Dufferin Street, North York, Ontario M3H 5T8, Canada.

The policy of Multilingual Matters/Channel View Publications is to use papers that are natural, renewable and recyclable products, made from wood grown in sustainable forests. In the manufacturing process of our books, and to further support our policy, preference is given to printers that have FSC and PEFC Chain of Custody certification. The FSC and/or PEFC logos will appear on those books where full certification has been granted to the printer concerned.

Typeset by Techset Composition Ltd., Salisbury, UK.
Printed and bound in Great Britain by Short Run Press Ltd.

Contents

1 Introduction: Extraordinary Journeys

'The world is a book, and those who do not travel read only a page'
St Augustine

The world is a book, and a book opens the way to a whole world. St Augustine, born in 4th century Roman Africa, was a teacher in Carthage, Rome and Milan, until his conversion to Christianity in his early thirties. He was an inveterate reader as well as experienced traveller throughout the ancient Roman world, and wrote several texts, including his *Confessions*. Augustine's metaphor works two ways. Not travelling and staying in one place is like trying to understand a book by reading only one page. While the world might be understood metaphorically as a book, conversely books can both inspire travelling and dreams about travel.

Readers may seek places and adventures specifically featured in a story, or destinations connected with an author. Such literary tourism has been the subject of much analysis, including its roots in the 19th century (Watson, 2009), tourists' motivations for visiting literary-related sites (Herbert, 2001; Smith, 2003), and the role of authenticity and social and cultural meanings attached to their experiences (Fawcett & Cormack, 2001; Squire, 1994). Various tourist attractions have been developed to meet the needs of this segment, such as writer's birthplaces and homes, theme parks based on literary themes and places associated with books or authors (Robinson & Andersen, 2002). Though an important influence, this is only one way in which books influence tourists.

Writers and philosophers have long recognised the appeal of armchair travel and dreaming about destinations (Dann, 2002; de Botton, 2002; Taylor, 1994). We acknowledge this body of work, but go further, by arguing that most travellers are *culturally acclimatised* to aspects of travel, before they even set foot outside their front door, through what they have read. The shaping of our ideas about travel through books might be subtle, but it can have deep and nuanced effects on the traveller. We might understand, to some degree, how we are supposed to behave when we travel and what the ingredients of a future travel experience might be. We may learn about the hardships and the 'hellish' side of travel, as well as experiencing the sublime, and observe that travel can change us, not necessarily in the ways we might foresee or desire. Reading books may transmit a form of cultural heritage. This might help us to anticipate contact with *the other* and the nuances of culture and tradition we might encounter through a journey, as well understanding our own culture more deeply. The tourist experience may seem more real to us because it is framed by what we have read. We might also be disappointed in experiences that do not resemble those we have read about. Thus books might predispose us towards a particular view of authenticity, which could be connected to the tangible and some form of objective reality, or alternatively a more existential form concerned with the authentic self (Wang, 2000).

Our research supports that of sociologist John Urry on the way the tourist gaze is constructed. Urry (2002: 3) observes that the tourist chooses places 'because there is anticipation, especially through day-dreaming and fantasy, of intense pleasures, either on a different scale or involving different senses from those customarily encountered'. This gaze can be 'constructed and sustained' through various mechanisms, including film, television and magazines, but also literature. These act as signs in constructing the tourist gaze (Urry, 2002), and thus might help to construct *ideas about travel* and frame the travel experience. We also acknowledge Reijnders' work on the influence of the media on 'places of the imagination'; locations or landscapes, which are the focal point or a 'symbolic anchor for the collective imagination of a society' (Reijnders, 2011: 8). He discusses the influence of texts such as *Dracula* and the Inspector Morse and Wallander crime fiction series on the way place is constructed by visitors, rather than in relation to the process or phenomenon of travel itself.

It has been argued that there is a reciprocal and symbiotic relationship between culture and tourism, with tourism 'an expression and experience of culture', which may also assist in 'generating nuanced forms of culture as well as new cultural forms' (Robinson & Smith, 2006: 1). Through considering how books as a cultural phenomenon affect our conceptualisation of travel, our research illustrates the interplay between these two concepts, as well as the continuing power of the printed word over other forms of media in shaping and framing the way in which we perceive the world.

Extraordinary Journeys

Books often make a promise to the reader that, if they travel, they too will have adventures and explore the world. Many fictional works and travel stories focus on journeys. These may inspire their readers to travel and seek out transformative experiences. In addition to their role in prompting visits to specific places, we need to examine and understand the ways in which books transport a reader to a world of their imagination and influence the general desires to travel and explore.

This process starts young. Many children's books have common themes of escape through travel. Children in routine and dull existences are transformed through their journeys. *Harry Potter and the Philosopher's Stone, Peter Pan* and *The Lion, the Witch and the Wardrobe* are all examples of books where children escape the everyday by travelling to magical worlds. As we get older, we turn to a wider range of genres that may inspire travel. Adventure, historical romances, science fiction and fantasy all commonly feature journeys and quests that transform the lives of the key characters.

These transformations are not just confined to fictional books. Real-life adventurers recount their treks to the North Pole, camel journeys across the Outback, romances in Tuscany and marriages to tribal leaders. These books can take a reader out of themselves and shape and frame their dreams of travel. We reflect in this book on the growing popularity and inspiration afforded by travel books, written by, about and for travellers. In some cases, the line between fact and fiction is blurred, which may perpetuate or add to a fantasy and contribute to our perceptions and attitudes about travel and our image of a destination.

This book complements other studies on the links between film and music and travel behaviour. However, our argument is that, while these areas overlap, books, by their very immersive nature, work differently to other media, in encouraging ideas of escape, quests, exploration and personal transformation. In reading books, we use our imagination to visualise the action, characters and setting. The imagined experience is different from reader to reader. Often a private and solitary activity, the reader is deeply absorbed, even 'lost', in the story. Specific genres or a series of books written by one author encourage the reader's engagement and immersion. This may have a deeper impact on the reader than a cinematic or televised treatment of the narrative. In this era of computer games, social media and 'connectivity', books still retain a powerful role in many people's lives, and the growth of book clubs, level of sales of new and back titles and popular interest in authors and literary events around the world are testaments to this. The launch of each new *Harry Potter* book became increasingly frenetic and attracted saturation coverage across the globe. Media convergence also means that there is an increasingly blurred boundary between new and old forms of media (Jenkins, 2001; Månsson, 2011; Månsson, forthcoming), providing new audiences for electronic versions of books through technology, such as e-readers and mobile phones. Merchandise associated with films of a book, such as *Mary Poppins* or *The Lord of the Rings*, including revamped or commemorative editions of the text, may also shine a spotlight on the original source of the story.

In this book, we aim to examine this social and cultural phenomenon, using a diverse and eclectic series of texts to illuminate and build on the central themes. While our common research interests as academics are largely in the tourism and events sphere, we do not feel constrained by these boundaries. We therefore draw upon theoretical perspectives from sociology, anthropology, literary and cultural studies, folklore, history and geography. In this chapter, we introduce some of the more important perspectives, with examples that we will expand upon throughout this book.

A Lexicon of Movement

According to Vogel (1974: 185), all fictional stories involve some form of *movement*, yet 'we know that not all journeys have precisely the same symbolic intentions'. He has identified six basic types of movement in fictional narrative. This typology is loosely applied, in that some books can span several types of movement, and there may be disputes over the subjective categorisation.

(1)   *The journey.* A character travels from one place to another, but there is no particular goal in mind, nor is any kind of meaning derived from the travel. These movements are essentially purposeless meanderings and tend to be found in the picaresque genre. Examples are *Little Big Man*, *Gulliver's Travels* and *The Sun Also Rises*.

(2)   *Wandering.* While this travel appears to lack purpose, there is a hidden mission underlying it that the reader eventually begins to understand, even if the central character is unaware of it. An example is *The Prisoner of Zenda*.

(3)   *The quest.* This travel is accompanied by a sense of mission, both on the part of the character and as understood by the author and reader. While the ultimate goal may not be clear, the sense of purpose (or *destiny*) is present from the very beginning of the narrative. Examples include the *Harry Potter* series and *Ivanhoe*.

(4)   *The pilgrimage.* This travel is purposeful, but aimed at a clear (spiritual) goal. An example is *The Lord of the Rings* series.

(5) *The odyssey*. This travel is underpinned by a purpose or goal, but no spiritual or moral mission is involved. Examples are *Sherlock Holmes* and *Around the World in Eighty Days*.

(6) *The going-forth*. The character starts travelling with a vague notion that their movement has some kind of purpose, mission or meaning, but they (along with the reader) only discover its precise nature at a later stage in the narrative. Examples are *The Lost World* and the *His Dark Materials* trilogy.

We have added two more types of movement in fictional narratives to Vogel's lexicon, drawing on the work of Adams (1983).

(7) *Flight/pursuit*. The character is forced from home or is running away from an unpalatable or dangerous situation (i.e. punishment, prison, marriage to the wrong person or the curtailing of freedom). The runaway may be followed and must evade capture. The tale may be told either from the viewpoint of the fugitive or the pursuer. Examples include *The Adventures of Tom Sawyer* and *True Grit*.

(8) *The search*. The hero searches for someone or something that is lost, or wishes to clarify or solve a mystery. Others may be trying to mislead them, to prevent this from occurring. Examples are *King Solomon's Mines*, *The Searchers* and *The Girl with the Dragon Tattoo*.

A Typology of the Quest

Many narratives have a *quest* embedded in them. Adams (1983) has identified seven types of quest and argues for a crossover that often exists between quests, odysseys and pilgrimages. The tendency of travellers to take on various roles has also been observed by Cunningham (1994: 228): 'The traveller [in most traditional novels] may be variously pilgrim, soldier, picaro, agent or imperialist expansion, detective'. Nevertheless, we feel that these typologies are helpful in the analysis of travel within texts, as well as contributing to a deeper understanding of the implications of different texts for travel behaviour. They can be applied to both fictional and non-fictional travel narratives. Given that they are meant to be true, the latter may have a particularly strong impact upon readers. The seven types of quests are listed here.

(1) *Religious*. Otherwise known as the pilgrimage – the search for a religious or holy object, place or person. An example is *I'm Off Then*.

(2) *A battle*. The travel involves searching out an enemy or going to war. Examples are *The Lion, The Witch and the Wardrobe* from the *Narnia* series and *The Three Musketeers*.

(3) *Utopias*. The search is for a utopian land or existence. Examples include *Lost Horizon* and *The Beach*.

(4) *Exploration*. A character looks for a new land or uncharted territory. Examples include *Journey to the Centre of the Earth*, *Little House on the Prairie* and *The Kon-Tiki Expedition*.

(5) *A fortune*. This involves travel for monetary gain. Examples are *Treasure Island* and *King Solomon's Mines*.

(6) *A person*. The character wants to find a missing person, perhaps a loved one. Examples are *The Searchers* and *How I Found Livingstone*.

(7) *Knowledge or wisdom*. The search is to know oneself better or to understand the world better. Examples are *Mediterranean Food*, *Harry Potter* and *Tanami*.

Two more quests can be added to this list. They are the *quest for love* and the *quest for healing*. Both are exemplified by the book *Eat, Pray, Love*. Many narratives based on one or both of these forms of quest involve women, often in exotic settings that encourage reflection, self-actualisation and emancipation (Wilson *et al.*, 2009). They combine the romance and self-help genres and travel plays an integral part in the storyline and is a catalyst for empowerment.

Quests are purposeful journeys and often appear to be predestined (Vogel, 1974). This gives the narrative *gravitas* and meaning and contributes to its compelling and epic quality. The reader is drawn in and gripped by the story, in their desire to see the quest succeed. Like the hero's journey, the traveller encounters obstacles and dramas, which must be endured and overcome, before the return home can take place.

Travel Tropes

Travel literature can also be analysed through uncovering the *tropes* that lay behind it (Adler, 1989; Bruner, 1991; Stanford Friedman, 2011; Zurick, 1995). This refers to 'enduring story lines' (Adler, 1989: 1375), but can also be understood as a literary convention where words are used in a different sense to their literal meaning. Metaphors and irony are examples of literary tropes. We are using the term 'trope' in the sense that Adler uses it, to describe narrative arcs concerning travel that have a long history and are still being used to this day. These tropes shape and frame our understanding of travel, and can be found in both fiction and non-fiction narratives. Travel tropes include the following list.

(1) *Voyages of discovery.* Exploring new worlds or territory. An example is *The Lost World*.
(2) *Promises of time travel.* Seeking a travel experience from an earlier time, 'going back in time' or catching a glimpse of the future. Examples are *The Kon-Tiki Expedition* and the *Nomad of Time* trilogy.
(3) *Seeking a 'homeland of the soul'.* Akin to a pilgrimage but focusing on a place that represents or symbolises one's values. There is a strong sense of nostalgia and yearning running through this trope. The traveller is looking for a place to belong. Examples are *My Family and Other Animals* and *A Year in Provence*.
(4) *Exploring paradise or hell on earth.* This travel can involve utopian or arcadian landscapes, which give us a glimpse of heaven. Alternatively, travel to 'dark' places, such as battlefields or places of suffering that can be likened to 'hell'. *Lost Horizon* could be described as incorporating both these tropes, based on the differing perspectives of its characters.
(5) *The noble savage/'vanishing primitive'.* The 'other' is exotic, praiseworthy and unspoilt, but on the cusp of change and thus required 'viewing' before it is too late to see them as they 'really' are. Examples include *The White Masai* and *Mutant Message Down Under*.
(6) *The world as a 'book'.* We can learn from travel – it is educational and helps a traveller grow and develop as a person. The Grand Tour was designed to improve minds. Examples are *The Brendan Voyage* and *Brideshead Revisited*.

The Hero's Journey

The hero's journey is a perennial theme in narrative, which has been identified across different cultures and epochs. So much so, that Campbell (1949) calls it the 'monomyth', following Joyce (1939). We have found it to be a useful way to understand the journey narrative in many books we have read. It drives the plot, and, like the quest narrative, gives the story an emotional pull and weightiness. Important matters are at stake. We generally care deeply about the hero and their plight, and identify with their struggles as if they were our own.

Three stages are involved in the hero's journey (Adams, 1983; Campbell, 1949; Hume, 1974). These echo the elements of a *rite of passage* – separation, initiation, return (Campbell, 1949). The hero leaves their homeland (*the hero's departure*) for unknown hardships and trials (*initiation*), perhaps involving some supernatural aid, before arriving home renewed and changed by the experience (*return of the hero*). This proves the hero's worth. As Van Nortwick (1992: 28) observes: 'To look death in the face and to return to the living is the ultimate proof of a hero's extraordinary stature'. The hero's journey is essentially the *odyssey* identified by Vogel (1974). We often think of this narrative in classical terms – Jason searching for the Golden Fleece or Odysseus finding his way home after the Trojan War – but overlook its importance in most of the books we read. It is as readily found in children's books as in crime or adventure fiction directed at adults, and we unconsciously absorb its conventions and structure as readers.

There are also overlaps between the hero's journey and the *pilgrimage*. Both involve similar stages (O'Guinn & Belk, 1989; Turner & Turner, 1978; van Gennep, 1909). There is a departure, and a form of penance, with pain, dangers and hardships involved, before the traveller achieves their goal. The hero/pilgrim is transformed by the experience, or undergoes a rite of passage, sharing the experience with their fellow travellers, which can develop into a special bond (*communitas*). Both journeys end with the traveller becoming incorporated back into society, including telling stories to others about the experience. Turner and Turner (1978: 23) note that pilgrimages 'tend to accrete rich superstructures of legend, myth, folklore, and literature' and have become the genesis for many books; from Chaucer's *The Canterbury Tales* to modern-day equivalents such as Tolkien's *Lord of the Rings* trilogy. The use of concepts such as the hero's journey and the pilgrimage in literary analysis might therefore help to explain why we gravitate towards certain stories and their enduring popularity across the generations.

The protagonist may sometimes be portrayed as an *anti-hero*, at least for part of the book. Their heroic qualities may be hidden or latent until something happens to trigger them. This story arc might be appealing to readers, who may see themselves and their own struggles reflected in the narrative. Rudolf in *The Prisoner of Zenda* is a bored and lazy young man who is asked to impersonate a king, his look-alike. This safeguards the throne, while the real king can be rescued. Rudolf grows in stature through his experiences, perhaps because he has at last found a purpose in his life, but also because he falls in love with Princess Flavia, the king's fiancée. Rudolf is tempted to continue in this role, but eventually decides to do the noble thing and restores the real monarch to his throne. The hero in this case was flawed, like Achilles with his heel, but overcomes his weaknesses. The anti-hero may display qualities we do not admire, but generally does the right thing in the end. Sometimes they break rules to succeed or are forced to hide their true identity to carry out their journey. A few become outlaws in society, like Robin Hood. They might be understood as an example of the trickster archetype (West, 2001). Other anti-heroes include Zorro in *The Mark of Zorro* and Amos in *The Searchers*.

The Katabatic Narrative

The term *katabasis* literally means 'the descent', and is a concept that originated in Greek mythology, describing the journey to hell and back. Sacrifices are often demanded and the 'other' is encountered (Falconer, 2005). The underworld might be understood as a 'sacred place or vessel of initiation', which has a 'transformative power' (Lansing Smith, 1990: 5). When the traveller returns, they are usually irrevocably changed by the experience.

While Falconer (2005) notes that the katabasis traditionally involves 16 steps, we distil them down to the following six, following Clauss (1999) and Holtsmark (2001).

(1) A journey is taken to the realm of the dead.
(2) The journey is necessary to recover someone or something.
(3) The entrance is over a river or through a cave and requires a guide, who may need to be paid or tricked into helping.
(4) The realm of the dead is more than dangerous. It is forbidding, nightmarish and haunted.
(5) One of the group must die as a sacrificial victim.
(6) The journey changes the hero. He is reborn or gains some other benefit.

Falconer (2005: 2) argues that Western culture is 'still very much governed by a "katabatic imagination"'. We react instinctively to these tales, which essentially involve journeys of self-discovery and identity.

> The descent requires the hero to undergo a series of tests and degradations, culminating in the collapse or dissolution of the hero's sense of selfhood. In the midst of this dissolution comes the infernal revelation, or the sought after power, or the spectre of the beloved. The hero then returns to the overworld, in some cases succeeding, in other cases failing to bring back this buried wisdom, love or power from the underworld. (Falconer, 2005: 3)

A katabasis may, therefore, involve failure. Falconer (2005) argues that the hero may not even be the one to return. Persephone could only return from the underworld for six months of the year. These narratives may be bleak, given the potential element of a sacrifice. Amos in *The Searchers* is forced to wander, unable to return to civilised society, to which he does not belong (Clauss, 1999). Wendy returns home to the nursery after her adventures with Peter Pan, but Peter is fated always to be the outsider looking in; the price he pays for never growing old. There are Freudian overtones that have been applied to the katabasis, which are clearly illustrated in the *Peter Pan* example. Freud was very interested in the idea of the *underworld*, and Alice's fall down the rabbit-hole into Wonderland can be argued to be a 'metaphor for the descent into the Freudian unconscious' (Falconer, 2005: 120). The element of a cave in the katabasis might also be a reference to hidden desire (Falconer, 2005) or sexual imagery.

Despite these adult themes, many children books are based on a katabatic structure, including the *Harry Potter* series. This gives these books a dark quality, which seems antithetical to the traditional concept of children's literature as cosy and comforting. This could be argued to be part of the reason that they are so beloved and memorable. We are attracted to, and thrilled by, the shadowy side of life, even as children, and the books we read at an early stage stimulate and encourage this interest. We also find this structure present in adult fiction. The colonial katabasis is one example, exemplified in books such as *The Lost World* and *Beau Geste*. More recent versions depict hell as something that exists around us – 'the descent occurs within a context which, unlike their classical predecessors, is already understood to be infernal' (Falconer, 2005: 41). Using this mythological concept to frame our discourse in this book allows us to penetrate to the heart of what makes these stories so captivating and enduring, including their influence and inspiration with respect to travel.

Travel Archetypes Embodied in Literature

Travel literature can also be analysed through the identification of *archetypes*. Archetypal criticism is based on Jung's theory of archetypal images (Campbell, 1949; Jung, 1938) and has been defined as 'an unconscious primary form, an original pattern or prototype in the human mind' and 'collective unconscious forces affecting beliefs, attitudes and behaviour implicitly and/or explicitly' (Woodside & Megehee, 2009: 420). They provide the constituent elements of myth (Campbell, 1949). Jung sometimes argued that there was a set number of archetypes in existence, but alternatively observed that it was a more fluid concept. The concept has been criticised, particularly for its attempt to link these images with the unconscious and the argument that archetypes are universal and span cultures. Lindenfeld (2009: 223), however, observes that Jung's contribution is his realisation that 'people think in terms of images much of the time, however culture-bound these might be'. Woodside and Megehee (2007) also note the utility of identifying archetypes within tourism narratives for the purpose of interpreting tourists' blogs and diaries. We also feel there is value in exploring how the use of archetypes in books influences travel imaginings.

Examples of common archetypes (see Hume, 1974; McNelly, 1973; Woodside & Megehee, 2009) are presented here.

- *The hearth*. This might be the home country, where the family resides. In children's books, such as *Mary Poppins or Peter Pan*, it might be the nursery. It represents security and safety.
- *The dark realm*. This is a place of evil; hellish and nightmarish. It is sometimes literally dark, such as forests, caves and dungeons, and always forbidding. The hero must tread carefully and may need the help of a guide to navigate their way through. An example is the land of Mordor in *The Lord of the Rings*.
- *The road of trials*. The hero must continue to put one foot in front of the other, through a path that is strewn with dangers and obstacles. Frodo and Sam take a torturous path to the slopes of Mount Doom in *The Lord of the Rings*, and face hunger, the risk of abduction, being killed or tortured by forces of evil, including a giant spider, and being tempted by the Ring that they carry.
- *Rescue of the lady*. The hero must find the heroine, who may be trapped or imprisoned. D'Artagnan tries to rescue Constance from Milady's clutches in *The Three Musketeers*, while Ivanhoe saves the life of Rebecca. This is often an important trial to be overcome and may lead to the reward or boon of marriage upon the hero's return.
- *The woman as temptress/siren*. These women are dangerous, often disguised by a beautiful exterior. In noir fiction, they are known as the femme fatale. They lure the hero with their charm, to their own ends. Examples are Milady in *The Three Musketeers* and Mrs Coulter in the *His Dark Materials* trilogy.
- *Confrontation with the evil one*. The hero cannot avoid the show-down or conflict with the villain, rogue or criminal. This is a common archetype in Westerns, with Mattie Ross stalking Tom Chaney, the killer of her father, in *True Grit*. There is an inevitability about Harry Potter's various confrontations with Voldemort, ending with the latter's final destruction. Aslan the Lion defeats the White Witch in *The Lion,*

the Witch and the Wardrobe through his own self-sacrifice, paralleling Christian narrative.

- *Crossing the threshold.* This is also part of the hero's journey, as explained by Campbell (1949). The threshold represents a transitional zone or portal into another world or to adventure, and is often associated with danger and magic. The nursery window is the threshold in *Peter Pan*. Sometimes it is a mode of transport – a train in Harry Potter or an airship and ship in the *His Dark Materials* trilogy. It might also be a hurdle or riddle that the hero needs to prevail over or solve. The hero may have to navigate their way past a 'threshold guardian', who might need to be cajoled, bribed or even tricked into helping the hero. An example is the hag or witch Gagool in *King Solomon's Mines*, who shows the heroes the way to the mines, but then tries to trap them before they can leave. Gagool is also an archetype of the Old Crone.
- *The trickster.* Clever, wily and often charming, the trickster beguiles and surprises us, but we wonder if they stand for good or evil. In some cases, they are an anti-hero. An example is Rupert in *The Prisoner of Zenda*. The hero may have to become a trickster on occasion, to achieve their desired ends. Rudolf in *The Prisoner of Zenda* takes on the guise of the king, to safeguard the Ruritanian throne. Zorro dons a disguise, as does D'Artagnan when he visits Milady in *The Three Musketeers* and Sherlock Holmes, in order to solve a number of crimes.
- *The wise old man.* This archetype is generally the opposite of the trickster. This is the guide who can be trusted and who can help the hero, if he is willing and not too proud to ask for help. Examples are Professor Challenger in *The Lost World* and Chang and the High Lama in *Lost Horizon*.
- *Atonement with the father.* The hero needs to make some form of rapprochement with their father or perhaps a father-figure. Cedric finally realises the worth of his son in *Ivanhoe*.
- *Attaining an ultimate boon or prize.* This might be an object or a desired status, including marriage, a throne or power. Galadriel bestows gifts on the Fellowship in *The Lord of the Rings*, which help them in times of trouble, while Aragorn wins the greatest boon of all – the hand of the woman he loves. Jane Austen's novels al. end with the longed-for marriage of the heroine to the man she truly deserves. For Professor Otto Liedenbrock in *Journey to the Centre of the Earth*, the reward is the recognition of his scientific peers and the public for his discoveries.

We consider these and other archetypes in this book, which we argue underpin mythic narratives across a range of different texts, and have a powerful link to travel.

Jules Verne and Travel Imaginings

To illustrate the promises about travel made by books, consider *Around the World in Eighty Days* by the 19th century French writer Jules Verne. This classic travel adventure is highly popular and still in print (and widely available on e-readers), nearly 140 years after its publication. It has been filmed many times, most recently in 2004 with Steve Coogan and Jackie Chan, but more memorably in the 1956 Oscar winning version directed by Mike Todd and starring David Niven. It has also been the basis for modern variations, such as Jean Cocteau's *Round the World Again in 80 Days* (1936) and the more recent documentaries *Around the World in 80 Days with Michael Palin* (1989) and Monty Don's *Around the World in 80 Gardens* (2008).

`Verne could be said to be the father of adventure travel, focusing on journeys to the frontiers of our world, including the depths of the oceans, and outer space. There are a number of Paris landmarks and sites named after the author, a testament to his enduring fame (see Figure 1.1). He published 54 novels during his lifetime, known as the *Voyages Extraordinaires*, or *Extraordinary Journeys*, and including such works as *Cinq Semaines en Ballon*

Figure 1.1 Jules Verne Librairie, an antiquarian bookshop near the Sorbonne in Paris. Photo by J. Laing.

(*Five Weeks in a Balloon*) (1863); *Voyage au centre de la Terre* (*Journey to the Centre of the Earth*) (1864); *De la Terre à la Lune* (*From the Earth to the Moon*) (1865); and *Vingt Mille Lieues sous les Mers* (*Twenty Thousand Leagues Under the Sea*) (1870). The public imagination was captured by these stories, and even Verne wished he could follow in the footsteps of his famous literary characters like Phileas Fogg and Captain Nemo. In a letter to his publisher, Verne wrote: 'I get caught up in all the extraordinary adventures of my heroes. I regret only one thing, not being able to accompany them *pedibus cum jambis*'.

We can visit the house of Jules Verne in Amiens or the Jules Verne Museum in his birthplace of Nantes, travel the route followed in the book, or even attempt a recreation suitably adjusted for modern life (as Jean Cocteau and Michael Palin did). However, relatively few readers go on to do these things. Rather, the inspiration is to emulate Phileas Fogg, a boring, comfortable stay-at-home, who embarked on an amazing trip. Reading the book, we hope that, as for Fogg, travel will redefine and transform our lives.

Around the World in Eighty Days (Jules Verne, 1873)

Life for Fogg is structured and predictable, as befits the stereotype of the uptight and formal British aristocrat. Richards (1997: 4) argues that 'Verne, who disliked the English, created his typical Englishman in Phileas Fogg'. Fogg dismisses his servant because his shaving-water had been provided at 84 degrees, rather than 86 degrees. His new servant, Passepartout, has left his old job as his previous master was always drunk. He likes his new master: 'This is just what I wanted! Ah, we shall get on together, Mr Fogg and I! What a domestic and regular gentleman! A real machine'. Fogg writes out his set program for the day on a card for his new servant:

> Tea and toast at twenty-three minutes past eight, the shaving-water at thirty-seven minutes past nine ... everything was regulated and foreseen that was to be done ... Each pair of trousers, coat, and vest bore a number, indicating the time of the year and the season at which they were in turn to be laid out for v earing, and the same system was applied to the master's shoes. In short the house in Saville Row, which must have been a very temple of disoLder and unrest under the illustrious but dissipated [former owner playwright Richard] Sheridan, was coziness, comfort and method idealized.

This state of affairs is, however, about to be overturned. Fogg is a member of the Reform Club, a refuge for gentlemen from the vagaries of a noisy and bustling London. A social card game acquires a twist, when Fogg takes on an absurd bet of the huge sum of 20 thousand pounds that he can go around the world in 80 days. Within moments, he is propelled into the wider world and his adventures begin. It is our first hint of his dual or divided nature and we realise that he is not as stable or as sensible as he previously seemed. Fogg resembles Verne, who was said to live through his creations (Butcher, 1990; Martin, 1990). Pressured by his father to embrace the security of the law, Verne wanted to be a writer instead, justifying his decision with the comment: 'I can make a good literary man, but I'll only ever be a poor lawyer' (quoted in Martin, 1990).

Though travelling the world, Fogg is determined to stick to his old routines. In Suez, the detective Fix tells Fogg that his watch is wrong. Fogg has been keeping London time and refuses to change it. It is this decision that leads to their failure to realise they have a day in hand when they arrive back in London. Whether in a train, carriage or boat, Fogg is cocooned from the world outside, and keeps to his cabin, playing his beloved whist ('As for the wonders of Bombay ... he cared not a straw to see them'). We are told that he 'was not travelling, but only describing a circumference ... traversing an orbit around the terrestrial globe, according to the laws of rational mechanics'. Passepartout on the other hand, once recovered from the shock at the journey, is enchanted by Mocha and Aden and 'lost in admiration' in Bombay. He takes every opportunity to immerse himself in his new surrounds, but like many travellers makes a cultural faux-pas. He gets in trouble for not taking off his shoes at a Parsee Temple. By the time they reach India, Passepartout is transformed: 'Now that they were plainly whirling across India at full speed, a sudden change had come over the spirits of his dreams. His old vagabond nature returned to him, the fantastic ideas of his youth once more took possession of him'.

The journey also becomes much more visceral for Fogg once he reaches India and things start to go wrong. His whole bet is based on newspaper reports that the railway now spans the sub-continent. However, this is not true; the railway track is not finished, and they are forced to hire an elephant, and cross wild lawless country. When they encounter a young Indian woman, Aouda, who is facing being burnt as a widow in the rite of *suttee*, it is Fogg who asks his companion Sir Francis Cromarty: 'Suppose we save this woman'. At one point, Passepartout is separated from his master, and Fogg is forced to manage things on his own. He becomes more outgoing, shopping with Aouda. At first there is a practical purpose for these trips, such as buying clothes or getting a visa in San Francisco, but by the time they reach Salt Lake City, they are simply 'promenading'. Fogg is thawing and becoming more human.

The journey through America is even more eventful. Fogg encounters a herd of buffalo, attends a Mormon lecture, takes part in a duel and must help to ward off attack from a band of Indians. He also saves Fix from a fight in San Francisco, actively stepping in instead of passively gazing at events. Once again, the train, symbolic of modernity and efficiency proves unreliable. When Passepartout is lost, Fogg does not hesitate to abandon his quest to lead the search.

At the end of the book, when Fogg thinks his bet has been lost, he is proposed to by Aouda. Travel has made her more assertive, while the confirmed bachelor Fogg is now able to drop his mask and ardently declare his feelings to the woman he loves. He later finds out that he can still make the deadline, and heads to the Reform Club with seconds to spare. He has achieved his goal, but saved himself in the process (Butcher, 1990). Passepartout observes that Fogg is a 'machine', 'neither restless nor curious', but the narrative proves him wrong, Fogg has rediscovered his humanity and feelings. Perhaps travel cannot help but bring those qualities out in many people, especially if they are there to begin with, but merely buried deepdown or hidden by a veneer of respectability or world-weariness. Wang (2000: 57) labels this 'existential authenticity' – the process of 'regaining authenticity of being' and finding your true self. In Fogg's case, he has also learnt the value of relationships and what is ultimately important to him.

> What had he really gained by all this trouble? What had he brought back from this long and weary journey? Nothing, say you? Perhaps so, nothing but a charming woman, who, strange as it may appear, made him the happiest of men! Truly, would you not for less than that make the tour around the world?

Scope of the Book

The thematic chapters that follow will explore the nexus between books and personal transformation or identity formation through travel; the contribution they make to a sense of place and destination image; and the part they play in imagined heritage and nostalgia. We also consider the role of books in empowering and inspiring the would-be tourist, creating tropes of travel, such as the pilgrimage, quest or recreated journey; shaping travel narratives and cultural memory; and offering avenues of escapism and fantasy. A variety of genres are covered, including children's literature, crime fiction, historical novels, fantasy, westerns, science-fiction and travel literature.

In this book, we are primarily concerned with fiction and travel books, rather than travel guides, as these are the two book types that most strongly have this inspirational aspect linked to travel. We are looking at books that are popular and widely-read, and our choices, reflecting our backgrounds, are firmly anchored in Western culture. Both of us are inveterate readers and travellers, which is the starting point for our exploration of this topic. We have deliberately selected books that we, as authors, have personally enjoyed or are memorable to us in some way, which allows us to augment our discussion with auto-ethnographic observations.

We are tourism academics. Like many of our colleagues we tend to research and teach tourism within a business paradigm, with an emphasis on marketing and management. In this book, we have chosen a very different direction, venturing far from our normal territory, and exploring theories and ideas from literary studies, sociology, history, folklore and geography. Many of the concepts we utilise have been thoroughly analysed within those disciplines. However, they have been given very little consideration within the mainstream of tourism studies. It is this marrying of different perspectives, from a wide range of disciplines, that we see as central to this book. To understand the phenomenon of tourism more deeply, it is important to explore what people imagine travel to be about, particularly the purpose of travel and its impact upon the traveller. By looking at a wide range of books, we aim to better understand their influence upon our imaginations.

2 The Gift Shop at 221B Baker Street

*'Don't talk rubbish', said Uncle Vernon, 'there is
no platform nine and three-quarters'.
'It's on my ticket'.
'Barking', said Uncle Vernon, 'howling mad, the lot of them'.
Harry Potter and the Philosopher's Stone,
J.K. Rowling, 1997*

The Sherlock Holmes Museum is in Baker Street, London. It has the number 221B, as that is the fictional address Arthur Conan Doyle used for the home of his fictional detective. Jennifer visited the museum in 2011:

A map or GPS is unnecessary for finding the museum. I just scan my eyes ahead and can see visitors in deerstalker hats posing and being photographed outside the entrance (the hats are provided by the shop). The first time I visited the Museum, a group of schoolchildren stood chattering excitedly outside the entrance and flocked into the gift shop. As I approached the counter to buy a postcard, these young tourists were quizzing the woman behind the counter, dressed in a Victorian parlourmaid's outfit, about the cost of a small glass vial containing one cigarette. Smash in case of emergency, I assumed, and perhaps a nod to Sherlock's prolific tobacco habit and the haze that often accompanies his brilliant deductions, as in *The Man with the Twisted Lip*. Were they real cigarettes? Did the schoolchildren want to smoke them? On the current visit, they were no longer on sale, but I noticed another tribute to a Holmesian addiction – a pen shaped like a hypodermic needle, but containing a harmless red liquid rather than the 'seven-per-cent solution' of cocaine Sherlock enjoys in *The Sign of Four*. Visitors were snapping up Sherlock magnets, key-rings, souvenir mugs and copies of the Conan Doyle books, tastefully arranged in a room bedecked with a potted palm and Victorian *chaise longue*. The sign outside, replicated in the souvenir business-cards on sale, read 'Sherlock Holmes Consulting Detective'. Upstairs in the Museum, a man dressed as Holmes greeted visitors, violin in hand, and bade them come closer to the fire. To fans, it was as if their consultation with the greatest detective of all time had just begun.

Our visits to 221B Baker Street illustrate what we term the 'conventional view' of literary tourism. This phenomenon of tourists being drawn to places associated with books has been well explored by researchers, both in general studies (Robinson, 2002; Robinson & Andersen, 2002; Watson, 2006) and through specific case studies (examples include Barnard, 2002; Fawcett & Cormack, 2001; Herbert, 2001; Light, 2007; Månsson, 2010; Reijnders, 2011; Squire, 1994; Tetley & Bramwell, 2002). This connection parallels similar phenomena of tourism based on films and television (Beeton, 2005) and music and musicians (Connell & Gibson, 2005).

Most studies of literary tourism identify it as having two dimensions. First, tourists are attracted to places depicted in books, 221B Baker Street is a good example of this. Second, they are drawn to places connected with the author. The balance between the two varies greatly. In some cases, the places depicted in books are the key drawcard; in others, the attention of tourists is mainly directed to places connected with the author. In the case of Sherlock Holmes, the Baker Street attraction is primary (Figure 2.1).

In contrast, there is no Arthur Conan Doyle museum. There have, however, been attempts to create one, utilising a house he lived in. In 1897 he built Undershaw, in Hindhead, Surrey and lived there until 1907. During that period, he wrote a range of books, including, arguably the most famous Sherlock Holmes mystery, *The Hound of the Baskervilles* (1901). Since 2006, there has been a campaign to restore the now dilapidated house and open it to the public as a museum. The campaign suffered a setback in 2010, when the local council issued a permit for it to be converted into a block of flats (Rayner, 2010). However, the campaign continues, recently gaining Mark Gatiss, the writer of the television series *Sherlock*, as its patron (www.saveundershaw.org.uk). A commercial tourist attraction that utilises its connection with Conan Doyle in its marketing is Groombridge Place in Tunbridge Wells, Kent (www.groombridge.co.uk). He did not live there, but was a frequent visitor and used some of the garden settings and stories associated with it in his works.

This interplay between the fictional and the real suggests Eco's concept of *hyper-reality*. An important aspect of hyper-reality is how tourism attractions mix both the real and fiction together, with little distinction. To

Figure 2.1 Commemorative statue of Sherlock Holmes, near Baker Street, London. Photo by J. Laing.

illustrate this, Eco provides examples of a California wax museum, where 'you see Tom Sawyer immediately after Mozart' (Eco, 1986: 14) and Ripley's Believe It Or Not Museum where 'everything looks real and therefore it is real ... and the thing is real even if, like Alice in Wonderland, it never existed' (Eco, 1986: 16). Eco famously played with this concept of hyper-reality in his own successful novel *The Name of the Rose* (1980). In this medieval mystery, the detective is a Franciscan friar using deductive reasoning. His name is William of Baskerville.

More recently, this interplay has been described as a form of *mediatisation*, 'where tourism and media consumption are becoming increasingly linked to one another' and 'the boundaries between imaginary, symbolic and material spaces are therefore dissolving' (Månsson, 2010: 169). These processes of imagining and imaging (and re-imagining and re-imaging) affect how we experience places linked to books and authors. Tourists not only travel to places where authors lived and worked, they travel to experience what they imagine that author was like, how they lived and how they worked. Likewise, tourists not only travel to places described in books, they travel to experience what they imagine those places to be. What was once a simple visit is now far more complex owing to the possible differences and conflicts between the imaginary realities of various tourists, marketing bodies, site managers and other stakeholders.

As with other forms of cultural tourism, the literary tourist may be a serious and highly motivated fan or an incidental visitor. Certainly there is a temptation to believe that all those who visit literary attractions do so because of a strong personal sense of engagement with the author or book, and this is the primary motivation for their trip. For many, this strong connection dates back to the profound effect of books read and loved during childhood (Fawcett & Cormack, 2001; Squire, 1994; see also Chapter 3). We may even go so far as to see visitors as literary pilgrims on a deep and profound, though secular, mission (Herbert, 2001). However, research in cultural heritage has tended to show that the great majority choose a destination and then visit a broad diversity of attractions (McKercher & du Cros, 2002). Arguably for most visitors, 221B Baker Street is not the main reason for visiting London, but provides a pleasurable experience for an hour or two that contributes to the overall satisfaction with a trip to London or the UK.

Baker Street also raises the issue of commodification of literary tourism. Many book-related attractions have shops and cafes attached and generate a proportion of their revenue from souvenirs. In many instances this is tasteful and appreciated by visitors, though in other cases it may be viewed by some tourists as excessive (Robinson & Andersen, 2002). The sale of the souvenir pen in the form of a hypodermic needle at the gift shop at 221B Baker St clearly pushes the boundaries of good taste. The issue of commodification is not confined to literary tourism, rather it is a major debate found in nearly every form of tourism.

In this chapter, we aim to illustrate and discuss this conventional view of literary tourism with a selection of examples. The cases we consider are drawn from around the world and are intended to cover a range of tourist attractions and experiences. Some instances are based on our field work, others drawn from a growing literature on this form of tourism. The examples we use are just a selection to illustrate key concepts and issues, we are not attempting a comprehensive survey of literary tourism sites or research. This chapter, however, is just a starting point. Books do attract tourists to specific places and we need to understand this phenomenon. In this study, our aim is to go well beyond that. In later chapters we will explore how books have a far greater influence on the motivations for travel and tourism. This is a more general inspiration, sometimes linked to a specific place, but more often to a general desire to travel.

In the Author's Footsteps

There is some debate over which sites associated with authors are the more attractive for tourists. Watson (2006) focuses mainly on places connected with the deaths of authors, either graves, memorials or the houses they died in. She argues that these were often better noted and maintained, as the authors were well-known at the times of their deaths. In contrast, many exact birthplaces are unknown or were demolished before their significance was realised. Robinson and Andersen (2002) lay greater stress on the writer's home. They see this as a focus for literary pilgrimage as the home life and surroundings were a central influence on the writer and the creative process. They note that many tourists gain an almost talismanic experience in seeing furniture, rooms and personal items that were actually used by their favourite author. Similarly, the research by Herbert (2001) focused on author's homes as attractions. Far less attention seems to have been paid to meeting places of authors, such as literary salons (whether in private houses or public places). Our concern is not to elevate one above the other in importance, but rather to provide a selection of examples of all three categories.

Graves, statues, plaques and other memorials

Many authors are commemorated through gravestones, statues and plaques. Watson observes that 'any literary tourist in Britain begins, in imagination at least, at Poets' Corner in Westminster Abbey' (Watson, 2006: 23). She also notes that the practice of visiting literary graves dates back to antiquity and became a common form of secular pilgrimage in 18th century Britain. Perhaps more prominent are public statues and monuments. The Walter Scott Monument in Edinburgh, at 61 metres high, is reputed to be the largest literary memorial in the world (Watson, 2006).

P.L. Travers, the author of *Mary Poppins*, is remembered in two statues. They are both of Mary Poppins, rather than the author, but they are located in Australian towns where Travers lived. The first is in Maryborough, Queensland, where she was born. The second is in Ashfield, a suburb of Sydney. The idea for the latter statue came from a nine-year-old Ashfield schoolgirl, Gracie Drew. Her mother was reading her the biography of Travers and they realised that she had lived nearby. They visited the house and were surprised there was no plaque. Gracie then lobbied the municipal council to recognise this local connection (Lawson, 2004). Two points of interest. First, even though *Mary Poppins* was written in 1934, these two statues were not erected until 2004 and 2005, respectively. Second, both statues are based on the drawings of Mary Poppins in the book, not Julie Andrews in the Disney film.

Many British authors are commemorated with the humble Blue Plaque attached to the outside of buildings. This scheme started in 1867, with a plaque for Lord Byron, and is currently administered by English Heritage. It is not confined to authors, though fictional characters are excluded. A blue plaque for Sherlock Holmes in Baker Street is not officially authorised. In the USA, the Association of Library Trustees, Advocates, Friends and Foundations has instituted the Literary Landmarks programme. Many of these are houses of authors or sites connected with their lives. Intriguingly, most Literary Landmarks are in Florida, followed by Oklahoma.

Houses

Robinson and Andersen (2002) note a wide array of tourism products associated with author's homes. Some are just marked by plaques and are not open to the public. Others operate as full visitor attractions, with a fee payable for entry and even gift shops and cafes. Interpretation ranges from a conventional museum approach with exhibits of labelled artefacts, to full recreations, with rooms curated to give a picture of how they looked when the author was alive. In such cases, tourists are presented with the illusion that the author might have just stepped out for a short time.

Perhaps the most well-known example is that of the Brontë Parsonage Museum in Haworth, Yorkshire. The Brontë sisters lived at the village parsonage and this is where they wrote their novels. Tourists started coming to Haworth from around 1850, intrigued by the mystery of who the writer really was (Charlotte Brontë used the asexual pseudonym of Currer Bell). In 1893, fans formed the Brontë Society and opened a small museum in 1895. In 1928, the Society was able to buy the parsonage and move their exhibits into it (Barnard, 2002; Tetley & Bramwell, 2002; Watson, 2006). This long-lived and substantial tourism flow was based entirely on the sisters as authors.

> Haworth itself, it should be remembered, features in none of the Brontë novels. Its appeal is as the setting of the Brontës' *lives*. (Barnard, 2002: 145)

Some aspects of visitors to Haworth are revealed in a survey by Tetley and Bramwell (2002). Over 85% of visitors surveyed were from Great Britain, with about 5% from North America. Surveys in the village showed that about two-thirds had read a novel by the Brontës, or seen a film or television series based on their works. At the parsonage museum, this was higher, at about three-quarters. While these are high levels of engagement and knowledge, it still leaves a large proportion of visitors with no direct contact with the Brontës' books. Furthermore, about 40% of visitors identified that they had little or no interest in the Brontës. Investigating issues of commodification, the research-ers found high levels of acceptance of the number of tourist shops in the vil-lage, with only 20% indicating that they would prefer fewer shops.

Similarly, visitors to Jane Austen's home at Chawton, Hampshire, were surveyed by Herbert (2001). This survey found visitors to be primarily middle class and over 80% were domestic, with North America at 8% being the largest overseas contingent. The great majority were well read and knowledgeable in relation to Austen, and nearly half identified themselves as 'fans'. Intriguingly, a third answered that they were just on a day out or had not planned the visit, but rather, merely noticed the sign in passing. As with the survey at Haworth, this is in line with the contention of McKercher and du Cros (2002) that, contrary to stakeholder expectations, many visitors at heritage attractions are incidental.

Two contrasting literary homes come from Nottinghamshire. Both are open to the public. Newstead Abbey was the ancestral home of Lord Byron. Typical of many grand homes and gardens, it attracts a steady flow of day trippers, but has the added appeal of this literary connection. Nowadays, Byron's appeal is primarily based on his scandalous Regency lifestyle, infa-mously described as 'mad, bad and dangerous' by his lover Lady Caroline Lamb. Lord Byron is a good example of where the reputation and extreme behaviour 'of some authors elevate them to a point where the tourist derives more pleasure from, and gives more attention to, their lives and times than from their works' (Robinson, 2002: 62). Nearby is the coal-mining town of Eastwood. One of its modest cottages is preserved and open to tourists as the birthplace of D.H. Lawrence. As with many literary homes, it is curated to appear as a reproduction of how it might have been in Lawrence's childhood. In stark contrast to the grandeur of Newstead Abbey, this attraction focuses on the author's humble origins.

In North America, there is a tendency for author's homes to be closely linked to the locations they wrote about. Canada's Prince Edward Island was both the home of Lucy Maud Montgomery and the setting for her *Anne of Green Gables*. Today, it contains three heritage tourism attractions cele-brating the author and novel. There is the site of her grandparents' house at Cavendish, where Montgomery grew up; another house at Park Corner, where she later lived with her cousins; and a third house owned by relatives, which she used as a model for the Green Gables House in the book (Fawcett & Cormack, 2001). In the USA, the Mark Twain Boyhood Home and Museum is at Hannibal, Missouri, near the Mississippi River that features in *Tom Sawyer* and *Huckleberry Finn*. Further west, near Independence, Kansas, is the Little House on the Prairie, both home and subject for Laura Ingalls Wilder.

Literary salons

Rather than their homes, some authors are better associated with places where they congregated with fellow literati. In such *literary salons* they drew their inspiration from the company and socialising. Tourists are then drawn to these locations.

In Paris, the bookshop *Shakespeare and Company* was a major literary gathering place for expatriates during the 1920s. These included Ernest Hemingway, James Joyce, F. Scott Fitzgerald, Gertrude Stein, William S. Burroughs and Ezra Pound. The bookshop was notorious for selling copies of books banned in the USA and UK, such as *Lady Chatterley's Lover*. Sylvia Beach, its owner, was the first to publish Joyce's *Ulysses* (Hussey, 2006). Today, it is a popular fixture on the tourist trail through Paris and featured in the 2011 Woody Allen film *Midnight in Paris*. We visited in 2011 (Figure 2.2) and Warwick recorded his experience.

Late in the afternoon on a beautiful spring day in Paris, tourists swarm outside the bookshop. The light is perfect for taking photos. A short time before we were probably all taking photos of Notre Dame, now we have crossed to the Left Bank to tick off another site. I am no different to the rest. Almost on cue, an ancient Bohemian wanders in and out amongst us. Wearing a beret and smoking a cigarette in a pearl shell holder, she glares at us. Perfect, just what we want, a real Left Bank experience

Figure 2.2 Tourists outside the Shakespeare Bookshop in Paris. Photo by J. Laing.

(though she could not possibly have been there in its 1920s heyday). I sit on a bench taking it all in. Behind me, a small tour group arrive. I sneak a quick look, but mainly try to be inconspicuous as I eavesdrop on the guide's commentary. He is an American in Paris, wearing tweeds, a man of letters. He explains how famous *Shakespeare and Company* is. Grace Kelly, on her way to Monaco, came here. Jacqueline Bouvier was a regular shopper. I didn't know any of this. I keep listening, but he is finished and they move on to their next stop. No mention of the 1920s or its radical past. With the success of *Midnight in Paris* he'll have to change his spiel.

In London, the Bloomsbury Set or Group is associated with the suburb of that name. This is the name given to a coterie of Bohemians, friends and like-minded souls who hit their greatest artistic and literary heights in the period between the early years of the 20th century and the beginning of the Second World War. The Bloomsbury Group chiefly lived in the area around Bedford Square, Gordon Square and Fitzroy Square (Nicholson, 2002; Seymour, 1992). At the time they moved there, Bloomsbury was considered to be 'inexpensive [and] unfashionable' (Dunn, 2000: 90), but gave the group a sense of liberation from the conservatism of the likes of Kensington and Mayfair (Dunn, 2000). Sexual and artistic experimentation was rife and they led a life of freedom from social restrictions. Conversation was open and ribald and nothing was off-limits (Dunn, 2000; Nicholson, 2002). The acknowledged leaders of the group were the sisters Virginia Woolf and Vanessa Bell, whose homes, particularly Charleston, the Bells' country house in Sussex, became a form of salon and 'epitomise the Bohemian lifestyle' (Nicholson, 2002: 29). The group also included artists (Duncan Grant, Roger Fry), writers (Leonard Woolf, Lytton Strachey, E.M. Forster), and the economist John Maynard Keynes. Their fascination is still evident in the popularity of tourist products, such as London Walks' 'Literary Bloomsbury and the Old Museum Quarter' tour, walks in the footsteps of Virginia Woolf (Plate, 2006) and visits to Charleston and Monk's House, the Woolf's country home. The National Trust attraction of Sissinghurst in Kent is also associated with this group. It was the home of Vita Sackville-West, who laid out its famous garden. In the USA, literary gathering places, such as the Algonquin Hotel in New York and the Hotel Monteleone in New Orleans, have recently been recognised as Literary Landmarks.

Further issues

These examples are instructive, but research into tourism and sites associated with authors needs to move on and investigate patterns. Clearly some authors attract tourists. However, not all authors get this attention. Why some and not others? For example, the Bram Stoker Experience was a Dublin museum celebrating the life of the author of *Dracula*. It was located in the suburb where Stoker was born and grew up. The museum opened in 2003 and was heavily featured in the destination marketing of Dublin. However, it was not a success and closed in 2008. *Dracula* is hugely popular (Reijnders, 2011). Why does that popularity not translate into interest in its creator? Similarly, there is no tourism product built around the homes or lives of J.K. Rowling or Stephenie Meyer. Will that come in time? The forces that drive tourism linked to authors need much further research.

Immersed in the Story

Real places featured in fiction often have a very strong appeal to readers. This is perhaps hardly surprising. These places have connections with key plot elements and characters. Visiting them transports readers back to the emotions they experienced in reading the book. These feelings may be reinforced by repeated readings and/or adaptations, particularly film or television versions. Personally visiting sites may be a form of pilgrimage. It may be a solitary venture or a shared experience. The latter seems particularly important for fictional works that have generated large-scale social worlds and fan sub-cultures. These places may either have been used in books as they were already famous, or have only come to the attention of tourists through that literary connection.

London and Harry Potter

A tourist in London can combine 221B Baker Street with a range of sites featured in popular novels. Just over 100 metres away is a statue of Sherlock Holmes outside Baker Street Underground Station. Nearby is King's Cross Station, a focal point for Harry Potter fans. Kings Cross is the site of Platform 9¾, the magical portal to the train to Hogwarts School. Paddington Station has a statue of Paddington Bear. Away in Kensington Gardens is a statue of Peter Pan, which was erected by the enterprising J.M. Barrie himself in 1912. London Zoo features a statue of Winnie-the-Pooh. Part of the inspiration for A.A. Milne's creation came from Winnie the Black Bear. In 1924, Milne told Enid Blyton in an interview that he had taken his son (Christopher Robin) to London Zoo for a birthday party and they had been allowed in the cage to pet the tame animal (Frost, 2011).

All of these are popular sites for tourists to take photographs. This hyper-reality of visiting the authentic sites of fiction is particularly strong at King's Cross Station. In 2011, Jennifer visited the station:

'Is it possible to go to Platform 9¾ without a ticket?' I asked the station guard. I half-expected a curt response like the one Harry Potter got from his uncle when he mentioned the magical platform in *Harry Potter and the Philosopher's Stone*. 'Well yes', he replied instead, 'We've moved it while we do the renovations. Turn left until you get to the street, then turn left again'. 'They've moved a *mythical platform* outside', I thought. And yet somehow it made perfect sense. All that demand, all that disappointment, if one came and could not see it! 'And of course it wasn't even filmed entirely at King's Cross Station,' I thought, 'In the film they use *St Pancras Station* as it is more gothic'. However, the books used King's Cross as the location, and so here I was. After getting lost, I found myself outside and facing a snaking queue. 'This is bloody ridiculous!' thundered an elderly man clutching shopping bags and his granddaughter, as I approached. At the end of the queue was a small enclosure framing a brick wall. There was a railway-style sign *Platform 9¾* and a luggage trolley, half embedded in the bricks. In the books and films, Harry enters the magical platform by running as hard as he can with the trolley at the wall between Platforms 9 & 10. For the tourists who had patiently queued, here was their opportunity to recreate that moment. They could place their hands on the luggage trolley and have their photo taken by friends as they pretended they were going through the portal and off to Hogwarts.

Rosslyn Chapel and *The Da Vinci Code*

Rosslyn Chapel is ten kilometres south of Edinburgh in Scotland. The 15th century building was famous for its intricate and mysterious carvings and used to attract around 10,000 visitors per year. In *The Da Vinci Code* (2003) by Dan Brown, Rosslyn Chapel is a key site, 'it is here that the narrative's turning point occurs ... as many of the mysteries in the story resolve and secrets unfold' (Månsson, 2010: 171). Within a few years of the book's publication, visitation to Rosslyn Chapel had increased enormously from 10,000 to 170,000 per annum. Once a minor attraction, it was now amongst Scotland's Top 20 tourist attractions (Månsson, 2010).

Dracula and *Twilight*

Bram Stoker wrote *Dracula* (1897); partly based on the Irish legends he was told when growing up. The research and writing of the novel mainly took place in the English seaside town of Whitby, and its harbour is included in scenes in the book. Today, Whitby attracts tourists through a number of sites connected to the book, has an attraction – the 'Dracula Experience' – and stages festivals on these themes (Reijnders, 2011).

To give his work an exotic flavour, Stoker based his vampire on Vlad Dracul and his son Vlad Tepes (aka Vlad the Impaler), 15th century Wallachian princes, and set much of the story in Transylvania. By Stoker's time, Wallachia had become part of Romania and the Balkans was often in the news as the Great Powers jockeyed for influence of this strategic region. Transylvania was an exotic borderland, the frontier between the Austro-Hungarian, Russian and Ottoman Empires. Stoker was also fascinated by the supernatural folklore of the region, which paralleled that of his native Ireland. However, he never visited Transylvania.

Stoker's inspired use of Transylvania as a setting has led to much tension. Romanian authorities have been bewildered by the desire of Western tourists to experience a fictional character based on a historical figure. This is compounded by the book being little known in that country until recently (Light, 2007; Muresan & Smith, 1998; Reijnders, 2011). Catering for tourists has led to some queer contradictions and instructive examples of hyper-reality. Just after the Fall of Communism, Warwick visited the town of Sigişoara, birthplace of Vlad the Impaler.

> Sigişoara is a beautiful and intact historic gem, justifiably deserving of its UNESCO World Heritage status. Established by the Germans in the thirteenth century (a series of such Carpathian border towns provides the location for where the Pied Piper led the children of Hamelin), it draws me with its magnificent medieval heritage. Juxtaposed with this, are its Dracula manifestations. I have not come seeking them, though they are interesting diversions. The house where Vlad was born is a tourist restaurant, a steakhouse to be precise, though not a theatre restaurant. We have to eat lunch there. In the square outside is a statue of Vlad. In the park down the hill, there is a moonlight cinema, showing *Dracula* (1992, d. Francis Ford Coppola). In the early twenty-first century there was a proposal to build a Dracula theme park at Sigişoara, but this caused an outcry and fortunately was eventually abandoned.

In the book, Dracula lives in a gothic castle. However, neither of the Vlads are associated with any real Romanian castle. To overcome this deficiency, Bran Castle is marketed to tourists as Dracula's Castle. Visually, it fulfils all our expectations of how a vampire's castle should look. It just has no historical or geographical connection with either Vlad. Recently, the Hotel Castle

Dracula has been built close to where Stoker located his fictional creation (Reijnders, 2011).

The success of the *Twilight* series has drawn tourists to the towns that are the settings for the novels. Christine Lundberg has been researching this phenomenon and she has kindly shared some of her data with us (see also Lundberg & Lexhagen, 2012). The American setting is Forks in Washington State. Based on information from the visitor information centre, Lundberg estimates that since 2005 (when the first novel was published), it has drawn 250,000 tourists to this small town. The other setting is Volterra (Tuscany, Italy). Here, Lundberg calculates that 20% of tourists are drawn by the novels.

Theme Parks

In some instances, books provide the inspiration for theme parks. Robinson and Andersen (2002) comment that theme parks chiefly look to children's literature, citing the example of a number of theme parks utilising *Gulliver's Travels*. The various Disney theme parks around the world draw on children's fiction, providing rides and shows based on *Tarzan, Winnie-the-Pooh, Mary Poppins, Alice in Wonderland, The Sword in the Stone* and *Huckleberry Finn. Jurassic Park* is recreated in a ride at Universal Studios and has strongly influenced how museums display dinosaurs around the world (Frost, 2010b). Two new theme parks utilise books and authors: one is the Wizarding World of Harry Potter at Orlando, Florida; the other is Charles Dickens World in Chatham, Kent. While Dickens is not usually regarded as a children's author, the format and marketing of this new venture is firmly aimed at children.

Missing Pages: Events Celebrating Authors and Settings

Much of the research into literary tourism has focused on visits to tourist attractions. Important as they are, this focus misses another dimension of how tourists interact with books and authors. This extra dimension is events, particularly festivals themed around books and authors. We provide a few examples of what seems to be an increasing trend, though it is an area that deserves far more research.

Authors are a common subject of commemorations. Such events focus on remembering and celebrating the author, combining a significant date, such as their birth or death and an appropriate number of years. For example, 2012 is the bicentenary (200th anniversary) of the birth of Charles

Dickens. Commemorative events may include re-enactments, readings, conferences, dinners and other functions, community festivals, publication of new editions and the dedication of statues or plaques. The date and anniversary are particularly important for the process of remembering. They have an almost talismanic quality in capturing the imagination of the public. Indeed, significant commemorations are attractive news stories for the media and present a rare opportunity to publicise authors and the activities of their fans.

Re-enactments often involve performances by actors in costume, playing the part of the author, recounting their lives and reading passages from books. Corryong, in rural Australia, stages an annual Man From Snowy River Bush Festival. It was originally held in 1995 as a centenary commemoration of the publication of *The Man From Snowy River* (1895, A.B. 'Banjo' Paterson). The event proved to be such a success that it was decided to hold it annually. The centrepiece of the festival is a re-enactment viewed by approximately 5000 people (the town's population is only 1200). An actor dressed as Paterson talks about his life and legacy and recites some of his poetry. This is followed by a spectacular re-enactment, by professional stuntmen, of the horseback chase that is central to the story of *The Man From Snowy River*. For this small and remote country town, this event is its major festival of the year and the main opportunity to attract tourists and reinforce its pioneer identity (Frost & Laing, 2011).

Re-enactments may also be participatory. Bloomsday is held annually on 16 June in Dublin. It commemorates the novel *Ulysses* (1922, James Joyce), which is the story of one day in the life of Leopold Bloom, that being 16 June 1904. Participants, often in Edwardian costume, follow Bloom's path through the city, with appropriate stops for readings and drinks at pubs. The event began with a 50th anniversary in 1954 (and note that it was the anniversary of the date of the action in the book, not of its publication). In 2004 there was a major commemoration for the centenary, titled ReJoyce 2004 (Frost & Laing, 2011).

Literary sites stage events as a way of attracting visitors, perhaps even broadening their appeal. For example, in 2010, the Brontë Parsonage Museum in Haworth held the first Brontë Festival of Women's Writing. A second was held in 2011 and it is intended to be an annual event. This event is not specifically about the Brontës, but uses them as a focal point to promote and celebrate women writers in general. It also provides an additional revenue flow for the Museum and the village.

Events may be popularised by books, in the same way that they attract tourists to places. In 1923, 1924 and 1925, Ernest Hemingway attended the Festival of San Fermin in Pamplona, Spain. In 1926, he published *The*

Sun Also Rises, a fictionalised account of his visits. It strongly featured the bullfights and the 'Running of the Bulls', which were part of the festival. Hemingway's book brought this local festival to the attention of an international audience.

Where fans of certain books have developed sub-cultures, these in turn have spawned events. Whitby, with its connections to Bram Stoker and *Dracula*, is now the venue for the Whitby Gothic Weekend. The growth of a 'steampunk' sub-culture is also reflected in events. The term steampunk was jokingly coined by K.W. Jeter, author of *Morlock Night* (1979) to describe science fiction and fantasy novels set in the Victorian era. This new trend, drawing for inspiration on Jules Verne and H.G. Wells, influences fiction, film, music and fashion.

Conflict and Gatekeepers

In a number of the above examples, we have touched upon potential conflict between the motivations and expectations of various stakeholders. To conclude this chapter, it is useful to consider this issue in some detail. Cultural heritage tourism is distinguished by high levels of dissonance. We preserve and value heritage as it has meaning, but those meanings often vary from person to person, from group to group (McKercher & du Cros, 2002; Tunbridge & Ashworth, 1996). Literary tourism is a subset of cultural heritage tourism and experiences these same disagreements and controversies.

For any author or book, there may be multiple places that could attract tourists. There is the potential for conflict as various stakeholders compete against each other, marketing their site as better, more authentic, or more iconic. On Canada's Prince Edward Island, for example, there are three heritage sites connected to Lucy Maud Montgomery and *Anne of Green Gables* (Fawcett & Cormack, 2001). In England, a number of towns claim strong connections with Lewis Carroll and *Alice's Adventures in Wonderland* (Robinson & Andersen, 2002). Tourists interested in *Dracula* have multiple sites in three countries to choose from.

The public commemoration of authors through statues, monuments or plaques involves subjective choices. Why devote resources and approval to one author and not another? This subjectivity is well illustrated in the Literary Landmarks scheme in the USA. Florida has, by far, the most Literary Landmarks. Does this signify that Florida is especially conducive to quality writing? Or is it that stakeholders in Florida are well organised and adept at having successful applications? To read the full list of Literary Landmarks is a fascinating exercise, both in terms of who has been chosen for inclusion and who is seemingly inexplicably not.

Dissonance comes to the fore where sites have other, competing meanings. This may lead to *gatekeeping*, as some stakeholders try to take charge, enforce their view and exclude others. Scotland's historic Rosslyn Chapel has long been a visitor attraction managed by the Rosslyn Chapel Trust. It perceives the building in terms of its art and history. With the success of *The Da Vinci Code*, visitor numbers have increased dramatically, with those new tourists (and tour operators) focused on the fictional mysteries in the book. The site is now characterised by contested authenticity, as different stakeholders hold different views of its true meaning. Indeed, the Trust would even like to see a large reduction in visitor numbers as part of a greater emphasis on historical interpretation (Månsson, 2010).

A similar problem occurs with tourists interested in Dracula visiting Romania. Reijnders (2011) dwelt on the disconnection between Western expectations of tourists and the Romanian tour guide's desire to contrast the historical and fictional realities. Reijnders notes that, for the guide, it was important to tell the true story of Vlad Tepes. However, few of the tourists were interested. They wanted the fictional version. Here was a strong and confronting cross-cultural clash. Some fans were upset with the guide's insistence. As one stated:

> My whole life I really thought that there were vampires out there and I needed to go find them. And now I've come here and heard that Vlad Tepes isn't ... The whole vampire theory is kind of shot ... He didn't bite anybody in the neck, he just cut their heads off. Which is still good, but it's different. (Reijnders, 2011: 93)

A final curious case of literary gatekeeping and demarketing relates to J.D. Salinger, author of *The Catcher in the Rye*. From the 1970s to his death in 2010, the reclusive Salinger lived in the small New Hampshire town of Cornish. Sympathetic locals helped him maintain his privacy. As reported in the *New York Times*:

> The curious descended on Cornish constantly, asking residents for directions to Salinger's house. Instead of finding the home, interlopers would end up on a wild goose chase. How far afield the directions went 'depended on how arrogant they were', said Mike Ackerman, owner of the Cornish General Store. Salinger, he said, 'was like the Batman icon. Everybody knew Batman existed, and everyone knew there was a batcave, but no one would tell you where it is'. (Zezima, 2010)

3 A Misspent Youth (Children's Fiction and Travel)

'Wendy, Wendy, when you are sleeping in your silly bed you might be flying
about with me saying funny things to the stars'
J.M. Barrie, *Peter Pan*, 1911

The first book we independently read as a child often sticks in our mind as something momentous, and might be potentially life-changing. For us, it was *The Adventures of Tom Sawyer* by Mark Twain (Warwick) and *The Enchanted Wood* by Enid Blyton (Jennifer). Blyton's book, with its recurring theme of children visiting magical worlds or 'dreamscapes' at the top of the Faraway Tree, planted the first seed of Jennifer's desire to travel as an adult. If the storybook children failed to leave a particular land in time, they would be stuck there forever. There was always excitement at seeing whether the children would manage to return home. The other novel aspect to the stories involved the various lands visited by the children. Benign places, such as the Land of Toys, were juxtaposed with more dangerous ones, such as the Land of Tempers (lose your temper and you are forced to stay there forever). Not all lands were fun to visit, but all were different to home and thus exotically desirable. This book was often re-read, like many children's books are, and was followed by discoveries of new favourites, including many of the works discussed in this chapter.

There is a paradox inherent in children's literature. Our recognition of its power to inspire imaginations and its enduring influence throughout our lives exists in tandem with its marginalisation as a body of literary work (Hunt, 2001). This is based, in part, on the notion that it is somehow less meritorious than works directed at adults. Even well-known children's authors such as P.L. Travers, author of *Mary Poppins*, may shy away from describing their books as aimed at children (Travers, 1975), for fear perhaps of being trivialised (Bergsten, 1978). Mark Twain, in the preface to *The*

Adventures of Tom Sawyer, notes: 'Although my book is intended mainly for the entertainment of boys and girls, I hope it will not be shunned by men and women on that account, for part of my plan has been to try to pleasantly remind adults of what they once were themselves, and of how they felt and thought and talked, and what queer enterprises they sometimes engaged in'. The tendency to refer to fairytales as naturally directed at or connected with children is also criticised by J.R.R. Tolkien, in his essay 'On Fairy Stories' in *Tree and Leaf* (1964). He observes: 'If fairy-story as a kind is worth reading at all it is worthy to be written for and read by adults' (Tolkien, 1964: 45).

This reticence to acknowledge children as a worthy branch of readership or to view them as just 'a member of the human family at large' (Tolkien, 1964: 34) undervalues the importance of embarking on the journey to becoming a life-long reader (Lowe, 2007) and the role that books read at an early age can play in our adult lives. Many of us read to our children the books we enjoyed in our youth, and receive a great deal of pleasure from re-living childhood memories in the process. These books shape us, even when we are not aware of it, and may lay the foundations of our worldview as adults. They expose us to different cultures, lifestyles, moral codes and values, thus opening our minds to the existence of 'the other'. Children's literature is dominated by themes of magical travel, adventure and escape, and the alternative worlds they offer up often provide a commentary on our own world (Hunt, 2001). They also introduce children to darker subjects and some of the less palatable sides of life, through the use of a katabatic narrative (Falconer, 2005). These tantalise and thrill readers. In many cases, they also reinforce the idea of travel as desirable and transformative.

In this chapter, we argue that the genesis of adult travel behaviour can be traced, in part, to the books we read as children, and their influence is both profound and long-lasting. We analyse the formative influence of children's books on travel, and consider the different ways that these texts may affect our mode of thinking and underpin a desire to see and experience other places, whether real or fictional.

We explore a number of themes in this chapter through seven texts that were published throughout the 20th and early 20th century, and have had, or appear likely to have, enduring appeal to a junior readership. They were all best sellers in their day (Griswold, 1992), although Twain's fiction initially did not sell as well as his travel books, such as *The Innocents Abroad* (Melton, 2002). Their legacy is, however, undeniable. Many have been turned into successful films and have entered the lexicon of popular culture, even if some of us have never read any or all of these texts. Most of us know that a 'Peter Pan' complex refers to a refusal to grow up, while characters like Tom Sawyer, Harry Potter and Gulliver have now been immortalised with their own theme park rides or attractions (Robinson & Andersen, 2002). Children's books appear destined to inspire another generation to travel, which makes the current absence of research on their link to travel even more curious. Before considering some of the travel-related themes inherent in these works, we start with a brief overview of the history of children's literature to frame the discussion.

History of Children's Literature

In this chapter, we suggest that the term 'children's literature' involves an eclectic mix of texts. We define it as an 'aggregation of texts with certain features in common, which enable them to establish meaningful transactions with child readers (and which incidentally may also enable them to do so with adults)' (Hollindale, 1997: 28). This definition acknowledges the appeal of many children's books to adults and focuses on the *texts* themselves, rather than arguing that they collectively form a genre or even a sub-genre. This makes intuitive sense to us, given we have read all of the books we use as case studies in this chapter, either as children or as adults (or sometimes both).

Our chosen definition also recognises that some of the texts we label children's literature today (*Gulliver's Travels*; *Robinson Crusoe*) were essentially written in the 18th century as satire for adults (Hunt, 2001), rather than being directed at a juvenile audience. It was really in the 19th century that the first books aimed at children were published. These can be categorised as follows.

(1) Fantasy tales (*The Water Babies*; *Alice's Adventures in Wonderland*; *The Adventures of Pinocchio*).
(2) Collections of fairytales or folklore (*Grimm's Fairy Tales*; *Perrault's Fairy Tales*; the tales of Hans Christian Andersen (i.e. *The Little Mermaid*; *The Ugly Duckling*) and Andrew Lang's *Fairy Books*.
(3) Adventure stories, often set in exotic locations (*The Jungle Book*; *Treasure Island*; *King Solomon's Mines*).
(4) More realistic tales depicting children who receive moral guidance in how to behave or undergo a journey towards self-improvement and self-knowledge (*Little Women*; *Tom Brown's Schooldays*).

The early 20th century saw some of the more celebrated children's books in print, including *The Wonderful Wizard of Oz* (1900) by L. Frank Baum, Beatrix Potter's animal fantasies, such as *The Tale of Peter Rabbit* (1902) and Grahame's

The Wind in the Willows (1908). Hunt (2001) argues that writers, scarred by their experiences in the First World War, created 'escapist worlds' – with examples including A.A. Milne's *Winnie-the Pooh* (1926) and Hugh Lofting's *The Story of Doctor Dolittle* (1920). Some fantasies included realistic elements for the upper strata of society, such as nannies (*Mary Poppins*) and servants (*Five Children and It*).

There was a growing demand for the school story, often set at boarding school, which led to Enid Blyton's *St Clare's* (1941–1945) and *Malory Towers* (1946–1951) series, the *Greyfriars School* (1947–1961) stories by Charles Hamilton, best known for the comic character Billy Bunter, and the *Chalet School* books (1925–1970) by Elinor Brent-Dyer, featuring a Swiss finishing school for girls. The *Harry Potter* series might be seen as the natural heirs to this tradition. The children leave home and enter a world that contains boundaries, and consequences for actions, yet they take part in various exploits and enjoy the opportunity to 'bend' the rules, through escapades, such as the 'midnight feast' and leaving the school grounds without permission. This is a gentle form of adventure, where risks are low, and comradeship is prized. The fear of leaving home is alleviated by a reassuringly structured environment, where teachers and fellow pupils provide social contact and cultural norms.

Another group of children's books in the mid to late 20th century focuses on children liberated from restrictive household duties or routines, and who take control over their own experiences. This might be the result of their possession of a magic device (*The Phoenix and the Carpet*; *The Magician's Nephew*); discovery of a magic portal or doorway such as a wardrobe (*The Lion, the Witch and the Wardrobe*) or a mirror (*Through the Looking Glass and What Alice Found There*); or simply possessing a boat or compass (*Swallows and Amazons*). They are often on holiday (Gilead, 1991) or have been sent to the country for health or safety reasons (epidemics, wartime) as a device to take them away from their normal 'home'. These children are not at boarding school, and thus often have time on their hands to explore different places, both in 'this' world (The *Famous Five* series) or in alternative worlds (*The Chronicles of Narnia*).

Many of these books feature maps (*Milly-Molly-Mandy*; *The Chronicles of Narnia*), which help the reader navigate through the world created by the author. Robert Louis Stevenson argued that the creator of imaginary places should start with a map (Hunt, 2001), although this does not always guarantee a sense of realism. Some children's narratives use an imaginary world merely as a space where things happen, rather than being 'a place of itself' (Hunt, 2001: 13). An example is Narnia, carefully mapped by C.S. Lewis, but often criticised for being nothing more than a 'place of ideas' rather than providing a feeling of real geographical existence. Middle Earth on the other hand, as imagined by Tolkien, is 'an historical land, meticulously conceived' (Hunt, 2001: 13) and its map gives us a sense of its solidity and great age.

The last sub-group of books we want to discuss are nonsense tales, where nothing is as it seems and the rules of this world are subverted or turned upside down. Cats talk and disappear and flamingos are used for croquet mallets (*Alice's Adventures in Wonderland*), while children romp with monsters (*Where the Wild Things Are*). The child is often forced to act as an 'adult', seeking a rational pathway through a world that is increasingly grotesque (Billone, 2004) and nightmarish. These journeys make a statement about the world in which we live, by contrasting it with the magic dreamscape. They may use satire to make a political point. Some of this is understood by the child reader, while other subtleties may go over their head but be appreciated by the adult reading the story. This is increasingly used as a device in children's films (*Shrek*, *Cars*), where 'in-jokes' are planted to amuse the adults.

We have not included some texts in this brief discourse on children's literature, based on their broad appeal across generations. We place Verne's novels in this category (*Around the World in Eighty Days*, *Twenty Thousand Leagues Under the Sea*). These texts are discussed in other chapters in this book. We only discuss *The Lord of the Rings* in a cursory way in this chapter for the same reason, but refer to it in more detail in Chapters 11 and 12. We also acknowledge that we cannot cover the full swathe of books we have collectively read, but have picked out salient examples that we feel illuminate some of the key travel-related themes found in children's literature.

The Call to Adventure

This is the first stage of the hero's journey (Campbell, 1949), where the protagonist is stirred to action (Hume, 1974). Many children's books have the word 'adventure' in the title (*Alice's Adventures in Wonderland*, *The Adventures of the Wishing Chair*), and point the way towards a tale where the protagonist is tested on a number of different fronts, not necessarily in a physical sense. Swarbrooke, *et al.* (2003: 14) observe in relation to travel: 'Adventure is a personal construct, based more on individual mental and emotional perceptions, than physical capacities'. Not all adventures are as we expect. We learn to be careful what we wish for. Alice has to deal with an increasingly bizarre dreamscape that 'torments and rejects her' and is 'driven from start to finish by women's fury' (Billone, 2004: 183). The Queen of Hearts wants to cut off her head and she witnesses the Duchess beat her baby. Alice can't even have a normal conversation with anyone and becomes increasingly exasperated at the nonsense she encounters. This is no bucolic paradise, but a nightmare, from which Alice eventually wakes. This represents Alice's 'growth out of childhood' (Billone, 2004: 178) although some argue that this occurred long before her fall down the rabbit hole, given her 'adult' reaction to the playful world in which she finds herself (Kincaid, 1992). The narrative arguably fits a katabatic structure, in that the rabbit-hole leads to a type of hell. Alice encounters guides (i.e. the White Rabbit and the Cheshire Cat), but they are often tricksters and fail to offer her a great deal of help. She returns home, older and wiser.

Adventures in children's literature might involve high danger or tragedy, rather than mere obstacles to overcome. In *Peter Pan*, one of the lost boys, Tootles, is told to be wary of adventures by the narrator – 'Take care lest an adventure is now offered you, which, if accepted, will plunge you in deepest woe'. In *The Adventures of Huckleberry Finn*, Huck finds a body in a house floating down the Mississippi River. He is acquainted with death, even though he avoids looking at the dead man's face. Harry Potter's adventures are ramped up through the series, through successive encounters with an increasingly powerful Lord Voldemort. We learn by the final book that once Harry reaches 18 years of age, he is no longer protected by the spell that the wizard Dumbledore has placed on his school, Hogwarts, to keep him safe from Voldemort's clutches. He must leave its sanctuary and defeat evil while on the run. The stakes are high – Harry finally learns that he must sacrifice himself to Voldemort to save his friends, in a Christ-like gesture that fulfils the prophesy that 'neither can live while the other survives'.

Some adventures are worth the angst, and take place amidst spectacular or poetically beautiful landscapes. *The Adventures of Tom Sawyer* is an example of travel that is motivated by the desire of Tom and his cronies for heroism, freedom and independence. Its setting, on the banks of the Mississippi, along with its companion piece, *The Adventures of Huckleberry Finn*, provide what have become enduring images of the 'great river' and the allure of the rafting journey.

The Adventures of Tom Sawyer (Mark Twain, 1876)

Tom Sawyer and his two siblings are cared for by Aunt Polly in the village of St Petersburg in Missouri, USA. Tom is a highly intelligent boy who is frustrated at his Aunt's attempts to discipline him. He dreams of escape, and takes a raft down the river, which he describes as 'just the life for me ... You don't have to get up, mornings, and you don't have to go to school, and wash, and all that blame foolishness'. The boys describe themselves as 'outlaws' and 'pirates', but have their own rigorous code of ethics, including looking after women and keeping each other's secrets. In Tom's and Huck

Finn's case, this prevents them from revealing the true facts behind the murder they witnessed one night, for fear of putting each other's lives at risk. Tom eventually unmasks the murderer, Injun Joe, in court, owing to a fear that an innocent man will pay for the crime. His devil-may-care exterior belies a strong moral core.

The river journey is portrayed as idyllic, a reverie without restrictions and pressures: 'It seemed glorious sport to be feasting in that wild free way in the virgin forest of an unexplored and uninhabited island, far from the haunts of men, and they said they would never return to civilization'. Eventually the boys succumb to homesickness, and gatecrash their own funeral, becoming heroes to their peers.

The denouement of the book involves a second adventure, when Tom and his sweetheart, Becky Thatcher, get left behind in a cave after a picnic excursion and are feared dead. The use of a cave is perhaps a hint at the use of a katabatic narrative. The pair eventually find their way home after Tom's serendipitous discovery of an exit, and take some time to recover their strength and health. The children were not alone in the cave – Injun Joe was hiding out with his stolen loot – and the decision of the town's mayor to block up the entrance to avoid further mishap leads to Injun Joe's death by starvation. When Tom hears the news after his recovery, he plans to revisit the cave with Huck Finn to recover the money Injun Joe had taken. The boys are now rich, a boon or prize from their travels, and Huck is taken in by Widow Douglas 'which introduced him into society ... the bars and shackles of civilization shut him in and bound him hand and foot'. Becky's father now considers Tom fit to court his daughter, as he has displayed courage, both physically and morally. Tom is transformed, which is the final stage of the katabasis. The sojourner is restored to everyday life, but is now aware of what else lies beyond their front gate. The next adventure beckons, to be continued in *The Adventures of Huckleberry Finn*.

Running Away – Flight and Pursuit

The motif of the wanderer (Vogel, 1974) or 'runaway' (Adams, 1983) is exemplified by *The Adventures of Huckleberry Finn* and *Peter Pan*, with the latter taking this to the ultimate conclusion – the boy who could never 'grow up'. These children are running away from something or someone, which Vogel (1974: 152) labels 'some kind of rejection'. Wandering is one of six forms of narrative movement identified by Vogel (1974). He notes that while it appears aimless, there is a purpose in a form of a hidden mission that the reader ultimately comes to appreciate.

These journeys take the children far from home, and may involve the realisation that one cannot escape from oneself or keep adulthood at bay forever. There may also be a form of transformation, as they make choices about their future and understand the consequences of their actions on others. Tom Sawyer learns how his flight down-river has hurt his aunt, who believes him to have drowned, and that his childish prank of 'crashing his own funeral' was cruel rather than comical. In *Harry Potter and the Deathly Hallows*, Harry Potter must leave his beloved school to track down horcruxes, pieces of Lord Voldemort's soul that must be destroyed in order to defeat his nemesis and thus prevent the triumph of evil in the world. Harry is on the run, with only his friends Ron and Hermione to help him, and displays courage when all hope seems lost, and self-sacrifice to save those whom he loves. These children may also be categorised as the *ingénu* – which Adams (1983: 276) labels 'a necessary character in both fiction and travels'. This is the naïve innocent, who 'nearly always grows in some important way'.

Freedom and Escape

In the following case study, we analyse *Peter Pan* in terms of its travel themes, while recognising that the book can also be understood in a psychological (particularly Freudian) sense as redolent of sexuality, which has been dealt with in a number of other studies (Hollindale, 1993, 2005). Clearly, some of the fascination with this book lies in its Oedipal motifs (Egan, 1982; Rose, 1994). It can also be conceptualised as fetishising travel as a way of escaping restrictions, rules and responsibilities. Robertson (2001: 198) notes that this is often the reality of children's lives and refers to the seemingly incompatible issues of control and powerlessness: 'being dependent on others for survival; having no say in the matter of having to grow up to responsibility and independence'. Like many travellers, freedom is simultaneously sought after and feared by the children in *Peter Pan*, and escape is seen both as a physical and emotional phenomenon (Laing & Crouch, 2005).

The metaphor of a Peter Pan figure has been applied to some modern travellers, who seek youthful pleasures (Loker-Murphy & Pearce, 1995). It has also been argued that young people on their gap years, backpacking around the world, are seeking to extend childhood and thus delay the transition to adulthood, characterised by jobs, mortgages and committed relationships (Maoz, 2004; Richards & Wilson, 2006). Travel might, therefore, be understood as a vehicle for suspending the passage of time and entering a liminal space; which is part of the hero's journey and the pilgrimage. Selänniemi (2003: 24) observes that the word *liminality* literally means 'threshold' in Latin – 'you are neither here nor there'. This may give the traveller the licence to do things that are dangerous, even subversive.

Peter Pan (J.M. Barrie, 1911)

This book was originally a story within a story aimed at adults. In *The Little White Bird* by J.M. Barrie, a boy is told the story of Peter Pan (Rose, 1994). It later became a stage play, again not necessarily aimed at children, and finally a book. This is pertinent because the book symbolises 'the problem of the relationship between adult and child' (Rose, 1994: 5), which starts with its very origins. Figure 3.1 depicts the statue of Peter Pan in Kensington Gardens, which attracts visitors of all ages, still fascinated with this strange tale of yearning and flight from the everyday (Figure 3.1).

Peter Pan enters the window of the Darling children's nursery (the threshold) and 'lures' them away to the magical island of Neverland, in a chapter headed 'Come Away, Come Away'. This is travel as a source of temptation, something desirable, even irresistible. Wendy is described as a 'stay at home'. Peter on the other hand is the exotic 'other' and she cannot resist his

Figure 3.1 Peter Pan statue in Kensington Gardens. Photo by J. Laing.

invitation. The children choose to venture into the unknown, even though they realise this could be dangerous. There are echoes of the legend of the children enticed away from the town of Hamelin by the Pied Piper. Even the name Neverland connotes something perilous or slightly subversive. Wendy feels a sense of power over Peter because she feels she knows more about the 'real' world than he does. For example, she is surprised that he doesn't know what a kiss is. However, she doesn't understand his world, until she visits Neverland. In this sense, Wendy can be likened to a tourist encountering another culture and having to realise how little she actually knows about their lives and customs, learning humility in the process.

Peter becomes the children's guide – they call him their 'captain'. At one point during the children's flight to Neverland, he leaves them, and they are frightened that they will not be able to find their way home. They are help-less without their guide. The children have encountered Neverland in their dreams, but it is now threatening for them when fantasy becomes reality: 'Thus sharply did the terrified three learn the difference between an island of make-believe and the same island come true'. The dream of travel is some-times enough whereas 'the real thing' can be confronting. Some people prefer being armchair travellers, and desire the comfort of home over the fear of the unknown. The children start to regret their hasty decision to leave home: 'In the old days at home the Neverland had always begun to look a little dark and threatening by bedtime ... it was real now, and there were no night-lights, and it was getting darker every moment, and where was Nana?'

Visitors are not welcome in Neverland ('They don't want us to land' says Peter, but as Wendy notes, 'Who are *they*?'). The island is not a benign paradise – it is full of dangers, both visible and invisible. Who are those who do not wish them to land? Groups track and later attack each other. It involves the stuff of childhood – pirates, Indian tribes, mermaids – but these things can leave a child vulnerable. Even the mermaids fail to help them in times of danger and we are told of their 'mocking laughter'. There is a con-stant motif of Wendy falling and dying. Tinker Bell is not the sweet fairy of most children's stories and the Disney film. She is jealous, vindictive and heartless when it comes to anyone but Peter. Neverland is thus a 'realm of death' (Nikolajeva, 2000: 72), one of the stages of the katabasis and a para-dox, given the children seek to escape 'growing old'. There are a number of references to 'caves' in the narrative, as fearsome places, and even Hook's mind is described as having 'subterranean caverns'.

Interestingly, Neverland is often used in modern popular culture as a term for a light-hearted dream world (see e.g. the lyrics of the 1981 J Geils Band hit 'Centerfold', which warns the besotted man: 'This ain't no Never-Never land'). Michael Jackson famously called his Californian theme park ranch 'Neverland', which Cirque du Soleil plans to recreate in Las Vegas in homage to the late singer. This misses the point of Neverland's seductive riskiness.

Wendy thinks of her life back home with fondness and we are told that she is 'absolutely confident that [her father and mother] would always keep the window open for her to fly back by, and this gave her complete ease of mind'. The traveller needs to know that home is still there and they will be eventually welcomed back home again. The children however, make plans to return, for fear that their parents will not keep the window open. Unlike Peter, they are not scared to lose their innocence and grow old, but they do dread losing a haven to retreat to: 'Off we skip like the most heartless things in the world … and then when we have need of special attention we nobly return for it'. This suggests that the traveller has to be selfish to 'leave home' and perhaps acknowledges that we are often in a state of conflict when we travel – trading home for adventure and leaving loved ones behind, or venturing to places where they can't follow. Peter on the other hand, is 'full of wrath against grown-ups, who as usual, were spoiling everything'. He will be 'forever barred' from the joy of home and hearth, which Wendy labels 'tragic'. He is the sacrificial victim. Tinkerbell is the second one. She dies in Peter's stead, taking the poison that Captain Hook had intended for him.

The return home for the children brings with it some readjustments, which fits the katabatic structure. They find it hard to remember 'the old life' and their father, says Michael, is not 'so big as the pirate I killed'. The traveller is sometimes disappointed when they return home – things are not as one remembered them during the journey. Travellers can romanticise about home, and the familiar routines may sometimes appear dull or commonplace after the excitement of being away. In time, the children cease thinking about Neverland – 'they no longer believed', which reflects the failure of memory. Not all travel experiences are unforgettable. Stories about travel however, often get passed on, in this case from parent to child. Wendy tells her daughter Jane about Neverland, and Jane eventually tells her daughter Margaret about it when she is herself a grown-up. The greatest transformation for the children is their acceptance of adulthood. Peter on the other hand is trapped in an 'eternal present', forced to go on reliving his story in an endless cycle.

The Childhood Quest

Quests are also a dominant theme in children's books. They sometimes involve finding something or someone, or returning something or someone to their rightful owner or domain, being two of the seven types of quests identified by Adams (1983). Most of the books discussed in this chapter fall into these categories. Another example is the spiritual quest, exemplified by *The Chronicles of Narnia*.

The Chronicles of Narnia (C.S. Lewis, 1949–1954)

The seven Narnia books collectively tell the story of the creation and end of the world of Narnia, an allegory of the Christian story that Lewis intended to precondition children to the Christian message. Their mythic dimensions, however, reflect common themes in children's literature. Lucy, Edmund and Eustace join Prince Caspian on the *Voyage of the Dawn Treader*, to find the seven lost lords, while Eustace and his friend Jill must seek out Prince Rilian in *The Silver Chair*. The children often come close to renouncing their quest, but ultimately remain true to their cause and persevere in the face of the 'easy option'. Their journey has heroic dimensions, in that it involves hardship and long periods of travel through harsh conditions. Apart from the land of Narnia and its adjoining countries, such as Archenland and Calormen, one character reaches the end of the world, while another civilisation is viewed under the water in *The Voyage of the Dawn Treader*. In *The Silver Chair*, Eustace and Jill visit an underground world, which Osborn (2001: 116) labels a 'spiritual proving-ground'. This is a type of katabatic hell. There are worlds within worlds; parallels of Verne's *Journey to the Centre of the Earth* (1864). The final book, *The Last Battle*, ends with the children defeating evil and entering Aslan's country. They have been reborn at the end of time itself.

Visiting Narnia from 'our world' occurs in different ways, which Hume (1974: 136) refers to as the 'threshold'. The four Pevensie children step through the wardrobe in *The Lion, the Witch and the Wardrobe*, and are summoned to Narnia from a train station on the way to school in *Prince Caspian*. Lucy, Edmund and Eustace enter a painting of a ship (The Dawn Treader) that comes to life. In *The Magician's Nephew*, Polly and Digory use magic rings and find themselves in the 'Wood between the Worlds', a series of pools that form a type of departure point to various places, including Narnia. Some of this travel is thus exploratory, like the children finding the wardrobe, and may involve making choices, like the pools in the Wood between the Worlds. Some of the pools lead to dangerous places, which the children discover. They don't have enough information, and must choose at random and hope for the best. In Narnia, they find a world that delights, but which they must fight for and ultimately die for.

The books have been criticised for mixing the Christian message with pagan and fantastical elements (Hunt, 2001) or being too ideological (Lowe, 2007). Nevertheless, the 'alternative world' Lewis created remains popular with readers (Hunt, 2001) and can be read for its folkloric elements (Sutherland & Arbuthnot, 1991) without making any connection with Christianity. We both enjoyed them as children, but never saw them other than pure fantasy. We can sometimes forget that children may read books differently to adults and take away different messages from them. That is part of the pleasure of re-reading children's books as an adult – you see them both as you did and as you now do – and the contrast can be staggering.

Strange Places and Encountering the Other

Another strong motif in children's books involves fantasy settings – places outside our known world. They may illuminate our understanding of our own world or simply show us a dreamscape, replete with enchantment and beauty. One of the songs in the musical *Mary Poppins* is titled 'It's a Jolly Holiday with Mary'. In fact, Mary Poppins is never a 'jolly' character in the book on which the musical was based. She is snappish, orderly and vain about her appearance. The holiday reference is however apt. She provides the opportunity for her charges to travel to strange places, usually via magic, and not surprisingly they find this exhilarating. Interactions with others may be challenging to the storybook children – some may not involve human beings, such as meetings with talking animals (*Chronicles of Narnia*), or mythical beings, such as giants, trolls, fairies or elves (*Harry Potter, The Magic Faraway Tree, Five Children and It*). These encounters may disturb the carefully constructed worldview of the children, and are often confronting or unsettling. They are akin to the tourist out of their comfort zone. The children learn, over time, to deal with the 'other', and in the process learn something about themselves.

Mary Poppins (P.L. Travers, 1934)

The Banks children live in the 'smallest house in the Lane' and endure a high turnover of nannies before Mary Poppins enters their lives. One of the grandest houses on the Lane is built like a ship and belongs to Admiral Boom. This seems to represent the lure of exotic places beyond the genteel comfort of Cherry Tree Lane. Mary Poppins arrives one windy night literally as if she has been blown in from another world, complete with a bang at the front door. They find her 'strange and extraordinary' – she is somewhat disquieting as one never knows what she will do next or where one will go. She merely says that she will leave when the wind changes. There is, therefore, a sense that these escapades have a finite time and, like all good travel experiences, leave the recipients wanting more.

Mary takes the children on a series of adventures, usually with very little explanation or warning. They need to make sense of what is happening to them through the use of their eyes and ears, rather than being told what they are to experience. There is no guidebook or guide to help them, other than their trust in Mary. Mary is the 'threshold guardian', who safeguards the entrance into the unknown (Campbell, 1949). Leaving the nursery is akin to crossing the threshold, which Campbell (1949) refers to as an important stage of the hero's journey.

They find a magic compass, which takes them 'round the world', to the four points of the globe. Their encounters with the 'other', including an Eskimo and an Indian chief, are unsettling, but wonderful to children used to a traditional life in inner London. The return home sees them tucked up in bed, in the comfort of fire light. Travel is seen as breath taking and mind altering, but it also makes the traveller appreciate the delights of home and hearth.

Even travel to the London sights takes on a magical quality. They visit St Paul's Cathedral to see the old woman feed the birds for 'tuppence a bag' and find out that their nanny can converse with them. They visit London Zoo, after an idle comment by Michael: 'I wonder what happens in the Zoo at night, when everybody's gone home?' The animals become the keepers, and sell the tickets. Eight monkeys ride on the back of an old gentleman at the Elephant Stand. The cages are full of human beings who had been left inside when the gates have closed. The old order is subverted and Jane refers to the evening as 'topsy-turvy'. She questions why the animals are dancing with each other, in friendship rather than enmity, and is told by a snake: 'We are all made of the same stuff, remember, we of the Jungle, you of the City'. The children learn that while travel shows us different people, with different customs, traditions and lifestyles, it also has the capacity to reveal things that are common across geographical and cultural divides and take away our fears of 'the other'. Returning involves crossing the threshold again, and reintegrating into life back home. The comforts of bed are manifest, but the children long for another adventure.

Nature is understood as mystical and awe-inspiring. The children often gaze on it at night, when they are supposed to be in bed. One night, they are privy to the sight of stars being painted on the sky by Mary Poppins, which she refuses to acknowledge the next day. Through their window, they see the final act of the wind taking Mary Poppins back to where she came from. Her note to them reads 'au revoir', which they find out means 'To meet again'. They take comfort from this, as they know that she always 'does what she says she will'. The promise of travel in the future is thus something to be looked forward to and cherished, along with the memories of journeys past.

The Magical Guide

Not all children's books involve a guide. In many cases, the children are left to their own devices and must find their way independently. Where there is a guide, it might be a magical being, even if outwardly they look ordinary. In the case of the nanny Mary Poppins, she is an 'eccentric intermediary' (Hunt, 2001: 19) who defies the conventions of this world and has become a mythical being or fantasy figure to the children she looks after. This person may offer assistance to the children on their travels. Hume (1974) notes that this is a hallmark of the hero's journey, where some sort of aid is proffered, sometimes from a magical source. In *The Lord of the Rings*, the Fellowship is given magical gifts from the elf Galadriel, such as a vial that would light up 'dark places', which Frodo uses to stop the advances of the spider Shelob.

The guide sometimes fulfils the role of a moral centre or 'compass', leading by example. This character might prompt children to think about things in a deeper way or prod their consciences. Mary Poppins offers moral guidance, using magic 'for punishment of moral lapses'. This didacticism is a feature of many classic children's writing (Griswold, 1992; Stewig, 1980). The children's book was used to instil a value system, even at a subconscious level. The books of Edith Nesbit often concern the dangers associated with satiating desire (Gilead, 1991). These moral lessons are told with humour, but their message is unambiguous.

Five Children and It (E. Nesbit, 1902)

This book starts with the typical convention of children's books – moving away from the known to the unknown. The five Bastable children, Robert, Anthea, Jane, Cyril and the baby (always referred to as the Lamb), are travelling to the English countryside, which leads to the 'first glorious rush around the garden' and the realisation that 'the house was deep in the country, with no other house in sight'. This is contrasted with two years in London 'without so much as once going to the seaside even for a day by an excursion train'. The prosaic takes on a romantic hue here for the children. The industrial buildings associated with the local quarry and lime kilns resemble 'an enchanted city out of the *Arabian Nights*' when the chimneys are smoking, and the country house is likened to 'a sort of Fairy Palace set down in an Earthly Paradise'. It even comes complete with its own sand fairy – It – who lies buried in the gravel pits until disturbed by the children. It grants them a wish a day, and has the foresight to arrange things so that the adults in the house (mostly servants) are not aware of anything strange going on.

Their first wishes are superficial – to be as 'beautiful as the day' and to possess golden guineas – and invariably turn out differently to the way they were originally envisaged. Being beautiful leads the girls not to be recognised by their baby brother, while the magical money is not accepted by the town's shopkeepers, who cannot believe the children could possess by honest means such ancient and valuable coinage. The sand fairy says that it will not give them advice, but notes that they should 'think before you speak' and approves of 'good solid everyday gifts'. Their wish to have wings to fly with appears to be more acceptable because it is less shallow than wanting good looks or wealth. The children fly over Rochester and Maidstone, which feels like 'looking at a beautiful live map, where, instead of silly colours on paper, you can have real moving sunny woods and green fields laid out one after the other ... It was most wonderful and more like real magic than any wish the children had had yet'. This was written in the days before air flight, when the thought of drifting 'between green earth and blue sky' was almost beyond comprehension for most people.

The children's final wish is the most altruistic. Their parents are returning home and they decide against wishing for a pony each: 'For everyone saw quite plainly that the wish for the day must be something to please mother and not to please themselves'. Their guide never travels with them, but shapes their characters through its responses to their different types of wishes and teaches them lessons about the true value of things.

Risk and Reward – The Allure of Danger

Many of these journeys thus involve dangers and temptations, in a form of initiation ('the Road of Trials') that reflects the middle stage of the hero's journey (Adams, 1983; Campbell, 1949; Hume, 1974). Belk (1992) refers to hardship during a journey that can 'transform' a person, and make them worthy of the challenges they face, as well as preparing them for reincorporation back into their home community (*liminal rites* or *rites of transition*). The dangers may enrich the experience and add to the sense of adventure. They are thus seductive, as well as repellent to the children in *The Magic Faraway Tree*, which mimics the way that many tourists embrace risky pursuits, particularly in an adventure context (Ewert, 1989; Ryan, 2003).

The Magic Faraway Tree (Enid Blyton, 1943)

The sequel to *The Enchanted Wood*, this book continues the story of Jo, Bessie and Fanny, three siblings, and their cousin Dick, who live close to a magical forest. The Faraway Tree is the focus of the adventures, with its top poking through the clouds and visited by a series of worlds or 'lands', which change constantly. The protagonists risk being left behind when the land at the top moves on, signalled by the blowing of a strange wind. They also experience magical events, such as the spell cast on Jo in the Land of Topsy-Turvy that makes him walk on his hands. Dick finds this new world exhilarating, despite the risks that it brings. The delights of the world visited and curiosity to see something new and exciting is accompanied, in some of the children, by the fear that one will remain trapped in another place 'forever'. Jo says to his cousin: 'We have to be very careful sometimes because there might be a very dangerous land – one that we couldn't get away from!' He eventually decides 'No more adventures for *me*!' Of course they succumb to temptation, and end up in the Land of Dreams, fighting to stay awake and needing to be rescued by their magical friends, elves and pixies. The lure of discovery is too great and outweighs their apprehension of the risks involved.

Like *Five Children and It*, there is often a moral message behind the magic. In the Land of Magic Medicines, they seek out a remedy for their sick mother, while the Land of Presents has a caveat – one can only get a gift to give to another person. They are told: 'This isn't a selfish land at all'. Some risks are seen as worth taking, but only for the right reasons.

Transformation: Self-Knowledge and Self-Acceptance

Children in books are often portrayed as outsiders – orphans like Oliver Twist, or mistreated by their extended families like Harry Potter. The child in fiction often journeys to a new family or life, which Griswold (1992: 11) refers to as a 'second birth' – the separation from one's parents and the going out into the wider world. They may also suffer the burden of being different than those around them. Tom Sawyer and Huckleberry Finn seek to escape from being made to conform to societal expectations and restrictions. This might be characterised as a quest to find 'knowledge or wisdom' (Adams, 1983) or the grace to accept ourselves as we are. Peter Pan can never overcome the burden of being different – he will always be the outsider looking in at the nursery window, while the children he observes and whose dreams he haunts grow up and have their own families. Harry Potter, after a long struggle, accepts his mantle of greatness – he is the Chosen One and his destiny is to kill Lord Voldemort. Hume (1974: 129) refers to transformation as an element of an 'archetypal romance pattern'. It is a higher state of being, where the ego is 'able to subordinate selfish concerns to the good of mankind as a whole'

(Hume, 1974: 132). It is also the final stage in the katabasis, where the hero is changed by their experiences.

These themes are not limited to children's literature but can provide a useful lens for analysing what appears to be a 'basic theme of our civilisation' MacCannell (1999: 5), which he characterises as the search for 'an absolute other'. Self-actualisation has been identified as a travel motivation (Crompton, 1979; Pearce & Lee, 2005) and is linked to a variety of tourism contexts, including adventure tourism (Walle, 1997; Weber, 2001), film-induced tourism (Frost, 2010a) and volunteer tourism (Wearing, 2002). Bruner (1991: 246) has examined the potential for tourism to transform the 'self', which he argues may be exaggerated in many encounters. Instead, the tourist simply 'confirms his or her view of the world and validates his or her social position in it'. Many books challenge this viewpoint, although it might be the case that these experiences are rare, rather than commonplace. We discuss the link between literature and transformative travel in more depth in Chapter 11.

Harry Potter (J.K. Rowling, 1997–2007)

The seven books that make up the Harry Potter series, beginning with *Harry Potter and the Philosopher's Stone* (1997) and culminating in *Harry Potter and the Deathly Hallows* (2007) were a global phenomenon. They attracted praise for the carefully crafted wizarding 'world', which is arguably edgy in its themes of racial and cultural prejudice and social injustice (Waetjen & Gibson, 2007), and their role in making reading 'cool again' for a young audience. At the same time, they were condemned for being sexist, with women having 'little power in Harry's world' (Billone, 2004: 179) or described as 'formulaic' and market driven (Zipes, 2001). It is impossible to ignore their influence however on popular culture. Collections of Harry Potter memorabilia are a popular tourist attraction (Figure 3.2).

Harry is an orphan, living with his relatives, the Dursleys, in a small village in Surrey evocatively named Little Whinging. He is treated as a menial, living in the cupboard under the stairs, and kept ignorant that his parents were a wizard and a witch. Harry was left there when he was a baby to keep him safe from the clutches of Lord Voldemort, who had killed his parents and left Harry with a strange scar on his forehead in the shape of a lightning bolt. Harry is 'marked' as something special, even if he is unaware of it. His uncle and aunt know about his magical origins (they are ordinary people – Muggles – and proud of it), but prefer to hide this secret ('their greatest fear was that somebody would discover it'). When Harry visits the zoo, he finds out that he has a magical gift – he can talk to snakes. Phipps (2003) uses this example to discuss the way that speaking a foreign language can have an impact upon

Figure 3.2 Props from the *Harry Potter* films displayed at the London Film Museum. Photo by W. Frost.

one's identity and influence our relationships with others. Harry is ostracised at school for this gift, which is seen as evidence of alignment with 'outsiders'; such as Voldemort. The desire to know one's place in the world is often relevant to a traveller in foreign territory. Phipps (2003: 12) labels these places 'boundaries ... sites where status, character, position and self change'. Harry is about to find this out, when he is accepted as a student at Hogwarts School of Witchcraft and Wizardry. His transformation is about to begin.

Despite his relatives' efforts to keep the news from him, Harry eventually makes the journey, by train from King's Cross Station (Platform 9¾), to his new school. The train journey and departure point is a nod to the fact that J.K. Rowling's parents met on a train travelling to Scotland from King's Cross Station and she came up with the Harry Potter concept while delayed for four hours on a train. The 'hyper-reality' of the platform number (Robertson, 2001) has been immortalised at the real King's Cross Station in London (Iwashita, 2006); an example of the tourism industry trying to make part of a literary 'shadow world' (Behr, 2005) tangible. Another way of doing this is the theme park attraction, with Universal Studios creating a replica train at the entrance to the *Wizarding World of Harry Potter*, but interestingly not the station, which is seen as 'elsewhere' (London). The train trip for Harry is a threshold, which marks his transition from the Muggle world to the magical world, and often involves important plot drivers, such as meeting new teachers or his first encounter with the Dementors – creatures that literally suck a person's soul from their bodies. The Hogwarts train station used in the Harry Potter films is located at Goathland in Yorkshire, previously a drawcard for tourists wishing to see the location of the *Heartbeat* television series (Mordue, 2001).

School is a refuge from Harry's dysfunctional family life and for the first time he feels that he belongs somewhere (Robertson, 2001). He will find out that this is illusory, and these feelings of security are threatened by his growing knowledge, both of himself and the world around him. As Harry matures in each year at school, he finds out more about his strange link with Lord Voldemort. The books become progressively darker and his travels become a katabasis as he 'moves gradually into a nightmare universe' (Billone, 2004: 192). Harry's scar created a form of bond with Voldemort, which allows Harry to literally see into his mind. Harry struggles to understand his growing powers as a wizard and what he must do to defeat evil. He must abandon childhood and a dreamworld for a terrible reality – that he will have to sacrifice himself in order to finally destroy Voldemort.

The katabatic structure can be seen particularly vividly in *Harry Potter and the Half-Blood Prince*. Harry and his headmaster, Professor Dumbledore, visit a cave by the sea. Harry's task is to find the various pieces of Voldemort's soul that the latter has hidden in various objects (known as horcruxes). Harry and Dumbledore are on the hunt for one of the horcruxes, which was believed to be a magic locket, hidden in the cave. Dumbledore is Harry's guide, as he knows about the cave and its association with Voldemort as a young boy. According to Behr (2005: 1118) 'Dumbledore is an archetype of the Wise Wizard, not just to Harry but to the wizarding world as a whole'. The locket is surrounded by a lake in which *Inferi*, or bewitched dead bodies, are lurking, waiting to attack anyone who tries to steal it. The locket is held in a basin filled with water and protected by a spell, which requires a willing victim (Dumbledore) to drink the water, causing him terrible pain and weakening him. He is eventually killed in a fight with Voldemort's henchmen back at the castle. In this way, Dumbledore sacrifices himself to aid Harry's quest. Harry must now continue the work Dumbledore began and destroy Voldemort on his own. He is transformed from a child to an adult.

Harry's final year at school is spent on the run. Once he has turned 18, the spell that was cast on Hogwarts School is broken. He must leave the safety of schooldays forever. He thus crosses a second threshold. His dilemma is that he does not know how many parts of Voldemort's soul are in existence and when he finds them, he is not sure how they can be destroyed.

Not even Voldemort is aware of the number of pieces his soul has been divided into. The twist in the book is that Harry himself is the final horcrux, created when Voldemort tried to kill him as a baby. Harry and his friends, Hermione and Ron, travel ('apparate') from place to place, trying to stay one step ahead of Voldemort and his followers. Hermione takes them at one stage to a place in the Forest of Dean, where she stayed on a family camping holiday years ago. This place represents safety and security to Hermione in a world turned nightmare.

In the final part of *Harry Potter and the Deathly Hallows*, Harry is killed and enters a strange limbo world, which looks like King's Cross station room, where Dumbledore gives him the choice to return and help to save his friends. Harry is 'reborn' and Voldemort is defeated. The katabasis ends with the triumph of the hero after many trials and sacrifices.

Robertson (2001) argues that Harry's quest focuses on identity – both his origins and his future. The books slowly reveal a succession of secrets to Harry, which help him to comprehend what he needs to do, and why he needs to do it. His character's transformation is accompanied by a narrative transformation (Behr, 2005: 113), where 'the story changes' and 'clues or references ... are only appreciated in the light of later events'. The rat, Scabbers, acquired by Ron in *Harry Potter and the Philosopher's Stone* turns out to be Harry's father's schoolfriend Peter Pettigrew or 'Wormtail' in disguise, a fact only revealed in a later book. The levity of the earlier books gradually changes to the darker narrative of the last few books, which trace Harry's journey from moody adolescent to a flawed but ultimately heroic character. Harry has the potential to become like Lord Voldemort, and must 'recognize, acknowledge and control the darker elements within himself' (Behr, 2005: 116). The books confirm that human beings are complex – neither wholly good nor wholly bad – but that we have choices in terms of the side of use we wish to hold sway. This is illustrated by Headmaster Dumbledore's comment to Harry – 'It is our choices Harry that show what we truly are, far more than our abilities'. Rowling has also transformed the school story (Behr, 2005), into a far darker mythic tale of a journey into and discovery of the self.

Returning Home

The final stage of the hero myth (Campbell, 1949) is the return, which is a powerful theme in children's books. Gilead (1991: 271) characterises it as the 'return-to-reality closure ... the adventurers return home, the dreamer awakens, or the magical beings depart'. All fantasies must end, but often in very different ways (Gilead, 1991). It also marks the end of the katabasis (Falconer, 2005).

The first example of the return home is one which 'makes reality tolerable' (Gilead, 1991: 279). The child has grown and matured and no longer yearns for a dreamworld. Dorothy is happy to return to Kansas and Harry Potter has defeated evil in the form of Lord Voldemort. The second type of closure in children's literature involves viewing the fantasy as an 'idyll' rather than a confronting experience. Gilead uses the example of *Alice's Adventures in Wonderland*, where Alice's sister dismisses her story as just 'a curious dream'. In these kinds of stories, the children are happy to return to familiar places – the ordinary becomes desirable. The third type of return is seen as tragic, as there is a sense of loss accompanying the homecoming. In *Peter Pan*, Wendy and the Lost Boys can't face remaining in Neverland and seek the comforts of the nursery and the arms of their parents. This leaves Peter to seek a new generation of children to tell him stories, in an endless cycle of denial of death (Gilead, 1991). In *Mary Poppins*, the children wait for Mary's return, so that fantasy can come back into their lives. Mary compensates for their unimaginative and selfish parents (Grilli, 2007), who cannot give the Banks children the same sense of magic.

Many children in books ache for a home of their own, and it may be a catalyst for a journey. Harry Potter is obsessed with the idea of having a home – the Dursley house where he lived until the age of ten and returns to during school holidays is no substitute for a loving environment. He ultimately gets a sense of home from his magical school Hogwarts, and eventually creates his own family when he marries Ginny Weasley in the final book of the series. In order to secure this future for himself and others, he has to confront and kill Lord Voldemort, which sets up much of the tense narrative in *The Deathly Hallows*. Harry is not just fighting for home and hearth, but those of others. He believes he will have to die in order to fulfil this goal, but ultimately triumphs over death and achieves his dream of a happy family. His journey is complete.

Some children reject 'the other', and pine for home. Tom Sawyer and his friends experience homesickness while running away, even when home life is not ideal in Tom's case, with an over-attentive aunt and differing expectations of how he should behave. The familiar wins out over the unknown. Susan, one of the Pevensie children, rejects Narnia, and we are told that she prefers 'nylons and lipstick and invitations'. This is an allegory for rejecting God over Mammon. The other children leave Narnia reluctantly but ultimately return in *The Last Battle*. We are told that they have entered Aslan's country and thus are now in a perfect world.

The concept of what is regarded as 'home' thus varies across literature. Watkins (1992: 184) distinguishes three different types. The first is a form of 'interior space', which compensates or allows for things that have no room in the real world. It is an internal construct. Harry Potter creates a notion of home in his imagination and it sustains him until he can create the real thing for himself. The second is the image we have of our 'homeland'. This is a cultural construct. Sometimes the homeland is imaginary and helps to 'sustain myths of national identity, community and common heritage' (Watkins, 1992: 184). The Shire in *Lord of the Rings* might fall into this category – it is a fantasy of rural England as it used to be before being spoilt by progress and modernity. Children's books that help to build images of a homeland include the *Swallows and Amazons* series, set in the Lakes District, or *Tom Sawyer* and *Huckleberry Finn*, set on the Mississippi River. The third concept of 'home' creates a fantasy of what it *could* be – or more precisely, the pinnacle that it is able to attain; a form of utopia. This is also a cultural construct. In the end, many of us want to imagine there truly is 'no place like home'.

4   Murder They Wrote

'Somehow one didn't expect that kind of thing in the placid backwater of
Lymstock'
The Moving Finger, A. Christie, 1943

The genesis of the crime novel is subject to dispute. Some, such as T.S. Eliot, have argued that Wilkie Collins and his opium-soaked *The Moonstone* (1868) take the honours. Others contend that it began with the Newgate Calendar series of stories in the 18th century and Defoe's *Moll Flanders* (1722). Crime fiction is a twist on the fascination held for the 'great rogues' in fiction, including Dick Turpin and Captain Kidd (Knight, 2004). The pick-pocket or the procurer lurks in the background of many popular novels of the 18th and 19th centuries (Knight, 2004). Dickens' works expose the Victorian criminal justice system, but crime is generally incidental to the main storyline, and used to highlight the need for social reforms. Later on, the criminal becomes the prime focus of the novel, and attention shifts to the person who brings them to justice. This takes many forms, ranging from a masked avenger in *The Scarlet Pimpernel* (1905) to the tracker in Fenimore Cooper's *Last of the Mohicans* (1826). There is broad agreement however, that Arthur Conan Doyle's creation of Sherlock Holmes remains the best-loved fictional detective in history. He was the first of the recurring fictional sleuths (Alter, 2011); a trend that is followed in modern detective series, such as the Inspector Wexford novels of Ruth Rendell and Colin Dextor's Inspector Morse. Beginning with *A Study in Scarlet* (1887), readers devoured stories of the ingenious ways in which Holmes solved various mysteries presented to him.

Sherlock Holmes: The Urban *Flaneur*

Place or location is very important in the Sherlock Holmes stories, as it helps to evoke an atmosphere of tension and is often integral to the narrative (Schmid, 1995). Hardyment (2000: 211) notes that the most memorable crime novels are those with 'vivid settings, as well as vital characters'. Conan Doyle provides many descriptions of turn-of-the-century London wreathed in fog, with gas-lamps dimly penetrating the gloom, which still colour our perception of the city to this day. In *The Sign of Four*, Conan Doyle writes:

> It was a September evening and not yet seven o'clock, but the day had been a dreary one, and a dense drizzly fog lay low upon the great city. Mud-coloured clouds drooped sadly over the muddy streets. Down the Strand the lamps were but misty splotches of diffused light which threw a feeble circular glimmer upon the slimy pavement. The yellow glare from the shop-windows streamed out into the steamy, vaporous air and threw a murky, shifting radiance across the crowded thoroughfare.

This is a London tinged with the infamy of the Jack the Ripper murders in the East End, where the veneer of civilisation masks a notorious underbelly of crime. As Margaret Harkness revealed, there is an unexplored jungle *In Darkest London* (1889). The Ripper murders led to an interest in more lurid detail in crime fiction – 'in the grisly and the sensational' (Knight, 2004: 64). The Sherlock Holmes books build on and extend this myth. This London 'does not exist. It never did. But Doyle managed to build it in the mind of his readers' (Watson, 1971: 24).

Conan Doyle also writes convincingly about the *bourgeois* London made possible by the Industrial Revolution and growing middle-class affluence – with its 'long lines of dull brick houses ... Then came rows of two-storied villas, each with a fronting of miniature garden, and then again interminable lines of new, staring brick buildings – the monster tentacles which the giant city was throwing out into the country'. These regions, Holmes tells Watson, are not 'very fashionable'. Holmes is more comfortable disguised as a working man, in the decadence of the opium den or the modest gentility of 221B Baker Street than in Victorian suburbia.

Holmes is aware that the most seemingly ordinary dwellings often hide 'the queer things which are going on, the strange coincidences, the plannings, the cross-purposes, the wonderful chain of events' (*A Case of Identity*). In *The Adventure of the Copper Beeches*, Holmes observes that 'It is my belief Watson, founded on my experience, that the lowest and vilest alleys in London do not present a more dreadful record of sin than does the smiling and beautiful countryside'. These mirror Holmes' physical disguises, such as the clergyman in *A Scandal in Bohemia*, and the old sailor in *The Sign of Four*. Schmid (1995) argues that Holmes is, in one sense, a *flaneur*, guiding the readers through the murky parts of London. But the detective goes beyond that. He can 'assert a sense of mastery' over the city, and gives the reader a sense of protection.

They are not directly exposed to the dangers they read about, and Holmes always solves the crime, tying up the loose ends in a neat package.

Conan Doyle introduces the idea of the detective as an obsessive loner in his *Sherlock Holmes* series. Holmes' frenetic work habits are, in part, linked to the adrenaline rush he gets when involved in a case. When he doesn't have this stimulation in his life, he substitutes injections of a 'seven-per-cent solution' of cocaine. As he explains to Watson in *The Sign of Four*: 'Give me problems, give me work, give me the most abstruse cryptogram, or the most intricate analysis, and I am in my own proper atmosphere. I can dispense then with artificial stimulants. But I abhor the dull routine of existence. I crave for mental exaltation'.

His detective work thus comes at a personal cost – Holmes lives alone at 221B Baker Street once Watson is married and when he dispenses with the cocaine at Watson's urging, he has little to alleviate his restlessness and possibly lonely existence, other than chain-smoking or playing the violin. Watson notes in *The Adventure of the Missing Three-Quarter*:

> I knew that under ordinary conditions he no longer craved for this artificial stimulus, but I was well aware that the fiend was not dead, but sleeping ... Therefore I blessed this Mr Overton, whoever he might be, since he had come with his enigmatic message to break that dangerous calm which brought more peril to my friend than all the storms of his tempestuous life.

As with Agatha Christie and her use of the allure of Egypt in *Death on the Nile* (1937) and the romance of the train journey in *Murder on the Orient Express* (1934), Conan Doyle weaves into his narratives various exotic places as a dramatic foil to London. These include the goldfields of Australia (*The Boscombe Valley Mystery*), the Andaman Islands (*The Sign of Four*), Utah (*A Study in Scarlet*) and the Reichenbach Falls in Switzerland (*The Final Problem*), where Holmes and his nemesis Moriarty memorably tumble over the edge, ostensibly to their doom. *The Sign of Four* incorporates an exciting boat chase down the Thames, complete with pistols blazing, which could almost be a precursor of James Bond. However, it is Conan Doyle's descriptions of London that are most influential on travel imaginings.

A Study in Scarlet (Arthur Conan Doyle, 1887)

The story that introduced Sherlock Holmes and his first meeting with Dr Watson, *A Study in Scarlet* also highlights the use of the 'science of deduction' to solve a crime. A body is found in a house at Lauriston Gardens in London.

On the wall is written a single word in letters of 'blood-red' – RACHE – the German word for revenge. This is followed by the murder of the dead man's secretary, accompanied by the same wording. The story takes a turn towards the American West, and we find that the two victims, Drebber and Stangerson, are linked by their Mormon faith, and complicity in the arranged marriage of a young girl Lucy Ferrier to Drebber. They were hunted down by Jefferson Hope in the guise of a London cab-driver, who had planned to marry Lucy himself and took vengeance on his two rivals. Holmes pieces together the story, and the reader marvels at how the various deductions are built on common sense and an eye for detail. The suburbs of London are portrayed in this novel as slightly sinister and the ideal place for malevolent wrongdoings.

As Holmes observes: 'There's the scarlet thread of murder running through the colourless skein of life, and our duty is to unravel it, and isolate it, and expose every inch of it'. This reference to thread calls to mind the labyrinth in the Greek myth of the Minotaur, where Theseus finds his way through to kill the beast using a linen thread (Campbell, 1949). Holmes is the hero who must take up the call to adventure again and again, and overcome trials using his gift of cool logic and calmness in the face of danger.

Most of the action in the Sherlock Holmes books takes place in the urban *milieu*, although one notable exception is the gothic tale of *The Hound of the Baskervilles* (1902), which is located in the wilds of Dartmoor; symbolic of the brutality of the crime (Clausson, 2005). It has been argued that the city is the authentic setting for detective fiction (Knight, 2004; Schmid, 1995). This ignores the contribution made to the genre by writers such as Agatha Christie, whose novels make great mileage out of the English country house as a location for crime (Schmid, 1995). She builds on Conan Doyle's premise that the benignity of the countryside often hides intrigue and misdeeds.

Behind the Well-Mannered Facade: Agatha Christie

The Christie novels form part of the 'mystery' genre according to Knight (2004) following Malmgren (2001). A simple version is the 'clue-puzzle', where death is the focus, and the reader picks up clues to solve the mystery. These were popular in the period between the wars and even the actor Errol Flynn wrote a clue-puzzle novel *Showdown* (1946). Settings for Christie's novels could be exotic, including the Simplon Orient Express train, bound for London via Calais from Istanbul. Train journeys are a staple of crime fiction, as in the films *The 39 Steps, Strangers on a Train* and *North by North-West*. However, it is *Murder on the Orient Express* that arguably makes the original and strongest contribution to the myth of the steam train as the backdrop for crime – redolent of mystery, confinement and intrigue. In this chapter however, we will focus on Christie's predilection for setting her novels in the English village and how this influences travel imaginings.

The idyllic country houses and village settings of Agatha Christie (Figure 4.1) have often been subject to criticism. The American crime writer Raymond Chandler was scathing about the English detective novel, which he regarded as having unreal plots and even less authentic characters. Watson (1971) labelled it 'snobbery with violence'. They offer 'not outward escape ... but inward – into a sort of museum of nostalgia' (Watson, 1971: 171). This is reflected in the popularity of the television and cinematic versions of the stories, with all period detail lovingly reproduced. The play *The Mouse Trap* is still drawing audiences in London and is the longest-running play in history. Hardyment (2000) describes Christie more sympathetically as an observer, providing a commentary on upper-class or middle-class social mores.

Christie offers a dream 'but not of marble halls' (Watson, 1971: 169). These villages offer a middle-class vision of a place to retire to; sleepy, comfortable and self-sufficient, and thus not requiring recourse to outsiders (Watson, 1971). Anyone could be a potential murderer and no one can be completely trusted (Knight, 2004). Conservative values are always reinforced.

Figure 4.1 Thatched cottage in Helston, reminiscent of Agatha Christie's idyllic English village. Photo by J. Laing.

Hardyment (2000: 222) observes that the ultimate aim 'is to reiterate the values of an ordered society, in which evil does not triumph over good and evil-doers are punished'.

W.H. Auden, in his 1963 essay *The Guilty Vicarage*, observes that the person who solves the crime must be aware of the social rituals in play, as must the murderer, in order to be able to commit the crime. This necessitates an outsider from the same social class as the murderer to assist the lower class police inspector or constable; a Miss Marple or a Hercule Poirot, who is aware of the subtle nuances of the social world within which the criminal moves (Watson, 1971). The quirkiness of these detectives reflects the pattern set by Conan Doyle. While Holmes plays the violin and takes cocaine, Poirot waxes his moustaches and Miss Marple does her knitting. They are either confirmed bachelors or an elderly spinster – which puts them on the fringes of society to an extent, and allows them to observe behaviour and sometimes to assume disguises. In Holmes' case, this is a literal masquerade, while Miss Marple takes on the guise of an innocent and batty old lady when it suits her.

The village is, in a sense, a 'locked room' (Hardyment, 2000). As Auden notes, everyone is a suspect and people are interrelated. At least one person will ultimately be guilty of the crime. This makes the setting claustrophobic and gives its ordinariness and insularity a sinister edge. In *The Murder of Roger Ackroyd* (1926), the village of King's Abbot is described as 'very much like any other village ... We have a large railway station, a small post office, and two rival "General Stores" ... Our hobbies and recreations can be summed up in the one word "gossip"'. This sleepy village becomes the location for murder and blackmail: 'Out of the economic mainstream, they were places where odd things happened simply because eccentricity and other odd things were expected to occur in such quaint places' (McManis, 1978: 323).

A Murder is Announced (Agatha Christie, 1950)

The village of Chipping Cleghorn is a slave to routine. Everyone receives their morning paper six days a week, between 7.30 and 8.30 am, and their local newspaper the *North Bentham News and Chipping Cleghorn Gazette* every Friday. Most residents read the personal column, which announces one week that a murder 'will take place on Friday, October 29th, at Little Paddocks at 6.30 pm'. It is treated as a joke or a game, but people eagerly make their way to the house of Letitia Blacklock at the designated time and date. Those who gather include the vicar's wife, a retired Colonel and his wife, and the family's Hungarian maid. The lights go out, an attempt is made to kill Miss

Blacklock, and the assailant is found dead from a shot wound when order is restored.

Miss Marple, who is staying at the Vicarage, helps to solve the murder. She is a self-confessed snoop and has a theory about villages like Chipping Cleghorn and the way 'the world has changed since the war'. As she observes:

> Fifteen years ago one knew who everybody was. The Bantrys in the big house – and the Hartnells and the Price Ridleys and the Weatherbys … If somebody new came to live there, they brought letters of introduction, or they'd been in the same regiment or served in the same ship as someone there already … But it's not like that any more. Every village and small country place is full of people who've just come and settled there without any ties to bring them. The big houses have been sold, and the cottages have been converted and changed. And people just come – and all you know about them is what they say of themselves. They've come, you see, from all over the world … But no one *knows* any more who anyone is.

Inspector Craddock agrees: 'The subtler links that had held together English social rural life had fallen apart'. This is perhaps a paean for an England in the past, and demonstrates a xenophobic edge that is present in a number of Christie's novels. In *A Murder is Announced*, Myrna Harris, who worked with the deceased man, refers to the fact that 'I'm always on my guard with foreigners, anyway. They've often got a way with them, but you never know, do you?'

Miss Blacklock is revealed to be the killer and has also disposed of her dotty best friend Dora, who inadvertently gives the game away. Her motive is to conceal her identity – she is actually Charlotte Blacklock and has taken on her sister's identity in order to inherit a large estate. The respectable matron, with her country tweeds, is revealed to be an imposter. The book ends with a comment by one of the characters about the *Gazette*: 'How else would they know what's going on round here?' The village is replete with the stereotypes of nosy neighbours, community gossip-mongers and a society obsessed with local trivia and their own shallow pursuits.

The modern visitor to the English village is thus confronted by this strange dichotomy. On the one hand, they see a place of tranquil prettiness, full of cricket pitches, the flower-box bedecked pub and horsy people wearing jodhpurs and quilted vests. There is an edge to this picturesque facade however, which can be traced back to the village crime novels of Christie and subsequent exponents, such as Dorothy L. Sayers and P.D. James. We suspect that all is not what it seems on the surface.

Wastelands and Labyrinths: The Bleakness of Scandinavian Noir

The growth of crime novels by writers, such as Stieg Larsson (*The Millennium Trilogy*), Henning Mankell (the Kurt Wallander series) and Jo Nesbø (the Harry Hole series), has given rise to the term 'Scandinavian noir'. In a similar way, the Scottish writer Ian Rankin's *Rebus* books have been dubbed 'Celtic noir'. This is an allusion to *film noir*, a genre mostly set in North America, which 'sees the city as a nightmare of corruption, crime and violence. In its most extreme form, the *noir* city is practically a void, a place of pure negativity with no room for positive values of any kind' (Schmid, 1995: 252). It can be argued to represent a form of nihilism. Edinburgh is, therefore, not portrayed in the Rebus novels as a cultural city, with its rich festival scene, heritage streetscapes and Castle. Rather, the stamping ground of Inspector John Rebus, as illustrated in *Knots and Crosses* (1987), is the curry house with its 'purple lighting, red flock wallpaper, a churning wall of sitar-music'; the housing estates and the drunken 'hazard' of Lothian Road, with people 'staggering in and out of clubs and pubs and take-aways, gnawing on the packaged bones of existence'. The Rebus walking tour deliberately takes visitors to the seedy side of the city (Figure 4.2).

In the Scandinavian noir genre, the detective is a loner and lives a solitary and often unhealthy life and is often separated or divorced and estranged from their children. Kurt Wallander fits this stereotype. The settings are bleak and can almost be understood as wastelands, both in a cultural and environmental sense. Readers expose themselves through this crime fiction 'to a fund of images of violent and disordered urban [and rural] spaces' (Schmid, 1995: 243). This contrasts with the more traditional view of Scandinavia evinced in the tourist brochures as the home of saunas, the Midnight Sun, and a fit, healthy and blond populace living a largely outdoors life.

Faceless Killers (Henning Mankell, 1991)

This is the first book in the Wallander series. Kurt Wallander is a mess when we meet him. He is separated from his wife and lives on a diet of booze, cigarettes, coffee and junk food. His life is lonely and empty, rather like the Swedish landscape we are introduced to at the start of the book. The only colour in his life comes from his love of opera. It is winter, and the town of Ystad, where Wallander lives and works, is painted as grey and austere. Wallander muses on the oppression and 'drudgery' of snowstorms, with their

Figure 4.2 Guide conducting the Rebus walking tour in Edinburgh. Photo by J. Laing.

'car wrecks, snow-bound women going into labour, isolated old people, and downed power lines'. Throughout the book, there are storms, and sub-zero temperatures. This is an atmosphere that breeds depression and in some cases despair.

Wallander is called out to a brutal murder of two elderly people on a farm. It is attributed to a foreigner and the news triggers a third murder, which is believed to be racially motivated. While working with his team around the clock to solve the murders, Wallander attempts to get his life back on track. His meeting and affair with a beautiful district attorney brings some comfort to an otherwise bleak existence, as does the first tentative meeting with his estranged daughter. The killer is brought to justice, but Wallander is in no mood to celebrate. His fellow detective, Rydberg, is dying of cancer, and Wallander muses on a world of increasing violence and fear.

Despite the cheerlessness of this narrative, tourism in the town of Ystad is now largely built around the links to the Wallander books and tourists seek out places or sights associated with the fictional detective. Guided tours around the television studios, where the series based on the books is filmed, attract many fans, and there are brochures that help visitors walk 'In the footsteps of Wallander' (Reijnders, 2010, 2011; Sjöholm, 2010). While the local tourist office encourages this form of tourism, it is also concerned that visitors see Ystad in broader terms than just the connection to Wallander (Reijnders, 2010).

Månsson (2012) refers to this as 'mediatised tourism', in that the reading of the books frames the way the tourist understands and interprets place. These shared imaginings are, however, complex. Reijnders (2010, 2011) labels destinations like Ystad 'places of the imagination' and the tourists 'become characters in a role play' (Sjöholm, 2010: 158), yet they are paradoxically drawn to the town as a highly authentic literary landscape. This blend of the 'real and [the] imaginary' allows the visitor to create their own fantasy (Sjöholm, 2010: 164). The wasteland becomes the dreamscape.

The Girl with the Dragon Tattoo (Stieg Larsson, 2005)

Larsson's *Millennium Trilogy* focuses on an investigative journalist, Mikael Blomkvist, who runs a magazine, Millennium, and a security expert, Lisbeth Salander. In the first novel, *The Girl with the Dragon Tattoo*, we are introduced to Salander as a loner, emotionally fragile and highly intelligent. She hacks into computers and has no scruples in her search for the truth. The two join forces to solve the mystery of the disappearance of the granddaughter of Henrik Vanger at a family gathering on a Swedish small island. The conventions of the crime novel are followed, in that a bad crash on the bridge connecting Hedeby Island to the mainland has stopped all traffic entering or leaving. Like Christie's passengers on the Orient Express or the Nile cruiser, the suspects are isolated and contained, 'cut off from the rest of the world'. But who is responsible for the abduction and possible murder of Harriet Vanger, and why did they do it?

The novel can also be analysed within the framework of the katabasis. Blomkvist goes to live on the island while he is collecting information, under cover of writing a biography on the Vanger Corporation history. He has to step down from his magazine in the wake of charges of libel made against a local financier, so his banishment to the island is a form of descent (Clauss, 1999). The island is claustrophobic and provincial. Blomkvist describes it as a 'backwater'. When he arrives, it is winter and he does not have the right sort of clothing for the intense cold. In the summer 'everything was closed. Hedestad was practically deserted, and the inhabitants seemed to have retreated to their Midsummer poles at their summer cottages'. This is the perfect location to commit and cover up a crime. It is also a kind of hell or realm of the dead, both figuratively and literally, as Blomkvist is later to find out. Blomkvist is never entirely sure whether his patron, Henrik Vanger, is corrupt or not and thus must rely on his own wits, with the assistance of Salander.

Salander is also a city dweller but lives a more solitary life than Blomkvist. The two gravitate together when they are brought together to find out the backgrounds of the Vanger family. Blomkvist is, however, unaware of Salander's background, which she takes pains to keep hidden. She has a history of aggression and instability, and has been brutally raped by her current guardian. These scenes are explicit and shockingly violent, as is the revenge she exerts on him. This is not a book that glosses over human nature or the things that people do to each other. Like Blomkvist, Salander experiences her own hell in a form of katabasis and is forced to seek out her own justice. Neither is a passive victim, and both characters take control of their own destiny.

It could therefore be suggested that both Blomkvist and Salander undergo a form of hero's journey, where they confront danger and return home transformed. Sampaio (2011: 73) argues that Blomkvist must journey through a *labyrinth* of falsehoods and cover-ups, like a 'modern Theseus', before finding his way to the source of evil and destroying it. Just as the Greek hero Theseus is helped by Ariadne to slay the Minotaur (Campbell, 1949), Blomkvist must join forces with Salander to bring wrongdoers to justice and escape death. Salander finds Harriet Vanger living on a sheep station in the Australian Outback, about two hundred kilometres from Alice Springs. She has also chosen an isolated locale in which to escape her family and fake her own death, for reasons she later reveals. She was the subject of abuse from her father and brother. The latter is now the CEO of the Vanger Corporation. He is a serial killer and was responsible for a series of murders of young girls. The pleasant and unassuming facade hid the monster within; just as the outward respectability of Hedeby Island masks a horrific secret.

The landscape and environment in which the book is set is almost an afterthought. It is briefly and perfunctorily described, with more detail with respect to the island. Mostly, however, the focus of the drama is on the psychological environment and what is going on in the heads of the various characters. The external environment therefore takes on characteristics of the psychological drama for the reader, with its inhospitable and lonely qualities reflecting the neurosis and isolation of various characters.

Blomkvist's work on the case rehabilitates his reputation, as he is assisted with information to demonstrate that his legal claims against the financier were justifiable. Blomkvist can, therefore, be reintegrated into society after his fall from grace; another classic element of the katabasis (Clauss, 1999).

He also becomes closer to his estranged daughter, who helps him with vital clues to find out the truth about Harriet Vanger's disappearance. This rapprochement helps Blomkvist to feel less alienated and depressed. He could be argued to be 'born again' with a new self-identity (Clauss, 1999).

City of the Angels

In the early 20th century, Los Angeles became the new American frontier, a Wild West Coast. Its population growth was phenomenal. In 1880, it was a sleepy town of only 11,000. By 1920, it had over half a million, ten years later that had doubled to 1.2 million and by 1960 it had doubled again. In such a city, nearly everyone was a migrant – restless, mobile and displaced as they strove to achieve their economic dreams. The lure of Hollywood added another layer; one could get rich and famous. Lana Turner was discovered by a studio sitting on a stool in a Hollywood soda fountain. Of course, few emulated such a transformation. The City of the Angels was the city of opportunities, but also of disappointments.

In a transient, booming frontier town, crime flourished. It was fuelled by passion, drugs, alcohol, gambling, ambition and most of all – real estate. The dark side of Los Angeles was crime and corruption. This spawned a genre of crime fiction set in the city. The hero was a detective. He was an outsider, often operating on the fringes of the law and society. He was hard-bitten and raw, tough, but vulnerable. Hollywood utilised this archetype for *film noir*. As exemplified by the work of Raymond Chandler, and more recently Walter Mosley and Michael Connelly, this crime fiction took the image of Los Angeles as a city of opportunity and wonder and turned it on its head. The fictional focus was on the dark underside, the hidden city adjacent to the tourist sites.

The Long Good-Bye (Raymond Chandler, 1953)

Private Investigator Philip Marlowe describes himself as a 'Lone Wolf'. Single, with few friends, cynical, an observer. Most of his business is small time; missing persons, minor thefts. He is smart. Marlowe is passionate about chess and he gets a kick out of pursuing clues and identifying the weak points in evidence. He is also tough. However, he is not as smart or tough as he likes to think he is.

One of his few friends is Terry Lennox. From time to time they drink together in high class bars. Lennox is married to Sylvia, an heiress who plays around a lot. When she is murdered, Marlowe helps Lennox escape to

Mexico. Pulled in for questioning, Marlowe holds out for three days, then the police let him go. Lennox commits suicide in a remote Mexican town. Marlowe does not believe that Lennox was the killer. When he is warned to mind his own business by the cops and some Las Vegas hoodlums, he becomes more suspicious.

Marlowe is hired to find missing author Roger Wade. He takes the job only because he is smitten by Wade's beautiful wife Eileen. He finds Wade and begins to spend time at his house in an exclusive Los Angeles suburb. Marlowe is both repelled and attracted by their wealthy lifestyle. While searching for Wade, Marlowe interacts with fellow LA fringe dwellers. The slimy Dr Verringer has gone broke setting up an artists' colony. The unstable Earl lives in a fantasy world and dresses like a Hollywood cowboy. The aspirational Marlowe thinks he is better than these losers; the reader sees similarities. They are all outsiders, hanging around the edges of fame and fortune. Marlowe, the quintessential outsider, is jealous of Wade. He yearns for Eileen and, like Wade, he begins to drink too much.

Wade indulges in violent alcoholic binges. Marlowe finds out he was having an affair with Sylvia Lennox. He is increasingly convinced that Wade is the murderer. As he delves more deeply into the case, he realises that Eileen was once married to Lennox. Wade is found dead, it looks like suicide. He confronts Eileen. She confesses that she murdered both Sylvia and Wade. Lennox took the rap for her. Marlowe carries the guilt for his friend Lennox, Wade (an innocent man he was convinced was guilty) and Eileen (the real murderer he was in love with).

Marlowe has a brief affair with Linda, Sylvia's sister. She too is rich and wild, but there is a sincerity and humour that he finds very attractive. She wants to marry him and go to Paris. Perhaps thinking how unhappy Lennox was being married to a wealthy woman, Marlowe says no. The archetypal detective, Marlowe has seen too much; he is forever tainted by associating with evil and corruption. He is fated never to find happiness.

He keeps digging into Lennox's death. The facts do not add up. One day he is visited by a Mexican who says he worked in the hotel where Lennox died. Marlowe realises it is Lennox. With the help of his friends from Las Vegas, he faked his suicide and has had plastic surgery. Lennox wants to have a drink for old times. Marlowe refuses. He will not say it, but this tough guy is deeply hurt. He should have gone to Paris, but is stuck in Los Angeles.

5　The Past is a Foreign Country

'The past is a foreign country: they do things differently there'.
The Go Between, L.P. Hartley, 1953

'A foreign country with a booming tourist trade'
The Past is a Foreign Country, David Lowenthal, 1985

The past fascinates us. Hartley's famous opening line cleverly links history with travel. The past is both different and attractive. We would like to travel to it, experience and enjoy it, just like an exotic destination. However, physically we cannot actually go back in time. What we do instead is embrace proxies for it, such as historic attractions (museums, restored buildings, re-enactments) and media (films, television series, historic novels).

Understanding society's interest in the past invokes the inter-related concepts of *history* and *cultural heritage*. Both can be applied to analysing re-creations of the past, such as visitor attractions and books. Within the field of tourism studies, there is a substantial literature on cultural heritage tourism and there is a value in applying some of its key concepts to historical novels. In turn, a consideration of the appeal and themes of fiction also aids our understanding of the cultural heritage tourism sector.

Much of the literature on cultural heritage tourism takes a positivist approach towards history. Lowenthal (1998: 112) argues that history is factual and 'real', that there is a fixed historical truth of what happened in the past. Timothy and Boyd (2003: 237) posit history as 'the recording of the past as accurately as possible'. History is pure and objective and unchanging. Its tangible nature is represented by key dates (1066, 1776, 1914) and the stones and mortar of castles and other historic buildings. In turn, this positivist approach is wary of heritage, which often it sees as a subjective twisting of history to satisfy modern needs. It can be, 'the recreation of a selective past' (Timothy & Boyd, 2003: 4), 'a distortion of the past' promoting 'fantasies of a world that never was' (Hewison, 1987: 10) and 'bad history ... a partisan perversion' (Lowenthal, 1998: 102–103).

The alternative view sees subjectivity as an important element of history and constructing meaningful heritage. As Julian Huxley argues in the introduction to his travel book covering the Middle East: 'the accumulation of brute facts is a prerequisite for history as it is for science; but the raw historical data are not history'. Instead he sees history as 'not merely a set of facts: it is also the building up of the facts into a comprehensible whole' (Huxley, 1954: 16). Tunbridge and Ashworth (1996) argue that heritage, by its very nature, is nearly always contested and that tourism attractions and interpretation need to recognise this.

Historical novels balance historical accuracy, historical interpretation and creative story telling. The novelist faces similar problems to film-makers in getting the blend right (Frost, 2006; Rosenstone, 1995; Slotkin, 1990). Novels (and films) are not history books, simply reproducing known historical detail, such as the speeches, may be quite boring in these forms (Rosenstone, 1995). A common temptation is to focus on getting the historical feel right, particularly the detail of clothes, weapons, artefacts and customs. Then, 'as long as you get the look right, you may freely invent characters and incidents and do whatever you want to the past to make it more interesting' (Rosenstone, 1995: 60).

Generally, readers are not particularly worried by such inventions as long as the fictional nature is clear. Consider, for example, the wonderful Harry Flashman, created by George MacDonald Fraser for a series of 12 historical novels (1969–2005). Purporting to be the authentic reminisces of a 19th century British officer, they recount the cowardly Flashman stumbling from one disaster to another, as he is improbably involved in military debacles including the Retreat from Kabul, the Charge of the Light Brigade, Rorke's Drift and Custer's Last Stand. This fiction works because of the meticulous historical research and as the reader is in on the joke.

What interests us more is how historical novels interpret the past. Just like the signage and guided tours at historic visitor attractions, historical novels provide underlying messages about the meanings of what happened in the past, particularly how it relates to us today. For many historical novels there is a conservative paradigm, which looks to the past as a 'Golden Age', when society, customs and morals were far better than in the modern world. By reflecting on the past, we may be provided with an antidote for the ills of modernity. Our society, as this view sees it, would be much improved if we could 'turn back the clock' and return to a simpler, more stable and ordered world. Heritage is often linked with snobbery, the valorisation of past social values and even political fundamentalism (Hewison, 1987). Similarly, novels may reinforce imagined traditional identities and hierarchies, thereby fuelling conservative fundamentalism (Robinson, 2002). However, this is not the only interpretation of the past to be found in fiction, some may take a revisionist stance, highlighting problems in the past that our present society need to remember and be aware of.

In this chapter, we want to explore how authors of fiction have reinforced, even created, popular views of history and heritage. In creating fictional works in a historical setting, they have also imagined what their view of the past means to their readers in the present. Furthermore, these interpretations of an imagined past have evolved over time, as society and its attitudes have changed.

To explore these views of the past, we have chosen nine novels. Each of them was highly popular. Indeed, they easily qualify as classics. The majority are British, though we have included an American and a French work for variety. We have grouped them under three headings, each comprising three novels. The first novels are set way back in history, during periods in which national identities were being formed. The second group of novels are drawn from the Colonial Period, a 'Golden Age' of European domination of the world. The final group look backwards at worlds of social elites; where the imagined society is defined by ordered classes, customs and good behaviour, all 'desirable' aspects lost to the modern world.

Historical Adventures

The first group is the most simple. These three books are set in an earlier period, in which the nation was being formed or had just entered into an era of greatness. This 'Golden Age' is well before the memory of any reader and is suitably mythologised. The development of the national identity and spirit is linked with and symbolised by the personal journey of the hero. Key attributes, such as loyalty, duty, civility, courage and honesty, are valued and are tested by the heroes' travels. All three books are classics of historical fiction, hugely popular and influential, with Scott and Dumas in particular having as great an impact on the general public's view of history as any historian (Lowenthal, 1985).

Ivanhoe (Walter Scott, 1819)

While it is nearly 150 years since the Norman Conquest, England is still divided and troubled. The French-speaking Norman nobles are rapacious and cruel, imposing heavy taxes and treating the Saxons as sub-human. In the face of this oppression, many peasants flee to the forests and live as outlaws. Exacerbating the disorder, King Richard has been captured in Austria, as he was returning from the Crusades. His brother John uses this as an excuse to further increase taxes, but uses the money to buy the loyalty of Norman nobles. Cedric is a Saxon noble. He refuses to adopt Norman customs or clothing. He dreams of a Saxon revival and destroying the Normans. He has disinherited his son – Ivanhoe – for joining King Richard on the Crusade.

Prince John holds a grand tournament. Robin Hood wins the archery contest, splitting his opponent's arrow (now a standard feature of the outlaw's myth, this was invented by Scott). A mysterious knight wins the jousting. He is revealed as Ivanhoe, finally returned from Palestine. Cedric still refuses to forgive him. The third part of the tournament is a general melee. Ivanhoe is outnumbered until he is joined by another mysterious warrior, the Black Knight. The tournament breaks up in disarray as news comes that Richard has escaped and is heading home.

Norman knights, masquerading as outlaws, capture Cedric and Ivanhoe, partly for ransom and partly in revenge for insults given at the tournament. The Black Knight and Robin Hood storm the castle and rescue the prisoner. Now it is revealed that the Black Knight is Richard. Impressed by his courage and chivalry, Cedric and Robin pay homage to him.

Ivanhoe is a tale of national reconciliation and the birth of modern England. Cedric has been living in the past, dreaming of reviving the Saxon line of kings. At the conclusion, he realises that this will never be achieved and the best course of action is to support Richard. His son has already chosen that path, becoming the Norman king's companion and adviser. Through his adventures while incognito, Richard has learnt about the plight of the ordinary folk. Rather than a Norman England or a Saxon England, the country is now unified and on the path of destiny.

Some curious aspects are worth noting. Scott's Richard the Lionheart is brave and chivalrous, but he is also foolhardy and impetuous. Prancing around as the Black Knight he saves the day, but is recklessly exposed to danger. Both Ivanhoe and Robin reflect that he constantly needs wise counsellors. Written just after the Regency and Napoleon's absolute rule in Europe, *Ivanhoe* reaffirms that the checks and balances of constitutional monarchy are essential for England's success. Furthermore, the Divine Right of Kings is discarded. Richard is only truly the king because Saxons like Cedric, Ivanhoe and Robin have judged him worthy to be their monarch.

The 19th century saw huge popular interest in the legend of Robin Hood. *Ivanhoe* was a major part of that evolution (Knight, 2003). Given the title of Scott's novel, it is strange that Robin Hood is given far more action than

Ivanhoe. According to Knight (2003), the title was chosen owing to the literary conventions of the day. These required that a noble hero marry the noble heroine at the end. As Robin was not noble, he could not play that role. Another likely explanation is that the outlaw hero is often cursed. To fight injustice, the hero paradoxically must go outside society, even be rejected by the community. Having taken that place, it is very difficult for the outlaw hero to step back into normalcy (Wheeler *et al.*, 2011). Ivanhoe can marry and settle down, Robin Hood cannot.

The Three Musketeers (Alexandre Dumas, 1844)

This is a spy thriller. It is 1626. D'Artagnan comes to Paris to seek his fortune. He befriends three musketeers in the King's Guard: Athos, Porthos and Aramis. They spend their time fighting, feasting, gambling and chasing women. Perpetually in debt, they are drawn into a world of international espionage. King Louis XIII and Queen Anne are distant. The Queen is wooed by the handsome Lord Buckingham, chief minister to King James of England. Cardinal Richelieu wants to reveal this liaison and bring on a war between France and England. D'Artagnan and his three friends are recruited to aid the Queen by battling the Cardinal's agents.

To the modern reader, the story follows the convention of *Film Noir*. There are also elements that suggest an influence on Ian Fleming's James Bond series. The musketeers are young and full of testosterone. Tough guys, they are brought undone by a *femme fatale*. This is the beautiful Milady or Countess de Winter. She seduces both D'Artagnan and the Duke of Buckingham. In best spy tradition, she *turns* her Puritan gaoler Felton, so that he assassinates Buckingham. The world of espionage quickly turns D'Artagnan. Recruited for his honesty and bravery, he becomes an expert in deception and trickery. The final twist is that Athos realises that Milady is his former wife and he takes the responsibility of killing her.

Their adventures take place in the border zones between countries. Their main escapade concerns a trip to England to retrieve some of the Queen's jewels held by Buckingham. Their cover story is that they are en route to recuperate at the spa at Forges. However, Richelieu knows their true mission and has sent agents to waylay them. A number of innocuous traveller situations (inns and roadworks) hide ambuscades. D'Artagnan is only able to slip across the Channel by stealing a passport from one of the Cardinal's agents. Further action takes place at the siege of La Rochelle (which has rebelled against the crown). Milady is captured just as she flees across the border into the German states. Even Paris is portrayed as a city of night rather than a city of light.

As with *Ivanhoe*, this is another tale of the birth of the nation. France has just come through a chaotic period in the 16th century of internal wars and religious struggles. La Rochelle is the last bastion of dissent. Louis XIII seeks stability and security, out of which will come greatness (his son Louis XIV will achieve this). Adversaries, D'Artagnan and Richelieu are both French patriots and the Cardinal recognises this in D'Artagnan and hopes to recruit him. It is important to understand that Dumas was writing at a time of uncertainty in France. The achievements of Napoleon were in the past; the monarchy was unstable and would be toppled by another revolution in four years time. At a personal level, Dumas was often taunted about his mixed race origins. By setting his adventure in the past, he was also able to allow readers to reflect on the present and the future.

Treasure Island (Robert Louis Stevenson, 1883)

Young Jim Hawkins works at his parents' inn. He looks after a crusty old sailor. When the sailor dies, Jim finds a pirate's treasure map among his belongings. He shows it to the local squire and doctor, who are convinced of its veracity. They mount an expedition to find the treasure that is buried on an island. Jim is invited to come along as cabin boy. He strikes up a friendship with the one-legged cook, Long John Silver. However, as they near the island, Jim overhears Long John Silver. He is an old pirate and is plotting with other former pirates in the crew to steal the treasure.

They arrive at Treasure Island. The captain, squire, doctor, Jim and loyal crew members barricade themselves in an old stockade and fight off an attack by the pirates. That night Jim slips out of the stockade and realises that the pirates are all drunk. He cuts the cable on the ship which drifts away. Going aboard, Jim is menaced by one of the pirates, who he shoots. Jim then runs the ship aground on the other side of the island.

Returning to the stockade, Jim is captured by Long John Silver. Now their ship is gone, the pirates are in disarray and blame Silver for their predicament. Silver changes sides, the pirates are defeated and the treasure found. Returning home, Silver slips away when they stop at a Spanish port, thereby avoiding being tried for piracy.

Treasure Island is a 'coming of age story'. Jim starts his adventure as just a boy, but it is his brave actions that repeatedly save his friends. As Parkes (2009: 78) comments, '*Treasure Island*'s great appeal is that it is a wish fulfilment; it allows a young boy to leave home, to run away from both his mother's authority and the drudgery of waiting tables in a tavern: it allows young Jim to break free of social constraint into the world of romance'. Part of Jim's rite of passage is the search for a father figure. At the beginning of the story his father is bedridden and he dies on the night Jim acquires the treasure map. Potential proxies come in the forms of Long John Silver, the captain and the doctor. Jim finds he is making choices as to which is the right one to follow.

Jim's coming of age parallels that of Britain. The story is set in the 18th century; Britain has achieved naval dominance. Boys like Jim have a role in becoming part of that colonial and naval service (Parkes, 2009). In contrast, the rugged individualism of the pirates has had its day and Britain is now mopping up this lawlessness. Stevenson constantly contrasts the dissolution and drunkenness of the pirates with the sobriety and good sense of British authority. Indeed, he seems to go too far. The pirates come across as a worthless bunch, with neither strategy nor discipline and are continually double-crossing each other.

Exotic Adventure Tales

The 19th century can be seen as a 'Golden Age' of adventure in exotic lands. Britain had carved out an empire spanning the globe and the other European powers were quickly following. The USA was pushing its frontier westwards (as will be discussed in Chapters 6 and 7). The world had expanded very rapidly and this was reflected in fiction. Heroes could board trains or steamers and within a short voyage be in previously impossible faraway lands. Travelling to the distant outposts provided glamour and colourful backgrounds. Most importantly it provided opportunities for fantastic encounters, for courage in the face of danger. These exotic locales provided a distinct contrast with the increasing security and comfort of urban Britain. As Robinson notes (2002: 60), 'the British Empire provided novelists with new dimensions of fiction ... bringing heroic adventure and exotic cultural encounters back to an increasingly literate Britain'. Many of these writers had been colonial officials (for example, Haggard), soldiers (Wren) or journalists (Kipling). They were conscious of a strong demand for stories of the empire and that many of their readers would potentially serve in the colonies. Their books about imperial travel provided the opening to adventures and experiences that could no longer occur in the everyday world of Britain.

In this section, we examine three popular novels depicting Britons travelling to the edges of the world and the adventures they have. The three are very much 'Ripping Yarns', nowadays popular targets for satire. However, when they were written they were moral tales, intended to improve young minds by mixing improbable travel tales with inspiring examples of correct and valiant behaviour.

The Prisoner of Zenda (Anthony Hope, 1894)

'Heaven doesn't always make the right men kings!'

Rudolf is the younger brother of Lord Burlesdon. Though comfortably well off, he lacks direction. His family want him to settle down and join the diplomatic service. He procrastinates by taking a trip to Europe, ostensibly to write a book. He is drawn to Ruritania, somewhere south of Dresden. A new king is about to be crowned. Rudolf is amused that they share the same name and that there is a family scandal of an ancestor having an affair with the Ruritanian king 150 years ago.

Strolling through a forest, Rudolf accidentally encounters the King. They are almost identical. Indeed, both Rudolfs have a love of drinking and roistering and desire to shirk their responsibilities. The night before the coronation, the King is drugged and kidnapped. The culprit is his more popular half-brother Michael. If the coronation is postponed, Michael will be able to seize power. Loyal aides convince Rudolf to pretend to be the King. He is reluctant, but knowing that Michael will kill Rudolf to take the throne, he agrees and is crowned.

Rudolf starts to warm to his role. Though only a stand in, he 'was playing the King's hand very well for him'. Knowing the King is distant and unpopular, he makes a serious of gestures to curry favour with the crowd. Courtiers and officials notice that the King is now more sensible, serious and manly, even suggesting appropriate new legislation. Rudolf is particularly taken with his cousin the Princess Flavia. They are to be betrothed. She notices a difference, querying 'surely it's not possible that you've begun to take anything seriously?' Soon they realise they are in love.

The real King is a prisoner in Zenda Castle. If they try to rescue him, he will be killed. Rudolf finds himself in a moral dilemma. It is a 'terrible temptation' leading to 'wicked impulses' that any slip up could lead to him becoming the King permanently and marrying the princess. Michael's lieutenant is Rupert. He functions as Rudolf's alter-ego. Like Rupert, he is a younger son, brave, charismatic, adventurous and headstrong. Rudolf feels drawn to him. Rupert makes him an offer, demonstrating he understands Rudolf's temptation. The Faustian bargain he presents is that working together they can kill both the King and Michael and thus achieve power.

Rudolf rejects the offer, though it tempts him. He must end the stalemate. He breaks into Zenda to rescue the King. Michael is killed, but Rupert escapes for a sequel. The King is restored and marries Princess Flavia. Rudolf has done his duty, demonstrating all the qualities supposedly held by royalty, but he is a broken man.

King Solomon's Mines (Henry Rider Haggard, 1885)

Allen Quartermain is a hunter in South Africa. He is approached by Sir Henry Curtis and Captain John Good. Sir Henry explains that he once quarrelled with his younger brother George, who ran off to Africa. He now realises how stupid he has been and wants to find his long-lost sibling. Quartermain has seen him; George was setting out across the desert for the legendary King Solomon's Mines. Others have tried and died. Quartermain has a map of the route, given to him by a dying Portuguese adventurer. Sir Henry wants Quartermain to guide them. Though he thinks it foolhardy and believes that George is dead, Quartermain agrees. However, he charges an enormous fee so that his son in England can continue at university. The exploring party also comprises two natives – Ventvogel and the mysterious Umbopa.

The first stage of their journey is across a hellish desert. They are on the verge of perishing when Ventvogel finds them water. Then they have to scale a massive mountain range. Here Ventvogel dies of exposure. Crossing the mountains they find Kukuanaland, a fertile plateau with a militaristic society. To avoid death they pretend to be from the stars, a deception backed by their powerful rifles. Twala, the tyrannical ruler and Gagool, the ancient and evil witch, are suspicious.

Twala came to power by murdering the previous king. Umbopa reveals that he is the son and rightful heir. Quartermain, Curtis and Good join the rebellion. There is a bloody battle and Curtis kills Twala. Now king, Umbopa confirms that no-one has seen George Curtis. He agrees to take them to King Solomon's Mines and forces Gagool to show them the secret chamber where the diamonds are stored.

However, it is a trap. Gagool has her revenge by releasing the mechanism which locks them in. They are rich beyond their wildest dreams, but doomed to a lingering death in the pitch blackness. Realising that air comes in, they search for and find the secret escape passage. Umbopa is sad to see them go, but warns them that he will allow no further expeditions. He has travelled widely through southern Africa and seen too much of rum and missionaries. They will not be tolerated. Umbopa tells them there is an easier route across the desert, with an oasis half way. When they reach the oasis, they find George Curtis. A leg injury has left him stranded there for two years.

Beau Geste (P.C. Wren, 1924)

Where do you go when your life is in a mess? When you have disgraced yourself or have a failed romance you want to forget? Where can you go to redeem yourself and rebuild your life? The best option, of course, is to change your name to John Smith and join the French Foreign Legion. That is what the Geste brothers – Michael (nickname Beau), Digby and John – all decide to do.

The three brothers are university students. Orphans, they live with their aunt – Lady Brandon – at her country mansion in Devon. She possesses a fabulous sapphire – the Blue Water. One night it is stolen. John (the narrator) thinks Michael may have taken it as a joke that got out of hand. Michael disappears, seemingly confirming his guilt. Digby and John follow, leaving notes in which they claim to be the thief. They hope to confound the police by deflecting suspicion from Michael.

Being English private school educated they fit snuggly in with the routines and discipline of the French Foreign Legion. All would be perfect except for Sergeant Major La Jaune. 'La Jaune had been dismissed from the Belgian Congo service for brutalities and atrocities'; joining the Legion, he was 'a relentlessly harsh and meticulous disciplinarian'. He is the textbook sergeant of fiction:

> To his admiring superiors he was invaluable; to his despairing subordi-
> nates he was unspeakable. He was a reincarnation and lineal descendant of
> the overseers who lashed the dying galley-slaves of the Roman triremes ...
> He would have made a splendid wild-beast tamer ... and it pleased him
> to regard himself as one, and to treat his legionaries as wild beasts.

Posted to isolated Fort Zindernouf in the Sahara, La Jaune's severity provokes a mutiny. At this critical point they are attacked by Touregs. One by one the legionnaires die. The inspired La Jaune props each dead body against the walls, fooling the attackers into believing the fort is still well defended. After Michael dies, they find a confession letter addressed to his aunt. John and Digby trek across the desert. Digby is killed fighting off another attack. Eventually, John makes his way home and delivers the confession. When opened, it reveals that Michael had found out that his aunt had sold the sapphire years ago. He stole the fake to protect her.

The Colonial Katabasis

All three of these adventures share common patterns. Duty and loyalty are paramount (shades of Captain Hook's 'good form'). Deceptions are reluc-tantly entered into, for they have dangerous consequences. All are set slightly in the past, for example, Ruritania is described as not as advanced as Britain and swords are preferred over pistols. The writers are aware they are part of a genre. Haggard wrote his novel after an argument with his brother over the merits of the recently published *Treasure Island*. This led to his brother offering a wager of one shilling that he could not write a story half as good. Wren satirises Haggard, having John describe the journey through the Sahara as: 'we encountered no Queens of Atlantis and found no white races of Greek origin, ruled by ladies of tempestuous petticoat, to whom it turned out we were distantly related'.

The most striking common feature is that all three novels involve a katabasis – a descent into hell that the heroes must endure in order to succeed. Wren even specifically uses the term to describe the trek across the desert by John and Digby. *King Solomon's Mines* features two descents into hellish environments (katabases?). The first is a similar crossing of the waterless wasteland to reach this lost world. The second is where the heroes go underground into King Solomon's Mines and are then trapped by Gagool's treachery. In the pitch black they face death. They escape through a further dangerous *descent* along narrow passages. In *The Prisoner of Zenda*, hell comes in the form of the repeated temptation for Rudolf to seize both power and the princess. The katabasis is a journey so severe, that it requires dreadful sacrifices (and that is part of the intended moral lessons for junior empire builders). Two of the three brothers die in *Beau Geste*. In the desert crossing of *King Solomon's Mines*, it is the loyal Ventvogel who perishes. In the second katabasis, their entrapment underground, it is the beautiful native girl who loves Good that dies. In *The Prisoner of Zenda*, Rudolf sacrifices his love of the princess in order to do his duty. The deception and temptation have taken a terrible toll, he returns to Britain a ruined and reclusive man.

Nostalgia for a Genteel Past

The three books in this section prompt readers to look backwards into the past. The view is not just towards a vanishing society, but also to one that is imagined as much more genteel and civilised than today. In this vision of history, the world is well-organised and stable, capably in the safe hands of an aristocratic social elite. Good manners and correct social etiquette are valued well above mere wealth and power. Parvenus and adventurers might seek out colonies and conquests on the periphery, but real society revolves around the landed gentry. Idyllic and ordered as this world is, it is also under threat; the possibility lurks that all that should be valued might soon be swept away. This view of England is well presented in the classic novels *Pride and Prejudice* and *Brideshead Revisited*. In addition, we consider an American classic in *Zorro*, which well illustrates how heritage is reimagined to suit contemporary purposes.

Pride and Prejudice (Jane Austen, 1813)

In *Pride and Prejudice*, Elizabeth Bennet rejects marriage to the obsequious Mr Collins but eventually becomes the chatelaine of Pemberley and wife to Fitzwilliam Darcy, one of the richest young men in the country. The novel traces her attraction to Darcy, who originally rejects her as 'not handsome enough to tempt me!' His pride in his background and disdain at her family connections starts to fade, as he becomes entranced by her. Elizabeth similarly undergoes a transformation, as she recognises his good qualities and strong character. Their growing attraction to each other eventually cannot be denied, and they are the perfect foil for each other, with her vivacity and charm and his integrity and honour, making this one of the most satisfying love stories in literature.

Through Austen, the reader enters a world where conversations are dissected at length, where social status is important, but money holds the key to marriage prospects, and 'a single man in possession of a fortune must be in want of a wife'. Austen disliked artifice and snobbery, and mocks the vagaries and foibles of her characters, including their preference for financial security over the delights of love. Yet her heroines end up marrying 'well', rather than remaining in genteel poverty.

Austen is not such a rebel as to ultimately reject the social mores she learnt as a young girl – that an unmarried woman in Georgian England risks ridicule and hardship, and if one must marry, why not aim high? Her vocation and talents make her unusual within her social circle, and none of Austen's novels deal with the life of a professional female writer or artist. The ideal is to be established in one's own household; preferably aristocratic. And the house in which one lives tells the world who we are – our tastes, our interests and our pedigree, as much as what we wear and what we eat (Hardyment, 2000).

There are few references to landscape or architecture in *Pride and Prejudice*. We never encounter a description of Netherfield Park or Longbourn, the Bennet family's residence. They start when Elizabeth arrives at Hunsford, to see her friend Charlotte's new situation. There are, however, plenty of allusions to the joy of travel. Elizabeth welcomes travel as a welcome diversion from her everyday life, musing that 'there was novelty in the scheme, and as, with such a mother and such uncompanionable sisters, home could not be faultless, a little change was not unwelcome for its own sake'. Travel takes her away from the enclosed, narrow life of Longbourn. Her sister Lydia similarly delights in a trip to the seaside resort of Brighton, with the potential of consorting with the encamped militia ('In Lydia's imagination, a visit to Brighton comprised every possibility of earthly happiness. She saw with the creative eye of fancy, the streets of that gay bathing place covered with officers'). Brighton was associated in the Regency period with Prince George and his Royal Pavilion, 'the most fantastic of all seaside extravaganzas' (Batey, 1996: 125). Elizabeth notes the danger of such a move, 'where the temptations must be greater than at home' and this is borne out by events; Lydia escapes to London with her paramour Wickham, and is saved from ruin and social disgrace by Darcy's efforts in effecting a marriage between the pair.

There is also an invitation by her aunt and uncle to visit the Lakes on a 'tour of pleasure', which fills Elizabeth with rapture and makes her forget concerns about men and their intentions: 'What delight! What felicity! You give me fresh life and vigour. Adieu to disappointment and spleen. What are men to rocks and mountains? Oh! What hours of transport we shall spend!' She also mocks:

> other travellers, [who return] without being able to give one accurate idea of any thing. We *will* know where we have gone – we *will* recollect what we have seen. Lakes, mountains and rivers, shall not be jumbled together in our imaginations; nor, when we attempt to describe any particular scene, will we begin quarrelling about its relative situation.

Travel is also a popular and *safe* topic of conversation, as when Elizabeth meets Darcy at his home in Derbyshire: 'At such a time, much might have been said, and silence was very awkward. She wanted to talk, but there seemed an embargo on every subject. At last she recollected that she had been travelling, and they talked of Matlock and Dove Dale with great perseverance'.

The modern tourist sees the Regency period as the height of graceful style and seeks out palatial mansions and honey-coloured streetscapes that mirror this ideal, epitomised by Bath and its Royal Crescent, Circus and Pump Room, but also found in Cheltenham, Tunbridge Wells and Brighton/Hove. Some have criticised this as 'a chronic nostalgia for a make-believe past' (Sargent, 1998: 177), although it arguably makes a change from a 'depiction of history as the biographies of Great Men' (Sargent, 1998: 178). Austen's world, created through her novels, is strongly feminine and domestic (Herbert, 2001), and thus inspires an alternative heritage narrative. Visitors flock to Lyme Park in Cheshire, which was used as a stand-in for Pemberley in the 1995 BBC television series of *Pride and Prejudice*, in search of a quintessential Jane Austen 'experience'. Lyme Park is famous for the scene where Colin Firth's Darcy emerges dripping wet from the lake in a white shirt; quickening the hearts of female viewers the world over. Sargent (1998) labels

Figure 5.1 Jane Austen Museum, Chawton, Hampshire. Photo by J. Laing.

this the 'Darcy effect'. The fictional mansion of Pemberley was supposed to have been based on the great estate of Chatsworth in Derbyshire, ancestral home of the Dukes of Devonshire, which is also a popular tourist haunt. There are Jane Austen Festivals, and even a Jane Austen trail leaflet, produced by Winchester Tourism to celebrate the 200th anniversary of the first publication of *Sense and Sensibility* in 2011. A new permanent exhibition on Austen and her life has been opened in Winchester Cathedral in anticipation of the bicentenary of her death in 2017. The Jane Austen Museum in Chawton is tucked away in rural Hampshire but also attracts its share of visitors (Figure 5.1).

The Mark of Zorro (Johnston McCulley, 1924)

A nocturnal vigilante is at work, seeking out corrupt officials. Dressed in black, he wears a cape and a mask disguises his face. No matter what the authorities do, he is able to escape their traps through seemingly super-human abilities. Sounds like Batman. No, it is El Zorro – the Fox. The similarities are not surprising; Zorro is the forebear of all masked superheroes. Bob Kane, who created *Batman* in 1939, was a great fan of Zorro and credits it with providing much of his inspiration. Originally a serial in a magazine, Douglas Fairbanks read it during his honeymoon and decided to make it into a movie. That was a great success, so McCulley reworked it as a book, wrote three more Zorro novels and 57 novellas and short stories (Morsberger & Morsberger, 2005).

The setting is Los Angeles, somewhere between 1800 and 1820. Senorita Lolita is eighteen. Her parents want her to marry and restore their fortunes. Don Diego Vega comes courting. His family is the richest in all California and his father has insisted that he should get married. For the noble families of Spanish California there are strict conventions about how courting should proceed. Lolita's mother explains:

> It is like a little game, a maid delights to be won, It is her privilege, *senor.* The hours of courtship are held in memory during her lifetime. She remembers the pretty things her lover said, and the first kiss ... and when he showed sudden fear for her while they were riding and her horse bolted.

However, the vapid and listless Diego is bored by the prospect of courtship rituals. He complains:

> I trust there will be no undue nonsense. Either the lady wants me and will have me, or she will not. Will I change her mind if I play a guitar beneath her window, or hold her hand when I may, or put my hand over my heart and sigh.

The parents beg him to indulge their daughter with a moonlight serenade. Diego responds that it is cold at night, so he will send his servant to play the guitar.

Lolita is upset with Don Diego. Later that day, she is visited by Zorro. She is enchanted by the dashing and mysterious stranger. Soldiers come and Zorro disappears. Captain Ramon leads a troop searching for the vigilante. He likes Lolita and asks permission to court her. Suddenly Zorro bursts out of the closet where he has been hiding. He fights Ramon, wounding the officer.

The rest of the book is dominated by the melodrama of Lolita's romantic triangle. She is impressed by Don Diego's wealth, particularly his library, but she finds him very dull. Fairly quickly, she realises that it is Zorro she loves. His daring and charisma are in stark contrast to Don Diego's languor. Captain Ramon turns out not to be a gentleman and Zorro kills him in a sword fight, after first cutting a Z into his forehead. Not surprisingly, Lolita eventually finds out that Don Diego is Zorro, who has been pretending to be a weakling to distract any attention.

Zorro's popularity was tied to the attractive fantasy it presented of the Spanish heritage of Los Angeles (Morsberger & Morsberger, 2005). For most of the 19th century, Los Angeles had been a small provincial town, missing out on the benefits and excitement of the Californian Gold Rush. However, around the turn of the century it experienced a spectacular boom. In 1880, its population was a mere 4000, by 1910 it was over 400,000 and it was soon to overtake San Francisco as the largest city on the US West Coast. In such an instant society, there was a strong tendency to romanticise the Spanish past, appropriating its heritage to give stability and gravitas. This fascination with the Spanish period ranged from the success of Helen Hunt Jackson's novel *Ramona* (1884), to the craze for Spanish style housing.

The Mark of Zorro emphasises the chivalry and ritual of the *caballeros* (Spanish for knight or gentleman). Los Angeles is presented as a simpler, rural society, in which the wealthy landowners have developed elaborate customs concerning courtship. Crucially (and most disturbingly for the modern reader), this is a white elite, obsessed with maintaining the purity of its bloodlines. Anglo Californians were comfortable with such a heritage based on European superiority. It is notable that in a recent re-imagining of the story – *Zorro* (Isabel Allende, 2005) – that many of these racial elements are inverted to suit modern tastes. In Allende's version, Diego is part Indian on his mother's side. Accordingly, he goes through an initiation ceremony in which the fox is revealed as his totem. To successfully straddle two cultures, he becomes adept at hiding his true feelings and persona. As Diego, he can be an effete white gentleman, as Zorro a mystical Indian avenger.

McCulley's book also promotes Yankee love of small government. The governor and his minions are corrupt, parasitically feeding on the hard-working graziers and farmers. The soldiers are drunken blowhards, a standing army with little to do quickly becomes a blight on society. Zorro urges the younger caballeros to join him and together, 'we shall drive the thieving politicians out and then you shall be cabelleros in truth, knights protecting the weak'. At the end it is the caballeros who rescue Zorro. Threatening to overthrow the governor, they extract his promise to give Los Angeles autonomy. It is a classic re-imagining of history, justifying separating California from Mexico.

Brideshead Revisited (Evelyn Waugh, 1945)

A company of soldiers during the Second World War is setting up camp in the grounds of an English mansion. Their captain, Charles Ryder, is disillusioned with army life and full of *ennui*. This is dispelled when he realises that he has been here before. The house is Brideshead, the seat of the Marchmain family. Its name is a siren call to Charles – 'a conjurer's name of such ancient power, that at its mere sound, the phantoms of those haunted late years began to take flight'. For modern readers, it is equally evocative, with associations of aristocratic country houses, boater hats and flannels, punts on the river at Oxford, strawberries, cucumber sandwiches, champagne and teddy bears. This is no accident. Evelyn Waugh specifically intended the book to be 'an elegy for the great house and its way of life' (Waterfield, 2007). To his surprise, as he explains in the preface to the book written in 1959, the advent of tourism and 'daytrippers' led to 'the present cult of the English country house ... Much of this book is, therefore, a panegyric preached over an empty coffin' (Figure 5.2).

Many of these magnificent country seats with their gardens by Capability Brown, sumptuous fountains and follies, and art collections have survived and are popular with visitors, particularly those with connections to popular books, films or television series (Higson, 1993). Yet, while the death of the country house might be premature, the era of its epoch remains tantalisingly out of reach. The book depicts a brief window between the two world wars where life, at least for the upper classes, exuded a brittle glamour and a luxuriant decadence. This nostalgia for a privileged existence forms the backdrop

Figure 5.2 Castle Howard, York, setting for the Granada television series *Brideshead Revisited*. Photo by J. Laing.

to our sojourns to these country houses, which have come to symbolise 'continuity, tradition and Englishness' (Su, 2002: 554).

When Charles Ryder first meets Lord Sebastian Flyte at Oxford, he is entranced by his lazy charm and eccentricity. Their first encounter involves a drunken Sebastian leaning into Charles' window and being sick. Sebastian spends his time at long lunches and carousing dinners, and carries a teddy bear with him named Aloysius. Charles also falls in love with Sebastian's family and, most enduringly, with his ancestral home. He describes it as 'that enchanted palace', which provides him with an 'aesthetic education'. While Charles never accepts the family's religious fervour, he has a self-confessed 'conversion to the Baroque'.

Arcadia does not last. Sebastian's life falls apart, the result of heavy drinking and an inability to cope with the restrictions placed on him by his family and their strong Catholic faith. He flees to Morocco and lives a life that appears to be increasingly fragile and doomed. Even while he was still at Oxford, 'The shadows were closing round Sebastian'. The gilded youth becomes a wreck, to the despair of those who love him. A parallel theme to nostalgia for the past in *Brideshead Revisited* is thus the mourning for the loss of youth; in particular the innocence of a time without care and responsibilities. The book is an example of a 'crisis of inheritance' narrative (Su, 2002: 553). What the characters have to console them is memory 'for we possess nothing certainly except the past'.

Charles becomes close to the eldest daughter, Lady Julia, and they begin a passionate affair. Both divorce their partners and make plans to marry. Lord Marchmain announces that he will change his will to leave Brideshead to Julia and Charles, as he does not approve of his heir Bridey's choice of a wife. For a moment, Charles is seduced by the thought of being the owner of the place he loves best, 'a world of its own of peace and love and beauty ... Need I reproach myself if sometimes I was taken by the vision?' Julia's guilt over the affair and the clash between her religious feeling and Charles' agnosticism ultimately forces them apart. The novel ends with his musing at the army camp, on the 'fierce little human tragedy' that had consumed him and the Marchmain family for so many years. Charles is strangely comforted by the thought that the house represents something more permanent – a talisman of what England represents to those soldiers fighting for her in far-away lands.

6 No Country for Old Men

'If I were an Indian, I think that I would greatly prefer to cast my lot among those of my people who adhered to the free open plains, rather than submit to the quiet, unexciting, uneventful life of the reservation'
George Armstrong Custer, *My Life on the Plains*, 1874

The Western is an enigma. An adjective that has become a noun, it can be applied to books, films, music, even clothing. For Kitses (2004: 1), 'the Western is one of America's grandest inventions'. Comparing it with jazz and baseball, he argues, 'it represents a distillation of quintessential aspects of national character and sensibility' and it demonstrates, 'the American genius for the popular'. Pilkington and Graham (1979: 1) similarly argued that, 'Westerns are America's unique contribution to that body of mythic lore familiar to most of the human race'.

Such analyses of the Western and its cultural contributions and impacts raise a posse of further difficult questions. Westerns are clearly and unequivocally located in the Western states of the USA. While we can have Western-style stories set in other frontiers (such as the Australian Outback, South America, even outer space), these are novelties, not the real thing. If, as Kitses argues, the Western evokes special American characteristics and sensibilities, if it allows Americans to reflect on their heritage, if it tells them something about their identity, how do those of us who are not Americans relate to it? Westerns are popular around the world, from Italian Spaghetti Westerns (filmed in Spain), to French graphic novels (e.g. the improbably named Lieutenant Blueberry), to Thai Western theme parks. Even setting aside these culturally modified versions of the West, the American West, whether through books, film, music, clothing or being a tourist, is immensely popular throughout the world (Caton & Santos, 2007; Pilkington & Graham, 1979). Indeed, it may be that non-Americans are more engaged. For example, Pitchford (2008: 91) notes that, whereas the average North American will spend only 45 minutes at a Native American heritage centre, German tourists will take up to two days.

How do we explain this appeal? A popular theory is that Westerns tap into universal myths that engage with all of us, despite any cultural differences. Accordingly, Westerns are seen to draw on narratives, characters and themes from Ancient Greek mythology and Arthurian romances (Clauss, 1999; Coyne, 1997; Pilkington & Graham, 1979; Winkler, 2001). Other theories point to Westerns propagating universal myths of transformative journeys through the wilderness, rugged individualism, the clash between modernity and tradition, and the 'good' bad man – who has to step outside society's rules to right injustices (Calder, 1974; Coyne, 1997; Hitt, 1990; Kitses, 2004; Kooistra, 1989; Wheeler et al., 2011). All of these undoubtedly contribute significantly to the enduring popularity of this genre. They also demonstrate that, while the physical setting is uniquely American, the ideas, storylines and messages are not.

How and why did the American West become the physical setting for such universal adventure stories? Part of the answer is to go back to the 19th century. The USA acquired much of its western half through the American–Mexican War of 1846–1848. This new territory included Texas, New Mexico, Arizona and California. The immediate discovery of gold in California provoked a rush westwards. The movement westwards had begun earlier and would accelerate greatly after the ending of the Civil War in 1865, but 1848 stands out as a pivotal date.

At that time, the USA suffered greatly from an inferiority complex in comparison to Europe. Educated Americans were very conscious that, while they were economically successful, they lacked the historical sites, monuments, ancient buildings and critical mass of literature and artistic achievement that defined civilised societies. All of that could be found in Europe, but not in the USA (Runte, 1979). Even the scenery of the Atlantic states paled in comparison to that of Europe. Writing in 1851, James Fenimore Cooper noted both the 'greater superfluity of works of art in the old world than the new' and 'it must be admitted that Europe offers to the senses sublimer views and certainly grander, than are to be found within our own borders' (quoted in Runte, 1979: 15, 17). However, he offered one qualification, the new acquisitions in the West, which he had not visited, might offer some grand scenery. This was to be the case; the USA would find outstanding scenery that would exceed Europe's and which it would preserve through its new invention of national parks (Runte, 1979). Furthermore, in addition to monumental scenery to match Europe's human monuments, the West would quickly provide a colourful literature that would become popular on both sides of the Atlantic.

The expansion westwards was matched by an extraordinary growth and transformation of the eastern economy. An agrarian economy rapidly became a powerful industrialised and urbanised behemoth. That society quickly became hungry for any news, whether by newspapers, illustrated magazines or books, of the adventures of pioneers on the frontier to their west. In essence, there were two Americas; one highly populated and urban, the other a wilderness in the process of being tamed. Factory hands, mechanics, shop-keepers and schoolchildren in the East fantasised about the West. The more that Americans worried that they were becoming too settled and sedentary, the more they romanticised the West (Watts, 2003). This insatiable demand to share in the action of the frontier, meant that, 'Kit Carson, Wild Bill Hickok, Buffalo Bill and many others – outlaws, sheriffs and adventurers – were sublimated into a superb fiction while they lived ... real men became immortal heroes of fiction' (Calder, 1974: xi–xii).

In the late 19th century, Western literature was dominated by the cheap *dime novels*. These were essentially little more than magazines, characterised by a lurid action picture on the front and simple and sensational stories about heroic adventures. They were particularly popular among the urban working classes. Nonetheless, there were also more serious novels, biographies and travel books. While the USA loved the Western, so too did Europe. Jules Verne, for example, incorporated gunfights, Indian attacks and train crashes into his *Around the World in Eighty Days*. When movies became popular, the Western was a natural source of plots and the new media drew heavily on established novels and writers (Hitt, 1990). Western books and movies were successful over a long period of time as they tapped into this popular urban yearning for an escape to the frontier. As with other historic novels (as dis-cussed in the previous chapter), Westerns provided an antidote to the ills of modernity. This fantasy of immersion in the freedom, simplicity and romance of the West is also apparent in tourism research studies (e.g. Belk & Costa, 1998; Caton & Santos, 2007; Frost, 2008).

Our intention in this and the following chapter is to explore the connec-tions between books and perceptions of a mythic West, characterised by attractive ideals of frontier quests and transformations. In this chapter, we explore how books represented real historical persons, travellers, explorers and adventurers in the West. In the next chapter, our focus is on fiction. That the West was (and still is) a distinctive actual place and that much of its lit-erature is based on real people and events, leads us to once again consider the hyper-reality of books, travel and cultural heritage. Unfortunately, within the confines of these two chapters, we are limited to only examining a small number of cases. There is a strong need for a more detailed and fuller analysis of the culture and myth of the West and how that affects tourism.

Five Roads West

A starting point for exploring the Western is to consider five iconic and historic figures and how they were represented in books. The five we have chosen are: Davy Crockett, Kit Carson, Buffalo Bill Cody, George Custer and Wild Bill Hickok. All followed a similar road, pushing the frontier from east to west and were flag-bearers of Manifest Destiny (the philosophy that the USA was clearly destined to expand out from the original 13 seaboard states and eventually dominate North America). All found their personal destinies entwined with how they and their travels were represented in contemporary books.

Davy Crockett

Though he preferred David, he was universally known as Davy. Famous as a frontiersman, backwoods philosopher and teller of tall tales, he rose to prominence when the westwards movement was accelerating and the new concept of Manifest Destiny was gaining adherents. He came to national notice as a US Congressman for Tennessee in the 1820s and 1830s. Originally a supporter of President Andrew Jackson, he became a fierce critic, consistently supporting the position of small farmers on the frontier. Defeated in the 1834 elections, he struck out west to make a fresh start in Texas, which had just declared its independence of Mexico and seemed to offer many opportunities. It is not surprising that his rise in notoriety was contemporaneous with the success of James Fenimore Cooper's *Last of the Mohicans* (1826). Both popularised the American ideal of the self-reliant and honest frontier pioneer. The big difference was that Crockett was real.

While in congress he penned his autobiography *A Narrative of the Life of David Crockett* (1834, the University of Nebraska Press republished it in 1987 and facsimiles were published in 2009 and 2010). Full of tall tales and homespun philosophy, it appealed to both urban and frontier audiences. While it added to Crockett's formidable reputation, it also soured his chances in politics. Loudly declaring to voters 'You can go to hell and I'll go to Texas', he struck out westwards for adventure (Davis, 1999).

Arriving in Texas, Crockett and his party blundered into the fortified San Antonio mission known as the Alamo (Figure 6.1) just as the Mexican army was commencing its siege. There may have been a temptation to slip away, but Crockett was a national hero, a living legend partly through his own writings. He joined the defence and was killed with the rest of the garrison. Six weeks later the Mexicans were surprised and defeated at the battle of San Jacinto. The Texan troops charged shouting 'Remember the Alamo'. That

Figure 6.1 The Alamo in San Antonio, Texas. Photo by J. Laing.

defeat is well remembered (and the site today is a major tourist attraction), the victory hardly known. Texas became independent and America started rolling westwards (Davis, 1999).

Kit Carson

Carson was a 'mountain man', roaming through the Rockies trapping beaver, well beyond the limits of the frontier. When, in 1842, the US Government commissioned John Charles Fremont to map the Oregon Trail from Kansas to Wyoming, Carson was recruited as a scout. A second expedition in 1843–1844 mapped the trail all the way to Oregon and then took in California. It earned Carson and Fremont national fame. A third expedition sent them to California again, ostensibly to map, though actually to foment rebellion. Texas had achieved its independence in 1836 and this was the source of growing tensions between Mexico and the USA. Expansionists were looking for an excuse to carve off great chunks of Mexico. Fremont's mission was to be in California when the fighting started. When war did break out in 1846, he was able quickly to take control of that thinly defended province. For the next two years, Carson had a key role guiding armies back and forth.

Carson's exploits made him newsworthy, one of the heroes of America's success. In 1849 Charles Averill wrote *Kit Carson: Prince of Gold Hunters*. Cheaply published at 25 cents a copy, it was a best-seller among an American public eager to share in the romance of conquest, adventure and westwards exploration. Completely fictitious, it had a super-human Carson discovering gold in California while battling Indians and white villains. As his biographer Hampton Sides (2006: 313) summarised: 'Carson hated it all. Without his consent, and without receiving a single dollar, he was becoming a caricature'.

Inevitably, the fictional and the real Carson would collide. In 1849, a wagon had been ambushed by Apaches near Santa Fe. A woman – Ann White – was kidnapped. Carson led a troop of soldiers in pursuit. Near the Texas–New Mexico border they caught up with them. However, their attack was bungled, they lost the element of surprise and Ann White was killed. Examining the camp, they found White's copy of *Kit Carson: Prince of Gold Hunters*. Carson would be haunted by the implications of the find. He later wrote in his biography that, 'knowing that I lived near, I have often thought that as Mrs White read the book, she prayed for my appearance and that she would be saved'. Offered a copy of the book by a friend, the enraged Carson threatened to 'burn the damn thing' (both quoted in Sides, 2006: 321).

Buffalo Bill Cody

William Cody earned his nickname as a buffalo hunter. There were others with the same alliterative moniker, but he eventually became the best known. In addition to hunting, he was a Pony Express rider and a US cavalry scout. In 1869, Cody was introduced to Edward Zane Carroll Judson, a prolific and colourful author of dime novels. Twenty years earlier, the adventures of Kit Carson sold for 25 cents each, but from 1860 onwards a number of entrepreneurs had tapped the market for even cheaper paperbacks. The Beadle Company sold yellow covered volumes with a reproduction of a dime on the front cover and the term dime novel quickly spread to all their competitors. Judson wrote under the name of Ned Buntline, like Mark Twain his pseudonym was a boating term, suggesting adventure and travel. In Cody, he found a fellow charismatic teller of tall tales (Carter, 2000).

Buntline quickly dashed off the serial *Buffalo Bill: The King of the Border Men*, the first instalment appearing in the Christmas 1869 edition of the *New York Weekly*. In 1870 and 1871, Cody focused on guiding hunting expeditions by rich notables. These included England's Lord Adair, a party of New Yorkers led by General Phil Sheridan and Grand Duke Alexis, son of the Czar of Russia. As well as leading them to game, Cody organised fake Indian attacks for their enjoyment. Eastern newspapers gave him extensive and effusive coverage (Sheridan's satisfied band included two New York editors).

Taking advantage of all this publicity, Buntline adapted his Buffalo Bill story for the New York stage. He persuaded Cody to make an appearance at the theatre; this was so successful that he offered to pay Cody to play himself in the play. Eventually Cody agreed. His shows toured extensively through the eastern states with Buntline regularly producing new plays based on his serialised novels. Cody was a natural self-promoter. His greatest triumph (or tackiest, depending on one's sensibilities) was linking himself with the desire for revenge for Custer's death (see below). As the Buffalo Bill phenomenon kept expanding, Buntline published four of his serial/plays as dime novels. Their success stimulated Cody to release his own line of dime novels, 25 being published under his name between 1875 and 1903. Most of these were probably ghost-written. In 1879, Cody released his autobiography, this coinciding with the development of his famous Wild West Show (Carter, 2000).

George Custer

George Custer's fame rests on his death at the Battle of Little Big Horn in 1876 (Figures 6.2 and 6.3). Leading a cavalry attack on a massive Sioux encampment, he divided his force. His vanguard of 225 men was wiped out, his reserve barely survived. Today the battlefield is a National Historic Monument, managed by the US National Parks Service in a remote part of Montana. Unlike many battlefields, it is little changed, with no buildings nor development on the site. Very few tourists walk its rolling grassland. Those that do can follow Custer's line of attack down to where it stalled and he chose to retreat. Fatally, this was not back towards his reserve force, but inexplicably westwards where he was trapped (Elliott, 2007; Willard et al., forthcoming).

Custer had a meteoric rise during the Civil War. He was a general, nicknamed the 'boy general', at the age of 23. However, after that war his prospects faded. A succession of frontier cavalry postings provided little opportunity for advancement. He did have aspirations towards writing and he was aware of the market for Western adventures. In 1874, he wrote *My Life on the Plains*, which was an account of campaigns against the Cheyenne in 1868–1869. It is a well-written episodic account. Though the commanding officer, Custer leaves the expedition to hunt buffalo by himself. His horse is killed and he is stranded on the prairie. Later, when Indians attack on horseback, he notes that none of his soldiers can hit a moving target. The culmination of the expedition is a dawn attack on the Cheyenne at Washita. In closing, Custer reflects that this is probably the last time that the Indians will ever congregate in such large numbers. The Indian Wars seem over, 'nor is it probable that anything more serious than occasional acts of horse-stealing will occur hereafter'.

The wiping out of Custer's command at Little Big Horn was an immediate sensation, especially as it came between elaborate ceremonies for the

Figure 6.2 The Custer Memorial on Last Stand Hill at the Battle of Little Big Horn. Photo by W. Frost.

Figure 6.3 Young tourists ponder the meaning of Little Big Horn. Photo by W. Frost.

Centenary of American Independence and upcoming presidential elections. A torrent of dime novels quickly flooded the market. Buffalo Bill stage-managed his own connection to the defeat. Upon hearing the news of Custer's campaign, Cody closed his show in Delaware and hurried westwards to enlist. After the defeat, Cody vowed to avenge his fallen comrade. Accompanied by reporters and resplendent in a suit of black velvet with silver trim and a red sash, Cody came upon a band of Cheyenne and issued a challenge for a single combat duel. His challenge was taken up by Yellow Hand (or Hair), who Cody killed and promptly scalped, proclaiming this was 'the first scalp for Custer'. Cody then returned east, incorporating this episode into his theatrical productions. A number of dime novels took up this theme, featuring Buffalo Bill as either the avenger or sole survivor (Hutton, 1992; note Carter, 2000: 199–203 confirms that Cody killed and scalped Yellow Hand, but contends that much of the story was embellished for Cody's autobiography).

Over the years a wide array of books on Custer were published. These included three by his wife Libby Custer (1885, 1887 & 1890), historical reconstructions and post mortems and many popular novels (Hutton, 1992). Many of the latter featured heroes who somehow are miraculously and secretly the 'sole survivor' (Hutton, 1992). Such a literary device is a major element of *Little Big Man* (discussed in Chapter 7).

For nearly 70 years, books posed Custer as a tragic hero. This changed with *Glory-Hunter* (1934) by Frederic Van Der Water. In this work 'the new Custer was an immature seeker of fame ... distrusted by most of his officers and men ... a callous, often sadistic egotist, he alone bore the blame' (Hutton, 1992: 408–409). This was followed by other anti-Custer historical analyses and novels. Curiously, while Hollywood still portrayed Custer as a hero (played by Errol Flynn for example), books fashioned him as a villain. It would not be until after World War Two that cinematic versions would also become negative. However, recently the pendulum has swung again, with books presenting more complex versions of Custer (Elliott, 2007).

Wild Bill Hickok

Two months after the Battle of Little Big Horn, James Hickok was killed playing poker in a saloon in Deadwood, Dakota Territory. He was shot in the back of the head without warning. His hand of Two Aces and Two Eights is now known as the 'Dead Man's Hand'. Deadwood was the Wild West frontier town *par excellence*, nowadays well known through the eponymous television series. Springing out of the Black Hills gold rush, it sat on Indian territory, a squatter town outside of US laws. Aptly, in frontier parlance 'deadwood' was the term for the pile of discarded cards in poker.

Hickok was the archetypal Western gunfighter. A quick draw and a deadly shot, towns hired him as a sheriff to keep the peace by shooting it out with troublemakers. Like Custer and Cody, he dressed the part with long hair and flamboyant outfits. His exploits brought him newspaper coverage and inevitably he began to star in dime novels. De Witt's *Ten Cent Romances* started the trend with *Wild Bill, the Indian Slayer* (1867). Initially, these books focused on his work as a cavalry scout, but over time switched to his role as a dead-shot lawman (Rosa, 1974).

Probably the most popular of the dime novel subjects, Hickok could not escape the infamy that they brought him. The archetypal gunfighter became the target for others aspiring for notoriety. Hickock had to be always on guard. In poker games he insisted on sitting with his back to the wall so he could see everyone in the room. He travelled to Deadwood to make a new start, but letting his guard down he never got to pan for gold.

A fistful of Western heroes

Books made these five Westerners into heroes. Their real exploits were only a starting point for a series of exaggerations and inventions that were avidly consumed by Easterners. Crockett, Custer and Cody wrote books about themselves, though these were more than matched by the flood of adventure literature written by others. To no avail, Carson wanted nothing to do with these books. Hickok grumbled that the dime novel writers had attributed some of his adventures to Buffalo Bill (Rosa, 1974). An army of readers were unconcerned. These exploits satisfied the yearning for tales of a frontier of heroic adventures.

Buffalo Bill stands out in this group of five as the one who did not allow these books to take control of his life. Unlike the others, he embraced the publicity, was totally shameless in his self-promotion and used a range of media to leverage more and more commercial opportunities. Buntline wrote the first stories, but then Cody took control and churned out an average of one dime novel per year. The publicity from the written words and his stage plays allowed him to develop his Buffalo Bill Wild West Show, which would play to large crowds around the world until nearly World War One.

Crockett, Custer and Hickok were entrapped by the public reputations that these books had earned them and all consequently died violently. Losing office, Crockett went West for adventure. Innocently wandering into the Alamo, he was duty-bound by his literary reputation to stay and fight. Custer was aware that the frontier was contracting, that Little Big Horn was perhaps the last opportunity to further enhance his reputation. His orders were to await the expected arrival of other columns, but they also allowed him the independence to engage if he felt the enemy might slip away. As everyone expected, he took the chance for glory. Hickok's infamy made him the target for every hothead who wanted to make a reputation by out-gunning him. Desiring to escape his literary-enhanced reputation, his past caught up with him.

The West Changes, the Western Changes

The golden age of the dime novels came to an end in the 1890s. While the collapse of this genre was swift, the demand for Western popular novels, short stories and magazine articles remained strong (Handley, 2009). In 1890, the US Bureau of the Census had announced that settlement was now so widespread that it could no longer identify the frontier. This was popularly interpreted as official recognition of the 'closing of the frontier', an end of an era and of possibilities for adventure. Nonetheless, the Western maintained its grip on the popular imagination. Some literature looked backwards at the heroes of the 19th century, other works invented new fictional characters, while others kept the Western in a contemporary time period. The last approach, seen among the works of such popular writers as Zane Grey, encouraged perceptions that the mythic West still existed and accordingly could be visited and experienced (Blake, 1995).

Popular Western writers provided story fodder for the developing media of films and radio. Western books were an obvious source of material, as they already had an existing audience who knew the stories and were familiar with certain authors (Hitt, 1990). The prolific Zane Grey not only sold millions of copies of his books, but his stories were filmed a staggering 104 times (Hitt, 1990: 126). As always, Hollywood did not feel obligated to follow the story exactly. The Cisco Kid, for example, came from a short story by O. Henry. His real name was William Sydney Parker, who adopted the name to hide that he was serving time in jail for embezzlement (however he could not resist the joke of his pen-name being a shortening of Ohio Penitentiary, where he was incarcerated). In Henry's story, the Cisco Kid was a villainous Tex Mex outlaw. Hollywood just bought the name and applied it to their latest fictional hero.

After World War Two, tastes changed again. As television became obsessed with Westerns, film makers and novelists would create the Adult Western. In the next chapter we explore examples of this new fiction.

7 Once Upon a Time in the West

'I realized that I had seen and lived it all – all the successive
phases of the frontier, first the frontiersman, then the pioneer,
then the farmers and the towns'
Laura Ingalls Wilder, quoted in Smulders, 2003.

The Wild Frontier

The American West is the archetype of the frontier (Figure 7.1). A frontier
is a 'dividing line between worlds', a zone for both travel and interaction
'between savagery and civilization' (Zurick, 1995). Rooted in mythology, a
frontier is a place 'of possibility, an open future, and uncertain outcomes ...
frontiers are stories being written' (Hains, 2002: 5). Being written and being
written about.

We see frontiers as fascinating both writers and tourists through their
multiple contrasts. Consider the following contests, which are a feature of
frontiers like the American West:

- Settlement versus lawlessness.
- Nation building versus individualism.
- Order versus violence.
- An empty land versus indigenous peoples.
- Outlaws versus community.
- Adventure versus danger.

In this chapter, we examine how these contrasting values were played
out in four Western books. The first three are novels from the second half of

Figure 7.1 The Ghost Town of Bodie on the Western Frontier, USA. Photo by W. Frost.

the 20th century. This was a period in which Westerns developed adult themes, shifting from romanticism to earthier and grittier approaches. In these, the frontier is not an escapist landscape, but one of hostility and violence. Travel to this West involves personal testing and transformation. In contrast, the fourth book is often considered as an example of children's literature. Nonetheless, it too grapples with the paradoxical nature of the frontier.

Three Adult Westerns

After World War Two, America was becoming even more urban and consumerist. The new media of television was dominated by Western series. The old fashioned Western movies rapidly lost their box office appeal and the fiction of heroic Western adventures seemed corny and out dated. This new environment resulted in the rise of the 'Adult Western'. Film-makers made movies that explored themes that could not be shown on television. 1950s Westerns had a much harder edge, heroes were now flawed and morally ambiguous, sharing similar qualities with the villains. Taking the cue from Film Noir, the authorities were corrupt or impotent, other citizens were cowardly. Sex and violence became the mainstay. Feeding these adult films were a new generation of adult novels (Coyne, 1997; Loy, 2004). Three of these novels, which all became major films, are worth analysing in detail.

The Searchers (Alan LeMay, 1954)

Texas, 1869. Commanches raid the Edwards homestead. Everyone is killed, except 10-year-old Debbie, who they carry off. Amos (her uncle) and Marty (her 18-year-old adopted brother) follow the trail. Marty quickly realises that Amos is obsessed with killing and mutilating Indians. He worries that Amos will blindly attack the Commanches (who will react by killing their white prisoners) or even kill Debbie himself.

Their search goes for years, as they wander through Texas, New Mexico and Indian Territory (now Oklahoma). They follow many leads, but they prove to be dead ends. They eventually learn that Debbie was taken by the war chief Scar, though no one is certain whether she is still alive.

Amos and Marty become traders in order to pick up information. As the years pass by they become more and more like the Indians. Marty learns Commanche, though strangely the hateful Amos is already fluent. Caught in a blizzard, Amos even sings a Commanche death song. Every year or so, they briefly return back over the settled frontier. Initially they are supported by the other settlers, but every year the welcome is less friendly. Some of the settlers blame their search for triggering retaliatory raids by the Commanches, others see them now as the hated Commancheros – white renegades who trade and consort with the enemy. Laurie, the girl Marty left behind wants him to quit and settle down. Eventually she gives up and marries someone else.

Following a strong lead they go deep into New Mexico to meet a Commanche chief who has taken a young captive white as his wife. They believe he is willing to trade her, but when they meet they realise the girl is not Debbie. Disillusioned they finally decide to quit and return home. It has been five years. However, on their return news comes from a settler who has seen Scar and Debbie, the search begins again.

They enter Scar's village. They realise that they have been there many times before as traders. For all their work in gathering information, the Commanches have successfully hidden Scar and Debbie from them. They talk with Scar, who hates whites as they have killed all his sons. They meet Debbie, now 16 years old. She tells them that Scar is her father, he brought her from some other Indians and has raised her as a Commanche. She can't remember being white. When Amos tells her that Scar killed her real father and mother she refuses to believe them.

Scar has only revealed himself as he is preparing for a decisive battle with the cavalry and Texas Rangers. While Amos and Marty have become like the

Indians, Scar has become like the whites, learning and adopting their tactics. After an epic battle, Scar is defeated. Amos and Marty ride into the village. Amos rides after a Commanche girl he mistakes for Debbie. She shoots him as he picks her up to take her home. Marty finds Debbie. She tells him she does remember, she remembers it all.

James Clauss, a Classics Professor at the University of Washington, argues that *The Searchers* follows the structure of the katabasis from Greek mythology. This is a dangerous and epic journey, which the hero must undertake. The katabasis, literally 'The Descent', has six features (Clauss, 1999: 4) (see Chapter 1).

Such a structure is certainly in evidence in *The Searchers*. Indeed it appears in many books, a most notable example is *The Lord of the Rings*. However, some qualifications may be made to Clauss' argument. The Indian side of the frontier is certainly depicted as the realm of the dead. It is also a forsaken zone, for during the period of the search for Debbie, the US has pulled back its troops. The area of conflict is expanding as the Commanches get bolder. Amos and Marty are conscious that they are racing against time, that a 'Day of Reckoning' is coming (a strong parallel with *Lord of the Rings*). The fighting between Commanches and whites is becoming more widespread and constant, and Amos and Marty know that soon the US will change its policy and send in troops, which will probably lead to the Commanches killing all their white captives. To journey through this realm, Amos and Marty must become like the Indians, learning and respecting their ways. This alienates them from white society. How will they ever be able to return and settle down? The abrupt ending avoids this issue. Marty and Debbie are reconciled – where will they go? While their quest has a definite objective, their journey meanders through the south-west. They follow many spurious leads, really taking them in circles. At the end they find that the Commanches had easily avoided them, even controlled their route. Their search only ends when the overconfident Scar chooses to reveal himself.

Written in the 1950s, *The Searchers* has obvious Cold War overtones. Debbie's captor convinces her that he has rescued her, that he is now her father and that her real relatives are liars. She tells Amos and Marty that their quest is wrong, they are wrong, she is happy with her new life. In the vernacular of the 1950s, she has been brainwashed. Nor is she alone, other children are being taken and similarly converted to an 'alien' way of life. Furthermore, the American authorities are powerless. Washington has been convinced by Quaker pacifists that they need to appease the Commanches and not use any force. It is only after five years of frontier warfare that this policy is reversed and the cavalry can literally ride to the rescue of the settlers.

Little Big Man (Thomas Berger, 1964)

Western antiquarian Ralph Fielding Snell tracks down 111-year-old Jack Crabb in a nursing home. The crotchety old man tells Snell of his adventures in the Wild West. In 1852, he was 10 years old and his family joined a wagon train from Indiana to Utah. Owing to a series of misunderstandings, the young Jack is separated from his family and adopted by a tribe of Cheyenne. For the next five years he grows up as part of the tribe, learning their customs and rituals and how to hunt and fight. In a battle with the Crow, he rescues another young Cheyenne named Little Bear. Recognising his bravery, Crabb is given the name Little Big Man.

At 15, Jack returns to civilisation. He finds that he fits into neither society. He becomes a bit of a drifter, wandering the West. He hops back and forth across the frontier. At times he lives with the Cheyenne, at others he is a white. Echoing (or parodying?) *The Searchers*, his white wife and child are kidnapped by the Cheyenne and he spends years looking for them. When he eventually finds them, they have no wish to leave. Rejoining the Cheyenne, he takes an Indian wife and has a child, but they are captured by soldiers.

The book's meandering structure allows the fictional Jack to be present at key historic moments and to meet real historical people. The two main story arcs concern Wild Bill Hickok and George Custer. Jack becomes friends with Hickok, who teaches him how to be a quick draw and accurate shot. Jack and Bill regularly play cards. One day Bill accuses Jack of cheating and challenges him to a shootout. Jack only escapes by trickery. It is a finely drawn portrait of Hickok as a man on edge – paranoid and oppressed by the constant pressure of being a renowned gunfighter. Wild Bill knows he is doomed, he just does not know when.

Jack hates Custer for the attack on a peaceful Cheyenne village at Washita. He vows to kill Custer, but cannot do it. He tags along with the expedition to the Little Big Horn, torn between protecting the Cheyenne and his white friends. Custer is portrayed as vain and reckless, but also as heroic. His soldiers hate him (and Jack identifies this as a factor in their defeat). During the battle, Custer goes mad. In the final stand (Figure 7.2), an Indian knocks Jack out and carries him off. It is Little Bear, who Jack saved when they were children.

Little Big Man is a book of its time. A revisionist Western, written just as Americans were starting to question their national histories and more. Reading it today, it comes across as an allegory of Vietnam, though it was written before that conflict was at an end. It presents a highly sympathetic view of Cheyenne culture and was critically acclaimed (Dippie, 1992; Hutton, 1992). The Cheyenne, who call themselves simply the 'Human Beings' are shown as human, with a full range of qualities and foibles. In

Figure 7.2 Looking down from Last Stand Hill, the white graves mark where Custer's men fell. Photo by W. Frost.

contrast, the whites are generally presented as comical, greedy, melancholy (Hickok) or plain mad and bad (Custer). Jack's Western journey is a rambling odyssey. It certainly is not a katabasis; his crossing over to the Cheyenne is pleasant and enriching, in no way a hellish descent.

True Grit (Charles Portis, 1968)

It is 1928. Mattie Ross is a revered Arkansas pioneer. Newspapers interview her about the old days, though she would rather write articles for them and get paid for it. She writes down the story of her adventures 50 years ago, when she was 14-year-old.

Her father has been murdered by the drunken Tom Chaney. Mattie travels 70 miles west from her home to Fort Smith on the border of Arkansas and Indian Territory (now Oklahoma). Fort Smith is touted as the new Chicago, but Mattie is unimpressed. Nothing is being done to track down Chaney, who has fled over the border. Mattie recruits Rooster Cogburn, a one-eyed US Marshall, to go after Chaney. They are joined by LaBoeuf, a Texas Ranger who also wants Chaney for a murder in Texas.

Journeying West introduces Mattie to new sights and experiences. In Fort Smith she sees three men hanged. She is fascinated by watching a

Chinese merchant eating with chopsticks. When she crosses the river into the Choctaw Nation, she enters a lawless frontier that is a haven for many fugitive desperados.

Chaney has joined with Lucky Ned Pepper and his gang of train robbers. As Mattie, Cogburn and LaBoeuf follow them deeper into Indian Territory, their past histories begin to emerge. All are Southerners, yet there are differences between them. Cogburn is from the Missouri–Kansas border, he rode with William Quantrill's guerillas during the Civil War, where he lost his eye. Since the war he has drifted further south to a new unsettled borderlands. He tells Mattie stories of robberies and fights he has been in. He tells her how he charged a posse of seven men, his reins in his teeth and firing his two revolvers. She doesn't believe him. LaBoeuf is unhappy that he enlisted when he was 15, but only arrived at the front just before the surrender. He wants to prove himself. Cogburn's teasing upsets him and he replies with insults about Quantrill being a cowardly murderer.

Their long journey is comprehensively described (unlike that of *The Searchers* it can be easily followed on an atlas). Finally, in the prosaically named Winding Stair Mountains, they catch up with Ned Pepper and Chaney. Cogburn charges the gang with the reins in his teeth, firing his two revolvers. LaBoeuf kills Pepper, saving Cogburn's life. Mattie shoots Chaney, yet there is no triumph in her revenge. The recoil of her gun flings her into a pit, where she is bitten by a rattlesnake. Cogburn makes a difficult journey back east to Fort Smith with the unconscious Mattie. She recovers, though her arm is amputated. When she awakes, Cogburn is gone. Years later she travels further east to find him, but he has recently died. She never sees LaBoeuf again.

The twist in the tale comes in the last few pages as Mattie tells the story of the rest of her life. She has never married. She is obsessed with money and business. We realise that it is this older Mattie who has been telling the story. As a 14-year-old, her wordliness and wordiness, her pedantry and meanness, were all engaging and amusing, but in a mature woman they take on a sadder aspect. Then we realise that while she talks of finding Cogburn and LaBoeuf, she has never tried to do so. She knows that they are just over the border in Texas, but she won't make that trip. The impact of these revelations are deliberately jarring, out of step with the rest of the book. Mattie Ross has had one adventurous journey in her life and that is it.

Cinema Adaptations

All three of these 'Adult Western' novels were quickly made into major films and consequently seen by a much larger audience than that which read the books. John Ford, the doyen of Western directors, made *The Searchers* in 1956, only two years after the book's release. The film version of *True Grit* (d. Henry Hathaway) came in 1969, the year after the book. It was also remade in 2010 (d. Joel and Ethan Coen). *Little Big Man* (d. Arthur Penn) was released in 1970.

The Searchers is widely regarded as one of the best Western films ever made and probably one of the best in any genre (Kitses, 2004). Ford provides a much more detailed and nuanced backstory for the key characters and delights in the sympathetic portrayal of frontier community life. This variance is probably why Kitses dismisses Le May's book as a 'crude novel' (2004: 100) and Winkler (2001) regards the film as greatly superior. We do not agree with that judgement, Le May's novel delves far deeper into important aspects than the film. Le May evokes a greater sense that Amos and Marty are 'lost' in their search, achieving little in five years except their own degeneration. When they eventually find her, she brutally rejects them and they are shocked as she calls Scar her father. Finally, Le May's battle scenes make more sense, as he takes pains to explain Commanche tactics. Our view is that while there are differences, the film and book are equally impressive and complement each other.

Both film versions of *True Grit* aimed to hold true to the novel. They both directly utilised a great deal of dialogue from the book and revelled in the use of arcane frontier slang and idiom. The first version jars with its happy ending and it seems a production specifically designed to win John Wayne an Oscar (which it did). By the time *Little Big Man* was filmed, its revisionist stance fitted in very well with the counter-culture and concerns about Vietnam. Today, it seems dated, mainly as its core ideas are familiar rather than shocking to audiences.

Little House on the Prairie (Laura Ingalls Wilder, 1935)

The Ingalls family's journey begins when Pa Ingalls decides that there are too many people in Wisconsin for his liking: 'In the West the land was level and there were no trees. The grass grew thick and high. There the wild animals wandered and fed as though they were in a pasture that stretched much farther than a man could see, and there were no settlers. Only Indians lived there' (Figure 7.3). This narrative marginalises the prior claim of the original inhabitants of the land and is one of the key sub-texts of *Little House on the Prairie* – that the West was ripe for the taking by white Americans because, as Pa notes: 'We get here first and take our pick'. Ingalls Wilder's writing, therefore, encapsulates the Manifest Destiny philosophy and perpetuates the idea that the pioneers were entitled to and even ordained to collect their share of the spoils.

Figure 7.3 Frontier landscape in southern Utah. Photo by J. Laing.

Laura Ingalls Wilder was acquainted with Frederick Jackson Turner's work (1893) on the importance of the frontier in 'shaping American civilization' (Fellman, 1996: 102), as she noted in a speech in 1937. Telling her personal history through a fictional work was Ingalls Wilder's way of keeping the dream of the frontier alive for a new generation (Fellman, 1996). She was extremely successful in this aim. *Little House on the Prairie*, one of eight popular novels written about her life on the American frontier, was made into a successful television series in the 1970s and starred Michael Landon, best known as Little Joe in the Western TV show *Bonanza*. It was also added to many school reading lists as an example of authenticity with respect to the American West (Fellman, 1996).

The family pack up their belongings in a covered wagon and brave several life-threatening moments, including escaping falling through the ice and a near drowning in a swollen river. They undergo these hardships and privation to reach a country that is described as looking 'as if no human eye had ever seen it before. Only the tall wild grass covered the endless empty land and a great empty sky arched over it'. This is the West as an unspoilt and uninhabited Eden. It also emphasises the isolation and independence of the family – pitted against all that the West can throw at them, but ultimately resilient. Ma and Pa worry about being 'beholden' to their closest neighbour Mr Edwards, by borrowing some nails to build a roof. This obsession with self-reliance is another important theme in *Little House on the Prairie*. It adds to the myth of the West as a testing ground (Anderson, 1992) and also reflects Laura Ingalls Wilder's opposition to the Roosevelt New Deal, which she felt was creating unnecessary dependence on government and subverting the freedom that was a cornerstone of frontier mythology (Fellman, 1996).

Liberties, however, are taken with the facts to 'advance the aesthetic and ideological premises for the series' (Smulders, 2003: 192). For example, the family returned to Wisconsin after the sale of their house fell through, yet Ingalls Wilder writes: 'They never saw that little house again'. This premature return from the West is not part of the heroic narrative that she wishes to portray through her *Little House* books. To be part of the grand sweep of Western adventure stories, the family must be shown to battle the elements without giving up, and thus remain outside the reach of civilisation. To this end, she exaggerates the distance the family lived from the nearest town (Fellman, 1996; Smulders, 2003). She also understates the degree to which they illegally encroach upon Indian Territory, as this might raise awkward moral as well as legal questions. The family were effectively squatters (Smulders, 2003).

Little House on the Prairie is unusual in the pantheon of novels about the West in that it was written by a woman about her childhood experiences (Mowder, 1992). The book, therefore, gives a distinctly feminine perspective on the hardships of pioneering. Domesticity and the creation of home and community are an important part of the narrative (Fellman, 1996). It also shines a spotlight on a close-knit and sober family unit, rather than a solitary man, such as the cowboy, renegade or soldier. Some of these characters make their way at times into the book, reflecting Laura's fascination with traditional images of the West. She describes cowboys with 'flaps of leather over their legs, and spurs, and wide-brimmed hats ... Their songs were not like lullabies. They were high, lonely, wailing songs, almost like the howling of wolves ...'. They are juxtaposed however with nostalgic vignettes from family life (Bosmajian, 1983; Mowder, 1992). Ma makes roasted prairie hen and Pa builds a house, complete with glass windows bought from a store. Ma places the dainty china figurine on the shelf that she carried all the way from Wisconsin; a symbol of civilised refinement in this 'wild country' (Bosmajian, 1983). Santa Claus arrives in the guise of their neighbour Mr Edwards, who brings gifts for their first Christmas on the prairie. These are cherished possessions in an otherwise simple life; stripped of luxury.

Landscape in *Little House on the Prairie* is portrayed as more than just a backdrop to events. It is akin to a character, quickly changing its mood and difficult to comprehend. The author eulogises the prairie, providing many beautiful images of its silence and the emptiness of the landscape; that is both terrifying and awe-inspiring at the same time (Bosmajian, 1983; Frey, 1987). The spiritual grandeur of nature is celebrated, evoked by lyrical descriptions of the birds, whose 'songs came down from the great, clear sky like a rain of music'. Ingalls Wilder embraces the vastness of the landscape, which is 'so free and big and splendid'. Its huge scale can, however, be threatening, almost sinister. At times the family feels dwarfed by its size: 'Laura felt smaller and smaller. Even Pa did not seem as big as he really was'. Part of this trepidation is associated with fear of 'the other' (Smulders, 2003). Towards the end of the book, we are told that the Indians have been gathering in the creek bottoms, seemingly to wage war on each other or the white settlers, and their war chants and drumming at night gives the day-time silence a menacing edge (Bosmajian, 1983). Laura notes that the prairie 'didn't feel safe. It seemed to be hiding something. Sometimes Laura had a feeling that something was watching her, something was creeping up behind her. She turned around quickly, and nothing was there'.

The West, like the Australian Outback, is unsettling and transcendent at the same time (Frost, 2010a). The Ingalls family are outsiders, despite their rhetoric of possession. They eventually move on, because they believe that the government is going to require white settlers to leave the Indian territories. As Frey (1987: 128) notes, this seems a somewhat spurious excuse, given the book has already described the exodus of the Indians, and he ascribes their hurried departure as 'an ethos of nomadism triumphant against agrarian rootedness'. Or perhaps a crisis of conscience? The difference from other Western tales, such as *The Searchers* and *True Grit*, is that the Ingalls family take strength from each other, as illustrated by the closing scene of *Little House on the Prairie*. As the camp-fire burns and Pa plays the fiddle, Laura drifts off to sleep, secure in the notion that 'they were all there together, safe and comfortable for the night, under the wide, starlit sky. Once more the covered wagon was home'.

8   The Explorer's Quest

> 'I looked upon Central Australia as a legitimate field, to explore which no
> man had a greater claim than myself, and the first wish of my heart was to
> close my services in the cause of Geography by dispelling the mists that
> hung over it'
>
> Narrative of an Expedition into Central Australia, Charles Sturt, 1849

The peripheries of our world are rapidly receding, as travellers penetrate into
the most inaccessible and remote places on the globe. Yet the possibilities for
exploration still remain, including to outer space and the depths of the
oceans. We remember the great feats of exploration, immortalised through
books, perhaps even dreaming of following in their footsteps. At heart, we
are all explorers. Allen (2002) attributes this, in part, to our insatiable curiosity, which appears to have biological origins, helping us to survive as a species. The impetus 'to go' is linked to the need 'to tell', which translates into
the creation of travel narratives (Campbell, 1988).

An explorer can be defined as someone with a distinct goal (the quest) and
a desire to document what they see and find (the story) (Allen, 2002). This
'storytelling' has been done in the past through books or journals, providing
accounts of the exotic and dangerous settings in which these explorers found
themselves, and providing a historical record of their motivations for undertaking these journeys. Without these documented travel narratives, many would
miss out on the opportunity to travel vicariously through the explorers' eyes.

A book can make an explorer a household name and, more importantly,
bring them financial rewards. These exploration narratives have a power that
resides in the first-hand experience that is presented – the explorer has seen
these things with their own eyes (Hulme & Youngs, 2002). In more recent
years, these accounts are often posted on the internet, through blogs or
online diaries. Websites allow 'virtual tourists' or 'arm-chair travellers' the
opportunity to follow expeditions all around the globe. Exhibitions are
staged about their findings (Gregory, 1999), presentations are made to various groups and documentaries broadcast of the journey.

Figure 8.1 Monument to the Discoveries in Lisbon, Portugal, depicting Henry the Navigator and famous Portuguese explorers. Photo by J. Laing.

This chapter examines accounts of explorers and their quests. Such adventures are commonly justified as valiant attempts to achieve a high and worthy objective. The drive to be first to set foot in a new place (Figure 8.1) has been replaced by other goals, such as record-setting (the first to climb the highest mountain on each continent); self-actualisation/self-discovery or achievement in spite of disabilities, ill-health or personal set-backs. These tales push the boundaries of factual knowledge, but also contribute to the mythology and mystique of the heroic journey.

Hallmarks of Explorer Tales

Explorer tales, whether fiction or non-fiction, tend to share a number of common elements.

(1) They normally begin with a clear purpose or goal for the expedition. Aimless wandering does not qualify one as an explorer. Their narratives can, therefore, be understood as quests or odysseys, as conceptualised by Vogel (1974).

(2)   Detailed information is provided on the preparation for the journey, including the clothes worn, provisions to be taken, logistics, sponsorship to be sought and training that is required. This level of detail is present even in fictional explorer tales, such as *King Solomon's Mines* (1885) and *The Lost World* (1912). Such detail reinforces authenticity. Polar explorer Ernest Shackleton in *South* (1919) lists the stores that the *James Caird* took when it set off with its crew of six for South Georgia, in a desperate attempt to rescue the rest of the men stranded on Elephant Island. This heightens the tension, as the reader notes that this amount was only enough to last for six months. The precision is telling – 600 biscuits are listed – and we realise that these items will be eked out for their survival. Modern travellers continue this tradition. Dervla Murphy provides a 'list of kit' carried on her bicycle in *Full Tilt* (1965).

(3)   Clothes are important. They might be protective, or act as a marker of identity. Isabella Bird's *mountain dress* is both practical and shows she is exploring. Some use clothing as a means of disguise, which might also be characterised as fantasy and role-play. Sir Richard Burton devotes a whole chapter to Hijazi Dress in his *Personal Narrative of a Pilgrimage to El-Medinah and Meccah* (1855).

(4)   The expedition team must be chosen. Shackleton famously used a newspaper advertisement to recruit for his Antarctic expedition. These choices might be ultimately a matter of life and death. Burke and Wills were chosen by a selection committee to make the first journey across Australia. Their selection seems to have been driven by class and cronyism, as much as ability (Conefrey, 2007). Burke was a military man with no exploring experience. He could not even record his position. Both died.

(5)   There is a ritual of departure. The place is significant and often symbolic. Mawson, an Australian geologist and polar explorer, departed for his expeditions to Antarctica from the Adelaide Museum. This gave his expedition gravitas and emphasised its scientific aims.

(6)   The explorer seeks the unknown. This might be understood in different ways. They might be trying to find someone (Dr Livingstone) or something (the source of the Nile). They might be seeking health (Isabella Bird and Edith Durham) or scientific knowledge (Charles Darwin). They are not necessarily the first person to have set foot in a place, but they may often be the first outsider (read *Westerner*) to venture there.

(7)   The narrative must be written down. In some cases, this is a requirement of sponsorship, but it may also be a function of ego. Writing the tale down helps the explorer in their claim to be 'first'. It may also make their fortune. Unwritten discoveries are of no account. Illiterate

'Mountain Men' saw the geysers of Yellowstone, but these were not 'discovered' until an expedition verified their claims and published its findings (Frost & Hall, 2009; Langford, 1905).

(8) The explorer often discounts the literary worth of their prose, arguing that they have just set down the facts as they occurred. Murray (2008) argues that this is a common trope, which glosses over the 'prejudices and partialities' that are often a feature of these accounts. However, exploration stories often interweave fact and fiction (Thompson, 2011).

(9) This narrative is often replete with myth. The hero's journey or the Greek katabasis are popular ways to frame exploration tales. Various myths of place might be present, including 'the Orient', the 'South Seas' and the 'Arctic' (Holland & Huggan, 2000). It could be argued that these narratives are male constructs and represent myths of conquest or 'phallic myths' (Holland & Huggan, 2000).

(10) Some explorers are embarrassed by the myth of conquest and may employ a fiction of trying to justify or rationalise their activities, a type of 'anti-conquest' (Pratt, 2008). This may manifest itself in self-deprecatory humour (Murray, 2008). Women often do this, particularly in the Victorian era, perhaps as a way of avoiding public censure for being a female traveller (O'Neill, 2009). It can also be seen in modern explorer accounts, including the work of Eric Newby and Dervla Murphy, and might be argued to be a conceit that makes the adventures of the explorer even more amazing for being played down (Thompson, 2011).

(11) There is some sort of contact with indigenous peoples (the Other). Pratt (2008: 7) labels this *transculturation*, defined as 'a phenomenon of the contact zone'. This is the space of encounters and potential relationships. It also brings to light issues of identity, as the explorer finds out more about themselves by comparison with others (Thompson, 2011). Conversely, some explorers ignore indigenous peoples, even imagining a *Terra Nullius*. The American explorers of Yellowstone, for example, wrote (quite erroneously) that it was not inhabited by Indians (Langford, 1905).

(12) The route or goal is marked in some way. It can be the carving of names or initials on a tree or rock, as in Lewis and Clark inscribing their names at Pompey's Pillar, Montana. It may be the naming of a place or natural feature, often commemorating a patron and dispossessing an indigenous name. Perhaps the most notorious example of this is William Gosse's renaming of Uluru as Ayers Rock. Sometimes the words said (or believed to have been said) become immortalised in print. Examples include Stanley's apocryphal 'Dr Livingstone I presume' and Howard

Carter's response when asked what he saw within Tutankhamen's burial chamber: 'Wondrous things'.

(13) The return home is cause for celebration. The explorer may present on their findings or travels, or publish a book or journal. In some cases, the reward was a knighthood, a seat in Parliament, fellowship of the Royal Society, an audience with Royalty or public notoriety. A few never made it home and this adds to the heroic explorer myth. Robert Falcon Scott's name will never be forgotten, yet it was Amundsen who reached the South Pole first. Some of these reputations were stage-managed. Burton's wife, Isabel, worked tirelessly to keep his memory alive (Murray, 2008).

The Age of Exploration

According to Goetzmann (1979), there are three Great Ages of Discovery, beginning in the 16th century, and each age has its heroes, characters and potential villains, all of whom can be found within the pages of the books written about the various journeys. His 'First Great Age of Discovery' covers epic sea voyages, such as those undertaken by Vasco da Gama, Vespucci, Magellan, Drake and Columbus. A typology of travel writers during this period, based on the different roles they adopt or their *modus operandi*, has been developed by Sherman (2002). This includes the editor (Richard Hakluyt), the pilgrim, the errant knight (Sir Walter Ralegh), the merchant (Marco Polo), the explorer (Ralegh), the coloniser, the captive or castaway, the ambassador, the pirate (Sir Francis Drake, William Dampier) and the scientist. In this chapter, we will characterise these various narratives as *explorer tales*, in that these individuals brought back stories of other worlds.

Many of the explorer journeys of this period were prompted by a desire for imperialist expansion and driven by soldiers or spies (Campbell, 1988). These books were, therefore, often written in the language of conquest. Other journeys contained elements of a secular pilgrimage, such as Sir Walter Ralegh's search for the legend of El Dorado (Campbell, 1988). It was difficult at times to separate fact from fiction in some of these narratives, even where the writer did not intend to mislead their public (Campbell, 1988). For this reason, the writer Joseph Conrad in his *Last Essays* (Conrad, 1926) refers to this era as 'Geography Fabulous'.

Possibly the first widely known account of an 'extraordinary journey' was written by Marco Polo, the 13th century Venetian merchant who travelled to the court of the great Kublai Khan in China. While he employed a ghost writer, Rusticello of Pisa, 'a writer of romances' (Hulme & Youngs, 2002: 3) it is arguably Polo's voice that we hear and it is through his eyes that the West takes its first glimpse of Asia (Campbell, 1988). *The Travels of Marco Polo* inspired other explorers, notably Columbus (Hulme & Youngs, 2002), but seemed almost too incredible to be true to the medieval mindset. On his deathbed, Polo was said to have replied to friends who asked him to set the record straight: 'I did not write half of what I saw' (Edwards, 2001). This concept of 'wonder', closely linked to the idea of the sublime, becomes a strong feature of travel writing (Thompson, 2011). It has been argued that the convention of the 'alien culture' of the East began here and persisted long after (Campbell, 1988).

The Travels of Marco Polo combines fantasy elements, such as his sighting of unicorns (changed to a rhinoceros in later versions) and tales of miracles and 'magical and diabolical arts', with observed facts, such as the detailed account of his time at the court of the Great Kublai Khan. It is thus 'neither geography nor a merely mercantile itinerary' (Campbell, 1988: 103). Another famous explorer and writer who combined fact and fiction was Richard Hakluyt, who published several books on exploration including *The Principal Navigations, Voyages and Discoveries of the English Nation* (1589). Hakluyt's work mostly relied on 'eyewitness accounts', although it did include 'Arthurian legends' (Hulme & Youngs, 2002).

The accounts of Polo and Hakluyt, while a blurring of fact and fiction, are generally aimed at being a truthful account of these explorer journeys. They can be contrasted with a classic satire of exploration, Thomas More's *Utopia* (1516), which tells the story of a fictional traveller who journeys to the New World (Hulme & Youngs, 2002). It included a map and alphabet for the Utopian language (Sherman, 2002). We see in *Utopia* the start of a new genre of travel fiction, as opposed to the (generally) strictly realistic accounts of exploration.

The Age of Discovery

The second wave of exploration is characterised by the great sea voyages of the 18th and 19th century, chiefly by the British and French (Goetzmann, 1979). This era also saw the opening up of the American West and travel within the African and Australian continents. These journeys might have had a mixture of mercantile, missionary or scientific motives, but, as with the previous age, were often underpinned by an imperialist agenda (Bridges, 2002; Pratt, 2008). This era is marked by the writing and publishing of journals; which are seen as a source of 'the truth' (Thompson, 2011). Joseph

Conrad in his *Last Essays* (1926) labelled this era 'Geography Militant', when the world began to be charted and claimed (Murray, 2008).

Captain James Cook spent almost three years conducting the first truly scientific expedition by sea, arriving back in England in 1771. He maintained a handwritten Journal during his voyage, describing significant events and activities in several lines of narrative each day. Bridges (2002: 58) argues that Cook 'set the pattern of supposedly "scientific" observation'. His journal was published in 1773; a delay of two or three years was common. In contrast, the journals of Lewis and Clark almost never saw the light of day. Returning in 1806, Merriwether Lewis, as expedition leader, took on the task of preparing the journals for publication. However, he became mired in delays. He was finding it difficult to adjust to civilian life, he was not a literary man, there were disputes over expedition payments and other members wanted to publish their accounts. In 1809, Lewis committed suicide. It was not until 1814 that his heavily edited journals were published. It was only at the Centenary of their expedition in 1904 that the complete journals were published (Ambrose, 1997).

The most dramatic explorer tales of this era, however, came from Africa and the Middle East. Africa was particularly the focus of obsessive attempts of discovery, such as the source of the Nile (Bridges, 2002). Limited access to and presence in Africa made it a blank canvas on which to paint lurid stories and mythical elements, including treasures of gold, silver and ivory. *King Solomon's Mines* (1885) illustrates this view of Africa as a repository of riches, but also of barbarity.

These journeys gripped the public because of the larger-than-life personalities and the personal dramas that took place in exploration of the so-called 'Dark Continent' (Murray, 2008). The disappearance of the missionary David Livingstone and his eventual discovery by journalist Stanley; Speke's alleged suicide when his discovery of the source of the Nile was disputed by Burton; and Burton and Speke's rivalry still fascinate writers (and readers) today (Bridges, 2002). The role that these expeditions and explorers played in the development of Africa and the Empire has received less attention (Bridges, 2002). Even where the explorer is not necessarily subscribing to an imperialist agenda, it is arguable that their mere presence, and the recounting of their story afterwards, helped to entrench and normalise the ideals of imperialism and colonialism, as Said points out in *Orientalism* (Said, 1978).

Joseph Conrad's novel *Heart of Darkness* (1899) provides a critique of colonialism and its excesses (Murray, 2008; Youngs, 2002), but also depicts an inner journey into a dark realm. The psychology of the explorer is of increasing interest to readers these days (Whybrow, 2003). In the next section we consider the writings of three of the most charismatic and complex explorers of the colonial period.

Personal Narrative of a Pilgrimage to El-Medinah and Meccah (Richard Burton, 1855)

Burton's stories of travelling incognito through the Arab world made him a romantic hero (Phillips, 1999). His use of Arab garb is a hallmark of a later traveller to the Middle East, T.E. Lawrence, who wrote the *Seven Pillars of Wisdom* (1926). Burton's disguises included a Persian Prince, a wandering Darwaysh and an Indian physician. He may even have had himself circumcised in his zeal for concealing his true identity (Whybrow, 2003), yet basked in his public profile back home. His books played a large part in this process.

Burton is clear that he is a traveller rather than a pilgrim, and he notes that his feeling on reaching Mecca was 'the ecstasy of gratified pride', rather than religious humility. He boasts of his skill in languages and his training in 'Oriental manners', where he observes the smallest cultural differences, including the way a glass of water is drunk. This allows him to blend in, such that people he meets are convinced 'that the sheep-skin covered a real sheep'.

Burton exhibits a contrasting mixture of awe and superiority. He refers to the 'Oriental barbarism' of iced claret and accommodations 'that would disgrace a civilised prison' and bemoans the fact that his disguise made it impossible to enjoy the society of his 'fellow countrymen'. Yet he admires the Arab 'facility for voluptuousness unknown to northern regions', and talks of the 'knightly care of arms' and a language replete with 'poetical exclamations ... deeply tinged with imagination'. The swagger of Burton's prose is toned down when he shifts his attention to the landscape. There is a lovely description of a quiet moment on a steamer, when he writes of the 'soft night-breeze wandering through starlit skies and tufted trees, with a voice of melancholy meaning'. He is sensitive to the unearthly beauty of old Cairo in the moonlight, or the desolate splendour of the desert.

For all his devil-may-care attitude, Burton is also meticulous about his tools of the trade – his dress and his provisions for the journey – and takes great care to itemise what he took and why, including a goat-skin waterbag, bright yellow cotton umbrella, a dagger, a Persian rug and that indispensable item, a medicine chest, packed into a 'peagreen box with red and yellow flowers, capable of standing falls from a camel twice a day'. The cost of living in Cairo is similarly recorded faithfully, including sundries, such as visits to the hammám or hot baths.

How I Found Livingstone (Henry Morton Stanley, 1872)

Stanley had grown up reading stories about adventure, particularly the works for boys written by Thomas Mayne Reid (Jeal, 2007). This must have been a form of escapism in a difficult childhood, as he was placed in a Liverpool workhouse at the age of five. His real name was John Rowlands and his change of name was characteristic of a man who wove stories about his life and sought to disown his origins. Stanley left for the United States in 1858, jumped ship in New Orleans, fought for the Confederate army in the Civil War, and travelled west to the goldfields, when he was still in his early twenties. He embarked on his first expedition to Asia Minor, and wrote regular pieces for the *Missouri Democrat*. His list of interviewees included Wild Bill Hickok (Jeal, 2007).

The New York Herald sent Stanley on his most famous journey with the exhortation – FIND LIVINGSTONE. David Livingstone, a Scottish missionary and explorer, was believed to have gone missing in Africa, while searching for the source of the Nile. Livingstone was a strange mixture of zeal and hubris, and his first book *Missionary Travels and Researches in South Africa* (1857) is described as putting the explorer 'as hero centre stage' (Murray, 2008: 299).

Stanley reached Zanzibar in January 1871 and proceeded to Lake Tanganyika, where he found Livingstone. His famous greeting 'Dr Livingstone, I presume?' as recounted in his book, is argued to be an invention, like so much of Stanley's life, aimed at making Stanley seem the coolly understated gentleman explorer. Instead, it made him the object of ridicule (Jeal, 2007). The phrase has now entered popular culture. His rapprochement with Livingstone was celebrated with champagne in silver goblets (Murray, 2008).

After Livingstone died in 1873, Stanley took up his search for the source of the Nile, which he established was indeed Lake Victoria. Stanley also followed the Lualaba River to the Congo, a journey of 'unrelieved horror' (Whybrow, 2003). He writes of a 'cannibal world' and 'these unsophisticated children of nature', in language that seems to evoke both the primitive 'Other' and the 'noble savage' tropes (Thompson, 2011). Stanley also writes in a manner that suggests the empowerment of the explorer, incorporating what Pratt (2008) calls a 'monarch-of-all-I-survey' scene, where the landscape is suggested to be under the dominion, metaphysical or otherwise, of the traveller (Thompson, 2011).

Stanley was a genius at self-promotion and portrayed himself as an adventure hero succeeding against all odds (Youngs, 2002). Like Sir Richard Burton, he was photographed in Arab dress, although he is best known for his 'exploring outfit of thigh-length boots and pith helmet' (Jeal, 2007: 151), and was fascinated by Burton's exploits and persona, which he tried to emulate. His two other books, *Through the Dark Continent* (1878) and the two-volume edition *In Darkest Africa* (1890) were destined to become classic tales of the exploration and adventure genre.

A Ride to Khiva: Travels and Adventures in Central Asia (Frederick Burnaby, 1876)

Fred Burnaby liked adventure. At 13 years of age, he rowed a boat, by himself, from Windsor as far as Shrewsbury and back, a distance of about 500 miles. He was known for a towering physique, and great athletic gifts, which stood him in good stead when he became an officer in the Household Cavalry. He also liked to write when he had the opportunity, usually about his travels while on leave from the army. The catalyst for Burnaby to travel to Khiva, now part of Uzbekistan, was a newspaper article, which stated that the Russian government had made an order that 'no foreigner was to be allowed to travel in Russian Asia'. This aroused Burnaby's self-confessed 'contradictorious spirit'. It was, in part, aimed at making Russia's aggrandisement clear to readers, from a writer who feared that the British would lose out to Russia in a grab for imperialist power. The result was a rollicking adventure tale that made Burnaby famous. The sad coda to his life was that he died at only 42 years of age, speared through the throat, while part of a force sent to Egypt to support the ill-fated General Gordon at Khartoum.

His book is written in the style of the romantic adventure tales of Conan Doyle, Kipling and Rider Haggard. This is no coincidence. Thompson (2011: 53) notes the symbiotic relationship between these books and explorer accounts. The former drew on the latter for 'their settings and plots', just as the latter borrowed from the literary conventions of these fictional adventures. The result was a myth of 'imperialism' (Green, 1980). Burnaby's prose is brusque and masculine, comparing the wind on the steppes to 'the application of the edge of a razor' and writing of his 'party' and his 'men' as if he were in charge of a military campaign. Yet he is quick to tell his host in Khiva that he is 'travelling at my own expense and for my own pleasure, and not in any way an agent of the British Government'.

Like all explorer tales, we learn what to take on the journey, and how Burnaby has taken the advice of 'Captain Allen Young, of Arctic fame'. His escapades include pole-vaulting across an icy water channel, dealing with the pain of frost bite and riding on a camel-drawn sleigh. The women he meets are mostly not to his liking and he notes the differences between his idea of beauty and those of the Kirghiz. He describes himself as being like an animal at the Zoo, on show or 'exhibit' to the strangers he meets. Meeting the Khan, he describes him as a 'cheery sort of fellow' and 'the least bigoted of all the Mohammedans whose acquaintance I have made during the course of my travels'. He compares him favourably with his treasurer: 'The hang-dog expression of the latter made me bilious to look at him, and it is said that he carries to great lengths those peculiar vices and depraved habits to which Orientals are so often addicted'. The meeting is reminiscent of Marco Polo meeting the Great Khan.

Third Age of Exploration: The Poles, Everest and Outer Space

The third age of exploration (Goetzmann, 1979) covers the race to the poles, outer space and the ocean depths. It could be argued that the end of this era will occur when the world is now 'safely mapped and ordered' (Murray, 2008: 221), what Conrad called the phase of 'Geography Triumphant'.

Once again, it is the failures that make the most spectacular stories during this era of exploration. Kelly (2003: 313), writing of the explorer Gregory, notes: 'He is like Roald Amundsen surviving and triumphing in the Antarctic, while Robert Scott killed himself and everyone in his party. But which one is taught at school? Bold Captain Scott, of course'. Scott's tragic tale (Figure 8.2) is immortalised in *The Worst Journey in the World* by Cherry-Garrard (1922), which surely wins the prize for the most evocative travel title on the shelves.

Many astronauts have written accounts of their travels to the moon, or about life on a space station. Possibly the most famous astronaut of them all, Neil Armstrong, co-wrote *First on the Moon* (1970) with his fellow Apollo 11 astronauts, but has rarely been cajoled back into print since, preferring a low profile. None of the astronaut's books are considered classics, perhaps the result of sending scientists and pilots to the moon instead of writers or journalists. Or is the problem that we all saw what they saw through our television screens? The unknown in this case did not need to be made real through print.

We consider two outstanding narratives of this era. One is a tale of courage – Ernest Shackleton's *South* (1919) – while the other is a story of reaching what might be regarded as the last great first on Earth, the scaling of Everest, immortalised in Edmund Hillary's *High Adventure* (1955).

South (Sir Ernest Shackleton, 1919)

Sir Ernest Shackleton's public lectures and books, such as *South* (1919), fed the public's appetite for heroic explorers and journeys to the icy landscapes

Figure 8.2 Commemorative statue of Robert Falcon Scott in Portsmouth's Historic Dockyard. Photo by J. Laing.

of Antarctica. Many current-day polar adventurers refer to the inspiration they derive from Shackleton's feats of courage and leadership (Laing & Crouch, 2011). His humanity and ability to keep his crew's spirits high, as well as decisiveness and determination in the face of terrible odds, are constantly referenced by those who follow in his footsteps. His advertisement placed in a London newspaper in 1914 said it all:

> Men wanted for hazardous journey. Small wages, bitter cold, long months of complete darkness, constant journey, safe return doubtful. Honour and recognition in case of success.

Polar narratives, such as *South*, emphasise the mythic dimensions of exploration and the necessity of patience and fortitude (Holland & Huggan, 2000). The choice of the name *Endurance* for Shackleton's ship was no accident. *South* tells the heroic story of the Endurance trapped by ice packs in the frozen Antarctic waters, with the crew stranded on Elephant Island, cut off from communication and with dwindling supplies. Shackleton makes the decision to set off on a small boat with five other hand-picked men for South Georgia, where there is a whaling community that can help to save the marooned crew. To reach them, he must sail over 800 miles in open and frigid seas, and then trek across South Georgia, a marathon of 36 hours across uncharted crevasses, mountains and glaciers.

This journey has all the ingredients of a katabasis – the frozen Southern Ocean and then the icy obstacles of South Georgia are a living 'hell'. The men have no choice but to keep going, and do not have the benefit of a magical guide to help them through; only the moonlight and an indefatigable and dogged spirit. Shackleton seems to know when to say the right thing ('Come on boys') and despite his nickname of 'Boss', does not ask his men to take on more than he himself is willing to do. Shared jokes help to keep morale high and Shackleton understands the importance of a hot drink at night, even when stores are low. He is not afraid to make hard decisions however, such as the order to kill the expedition's dogs and sole cat, Mrs Chippy, when the Endurance is abandoned (Conefrey, 2007). Survival outweighs all other considerations.

The moment they reach the whaling station, marked by the sound of the whistle calling the men from their beds, is described simply but vividly – 'Pain and ache, boat journeys, marches, hunger and fatigue seemed to belong to the limbo of forgotten things, and there remained only the perfect contentment that comes of work accomplished'. They find out that the Great War is not over and hear stories of Gallipoli, poison gas and trench warfare that shock and stun them. This puts their struggle in perspective, but also contrasts their indomitable will to survive with the senseless slaughter that is happening elsewhere in the world.

High Adventure (Sir Edmund Hillary, 1955)

Mount Everest was first climbed by Edmund Hillary and Sherpa Tenzing Norgay in 1953. The statistics of death rates for would-be Everest climbers tells a stark story. This factor may even be a source of motivation for this type of travel, which is the ultimate in physical and mental challenge, and could paradoxically lead to this peak becoming less of a frontier, as it becomes over-popularised and crowded by would-be mountain climbers. Like many explorer narratives, Hillary starts his book with a caveat, that it is a 'personal record' of his part in climbing Everest, rather than an official record. Indeed, Hillary was not the expedition leader. That was John Hunt, whose excellent *Conquest of Everest* (1953) is now unfortunately largely forgotten.

Always a private and humble individual, Hillary was notoriously embarrassed at his feting and prominence as the 'first man to climb Everest', rather than the world seeing it as a joint achievement with the Sherpa Tenzing Norgang. *High Adventure* is simply written, rather like the man himself, but there are glimpses of what made him such a legendary mountaineer. His curiosity is apparent from a youth, when he explains about his first visit to Mount Ruapehu in New Zealand 'All I wanted was a chance to see the world . . . I felt I was in a strange and exciting new world'. He has a proper respect for the mountains, and for their power. Hillary was a beekeeper, and was used to working outdoors and dealing with the 'vagaries of the weather', and the adrenaline rush of a swarm of bees. He talks about the 'subtle science of snow and ice-craft'. This was no mad tearaway, itching to conquer a peak. Hillary's ascent up Everest started slowly and carefully, ensuring his success when others had tried and failed. In some ways his story lacks the romance of a Mallory or Irvine, gentlemen climbers who fuelled a myth. Hillary notes in his book that he thought of them as he stands on the summit, and even tries to find some evidence that they had reached there before he did, evidence of the same gentlemanly tradition.

Hillary mentions reading two books that inspired his career as a mountain climber – *Camp Six* by Frank Smythe and *Nanda Devi* by Eric Shipton. Explorers and adventure travellers often refer to the handing down of tales, from generation to generation (Heller, 2004; Laing & Crouch, 2009a). They become a form of *communitas*, binding people together through shared myths and stories. Hillary refers to the visceral quality of these books. His own book is less successful. Perhaps it takes a writer who is a less proficient athlete and is able to articulate the fear that most of us would feel in such an undertaking, to move us. Hillary is perhaps too stoic to grip his readers to the same degree.

The 19th Century Female Explorer

In this time of greater mobility, female explorer narratives start to be heard and there is a growing interest in personal stories, or self-discovery (Thompson, 2011). More of the earth's surface is mapped than ever before, but there are still places that are 'off limits'. Isabella Bird and Edith Durham accepted the challenge to overcome societal restrictions on women travelling alone and to places that are isolated and dangerous. Bird (1879) takes her carpetbag to some of the most iconic parts of the American West, and faces tremendous risks, being thrown off horses and surviving rattlesnakes. It took doctors' orders for both women to venture abroad, both comparatively late in their lives, but once there, they blossomed and their accounts of their journeys are as fresh today as when they were first written.

The role that these women travellers played in 'racist and oppressive policies', partly derived from exploration and the various narratives brought home by explorers, is the subject of much debate (O'Neill, 2009; Thompson, 2011). It could be argued that their accounts helped to perpetuate myths about the superiority of Western culture and stereotypes about other races and societies. Yet their books also opened people's minds to a world beyond their shores, and in some cases helped to develop new branches of science and social inquiry.

High Albania (Edith Durham, 1909)

Edith Durham is identified most closely with the Balkans, particularly Albania, where she was a trailblazer, not just for women but for Western travellers. Venturing among the mountain tribes, with one boy to tend the horses and a 60-year-old local guide, she describes in *High Albania* a series of journeys over a seven-year period. Her doctor's advice of a complete change (Hodgson, 1985) was taken to extremes. To travel where she did was believed to be impossible. Durham is told that official requests for papers to travel would be denied, and advised that if she wants to travel up-country, she will have to do so by stealth, to 'slip off quietly – or give up'.

Durham is keen to acknowledge her status as 'the Other', even though she was much beloved by the Albanians and dubbed 'Queen of the Highlanders'. In the preface to *High Albania*, she observes that she has 'reported what the people themselves said rather than put forward views of my own – which are but those of an outsider'. She starts with an account of their history, to highlight their 'stubborn individuality' in the face of invasion and conquest. Durham is keen to give the Albanians a status and a heritage that explains their current political situation and, in the case of the mountain tribes, their lifestyle and distrust of outside influences. She believes however, that knowledge of their history is not enough. One cannot start to understand them without experiencing their present lives for oneself.

The minutia of this life is covered in subtle detail. Durham refers to the food they prepare and eat, and the women's work in the house, which appears to be onerous and exhausting. There is a heartrending description of a small child buried with three green apples on its breast, which she learnt was an old custom. The small amount of sleep the locals can survive on in summer elicits her astonishment, while she is honest about her hunger, when faced with the local tradition of eating the evening meal only after sunset. We also find out about tribal laws on marriage, punishment for stealing, rules of hospitality, and beliefs about the 'Evil Eye' and 'blood vengeance', where only the spilling of blood can cleanse one's honour. Durham makes the point that, far from being lawless, these people are heavily subjugated 'under the tyranny of laws'. She tries to write about these things dispassionately, not making judgments but letting the reader make up their own mind about them. On occasions, however, her true feelings are revealed. When describing the blood vengeance, she writes: 'lest you that read this book should cry out at the "customs of savages", I would remind you that we play the same game on a much larger scale and call it war. And neither is "blood" or war sweepingly to be condemned'.

Durham also makes wry observations about various cultural differences. One can almost hear her snort when she observes that one of the men she met 'suggested that a "writing woman" would be a good sort to marry, but Marko said that kind would not fetch wood and water, which damped the enthusiasm'. Her descriptions of the men 'peacocking' in their best clothes at a feast are evocative, but there is no sense of sneering or snobbery. Drawings are interwoven among the text, to aid the reader and bring a scene to life, such as a depiction of a home, an old man and the various ways men shave their heads. She also includes her own photographs, such as an 'Albanian virgin' dressed in male garb and looking directly and defiantly into the camera lens. Durham appears to be a social person, describing the 'visits' she makes to various homes, and the kindness and hospitality she experiences, even among those with little to offer. She laughs of a meal where guests are greeted by gun-shot: 'I thought how dull London dinner-parties are ... This was as good as being Alice at the Mad Hatter's Tea-party'. Nevertheless, there is something self-contained about her, as there is perhaps about all explorers, at heart. She notes a touch wistfully: 'Never before have I been so popular; never in my life shall I be so again'. At one stage she attracts attention from a group who ask her questions about her life back home, and she is uncomfortable: 'now I was myself the victim'. Durham prefers to blend in and observe unnoticed and unheralded. She also finds the constant round of new experiences can be exhausting, making her 'glad to turn in early'.

Her account of her travels is not white-washed – she acknowledges her disappointments, and her struggles. Wading through freezing water on a bed of sharp shingled rocks, she notes without sentiment: 'It was one of the occasions upon which I wonder why I have come'. She refers to the endless patience and resilience of her guide, who never lets her despair, and tells her the tale of the wolf and the fox, with the moral 'However bad things are, they might be worse. It is as well to remember this in the Albanian mountains – and elsewhere'.

Modern Odysseys

Modern-day explorers are now focusing on the 'inner journey', given the world's frontiers are increasingly mapped and 'paved over' (Hulme, 2002: 94). They are essentially *memoirs* (Hulme, 2002). The focus is often on challenge – both physical and mental, with undertones of health, wellness or spirituality. These books explore the capacity of travel to change and renew us. This theme is expanded in Chapter 11 on transformations.

In Search of England (H.V. Morton, 1927)

Morton spent much of his life on a quest – to find the quintessence of a country. His books, often titled 'In Search of' (such as *In Search of Ireland*) or 'A Traveller in' (such as *A Traveller in Italy*), are wistful journeys that provide a snapshot of a world that has now gone, and perhaps was already gone by the time Morton wrote about it. While commercially focused and perhaps rather 'middle-brow' (Thompson, 2011), he captured the mood of the times and was a pioneer of travel writing (Knights, 2006).

Suffering from illness in the Middle East, Morton vows to return to a green England. He is searching for an England that is fast disappearing, a country of thatched villages, wooded coppices, shaded laneways, tearooms and welcoming inns. He recognises this, noting in his Introduction of the danger of the 'vulgarization of the countryside'. Morton understands that he is exploring the past, given that 'behind the beauty of the English country is an economic and a social cancer', and that the days of the sanctity and pre-eminence of the English village are 'now gone'. What he gives to posterity is a gorgeous and glowing tribute to an England that was, and will never be again.

Morton writes conspiratorially, as if he is writing just for his reader. 'Lady Godiva has always attracted me' he declares, and 'if we could see this ride', it was probably no more shocking 'than a modern girl catching an omnibus'. He asks the reader at one point: 'Have you ever tried an arrowhead of flint?' 'No', we are tempted to say, as we read on enthralled. His visit to Wells is prefaced by the following: 'How can I describe to you the whisper of the water that runs in gutters, musically tinkling past the steps of old houses?' It is as if we are sitting by the fire, as Morton spins his tales of the England that we all want to visit – and probably have in our dreams.

Full Tilt: Ireland to India with a Bicycle (Dervla Murphy, 1965)

Murphy is another traveller who chooses a disguise, wearing men's clothes and her hair short, which Holland and Huggan (2000: 20) suggest 'pokes fun at the male bravado associated with the figure of the explorer'. Yet this mas-querade is hardly a matter of mere 'amusement' for Murphy, given the warn-ings she is given about the dangers of a woman travelling alone through central Asia. It effectively becomes a form of armour, however lightly she dismisses it. Her bicycle, which she christens Roz, is like a companion, and seems to pro-vide her with support and comfort when times are tough. She laughs at Roz feeling 'jilted' when she travels in a Jaguar and constantly refers to 'Roz and I'.

Travel becomes a 'medium of emancipation' for Murphy (Holland & Huggan, 2000: 20). It also offers her moments of *anagnorisis* or recognition (Thompson, 2011), where she realises how strong her instinct is for self-preservation. We are told of incidents where she fires her gun at a pack of wolves, a group of men about to steal her bike and threaten her safety, and an uninvited man in her room in the middle of the night. She is no light-weight and this trip is no jaunt, no matter how hard she tries to adopt the comic role of the innocent abroad. Her journey is also conceptualised as a quest for understanding, both of the self and of others (Holland & Huggan, 2000). Murphy sadly writes of the typical young person she encounters, who travel as a means of *'going away from* rather than a *going towards'*. In contrast, she embraces the diversity of different cultures and sees travel as a privilege and satiation of curiosity.

This book is avowed to be based on her journals, without embellishment. In this way, Murphy harks back to the classic explorer accounts, which were based on notes kept on the ground, providing a sense of realism for the reader (Thompson, 2011). A confessional style is used (Holland & Huggan, 2000). Like many modern travellers, she expresses 'anti-colonialist sentiments' (Holland & Huggan, 2000: 115), while operating within a sphere of privilege. Her comment regarding India ('No amount of good done to a country by a conqueror can quite compensate for the loss of national freedom and the dignity that goes with it') sits uneasily with her views on life under com-munist rule. She observes that her expressions of admiration about life in communist Bulgaria will not be popular 'with Western propagandists', while noting that the improved standard of living 'has been gained at the cost of religious and intellectual freedom'. She fails to acknowledge that the very freedom she is enjoying – the right to ride a bicycle half-away across the world – is denied to many of the people she meets, whether from economic, political or socio-cultural reasons. Murphy is not totally unaware of the para-dox of her travels and does display sensitivity to the realities of life for those she passes by. She refers to the beauty of the countryside between Teheran and the Afghan border, while noting that 'as a background to daily life it's cruel and contemptuous country where cultivation is a fight all the way, with victory not worth much'.

There is an elegiac quality to this book, read in the knowledge that such a journey could almost certainly not be attempted in the current time, given the route would take in several war zones. Some of Murphy's comments, such as the one about how people she meets in Persia 'genuinely love their Shah – and would you blame them!' need to be read in context – this is a different time and world to our own. The ending is oddly abrupt, even more so than Eric Newby's *A Short Walk in the Hindu Kush*, as if Murphy is embarrassed to embrace the big denouement, complete with joyous arrival home. Her final sentence reads: 'So tomorrow, with Mrs Haddow's help, I shall look for some form of voluntary work here in India to keep me happy until Roz and I can get going again'. This is as far from the hero's return as it is possible to get.

A Time of Gifts (Patrick Leigh Fermor, 1977)

Patrick Leigh Fermor is regarded as one of the eminent travel writers of the 20th century, yet his famous depiction of a walk across Europe when he was eighteen in 1933 was not published until 1977. He wrote other books in the meantime, including portrayals of his time in Greece in *Mani* (1958) and *Roumeli* (1966), but it is his acknowledged masterpieces, *A Time of Gifts* (1977) and its sequel *Between the Woods and the Water* (1986), which provide a glimpse of a world that is now lost. Holland and Huggan (2000: 15), following Rosaldo (1989), labels it 'imperialist nostalgia', but this is perhaps unfair. Leigh Fermor is being true to the world he saw with teenage eyes and from his particular socio-cultural background and standpoint. There was to be a third book, eagerly awaited by his reading public, but although he promised it for many years, he passed away in 2011 without completing the trilogy.

A Time of Gifts traces the first half of a journey towards Constantinople, starting in London and ending with Leigh Fermor's arrival in Hungary. It is essentially a pilgrimage; based on a personal vision of travelling rough, adventuring on foot, and sleeping where he could find accommodation. He declares that he will 'sleep in hayricks in summer, shelter in barns when it was raining or snowing and only consort with peasants and tramps'. Leigh Fermor has a romantic streak and likens his journey to the travails of a 'broken knight or the hero of *The Cloister and the Hearth*'. Leigh Fermor's journey was also pre-empted by his expulsion from school (which he labels 'the sack'). This trip proves to be a rite of passage, where he is forced to rely on his own wits, but also becomes less selfish in the process.

Despite his desire to travel like a tramp, Leigh Fermor falls on his feet, a tribute to his great personal charm, but also to his networks, contacts and family connections. This is a man who, later in life, spent time on the set of

The Roots of Heaven with Errol Flynn and regularly corresponded with Deborah, the Duchess of Devonshire and the youngest of the notorious Mitford sisters (Devonshire *et al.*, 2010). While he does sleep in barns and is constantly overwhelmed by people's generosity, he also stays with Counts and Barons in castles and country houses, and describes evenings talking of art, culture and history over glasses of brandy, discovering the treasures of ancient libraries, and visiting heritage in cities, such as Cologne, Salzburg, Vienna, and Prague. He also has a marvellous way of describing the country-side he ventures through, with descriptions of the unfolding of the various seasons. Phrases like 'the hemispherical ghosts of weeping-willows' are evoc-ative, and he notices the smallest detail, such as the heron that 'sculled upstream, detectable mainly by sound and the darker and slowly dissolving rings that the tips of its flight-feathers left on the water'. Even his descrip-tions of architecture borrow from nature. His observations about the Nazi presence and sympathies towards them in Europe offer portents of the war that was to follow. Leigh Fermor spent much of that war in Greece, and his daring exploits as an agent against the Germans on Crete were immortalised by W. Stanley Moss in his best-seller *Ill Met by Moonlight* (1950).

Journey to the Centre of the Earth (Richard and Nicholas Crane, 1987)

Nicholas Crane belongs to one of the current generation of explorers, who accompany their travels with a tie-in television series and book con-tract. His journey by bicycle, with his cousin Richard, to the 'centre of the earth' refers to the point on the surface of the earth in central Asia that is the farthest away from the sea in all directions. This kind of geographic milestone echoes the drive to climb the highest mountain or reach the poles. As they write: 'No one has ever been there'. They also like the fact that it gives the expedition 'an objective and what you might call a reason'. Their parameters were clear – 'fresh and challenging' but not 'impossible'. When they find a reference in the *Guinness Book of Records* to the place remotest from the ocean, they are elated: 'It seemed that we might have stumbled on one of the very few 'pure' places in the world which are truly international and timeless'. The reference to *purity* is interesting – they also maintain this quality in their minds by cycling – 'going man-powered all the way'. This is a word often used by adventure travellers to describe their journeys (Laing & Crouch, 2009b, 2009c), and suggests something that is authentic, untouched and prestigious.

Like all explorer tales, the journey would not be possible without spon-sors, and they are effusively thanked at the start of the book. The ending is also ubiquitous, an exposition about the money they have raised for their chosen charity – Intermediate Technology – which helps people in developed countries with various equipment they need, including pumps, ploughs and building materials. This is not said to denigrate these efforts, but points to the need for modern exploration to have a moral purpose; a goal above and beyond the desire to discover more about the world in which we live in. While the tone of the book is generally light, occasionally there is a reference to the responsibility of the traveller in these places, as exemplified by this comment by Richard: 'The Tibetans, new to trade, were prepared to sell anything to acquire cash. Any money is good money when you have none, but for tourists to capitalize on this innocence is rape'.

The cousins travelled light – no change of clothes, no tent, no provisions. Food and water were all gathered on the way and they trusted to the generosity of those they met on the way. Again, this could be criticised as Westerners who have it all, taking the scarce resources of locals, ironically to raise awareness of their plight and help them down the track. We think, however, that in this age of fortress homes and preponderance of technological 'friendship' across the developed world, some feel the need to experience a different kind of culture, one more open, kinder to strangers and less materialistic, at first hand. They were also longing for adventure, in a kind of primeval way. As Nicholas describes it: 'problems we couldn't predict yet which we could survive'. Travelling so light made life simple, stripped down to the basics.

Both had grown up with family holidays in the mountains, led by their respective fathers, and were constantly departing on various journeys. Nick is described as 'always on the lookout for something a bit different'. No doubt the goal of reaching the 'centre of the earth' appealed as being a bit quirky, but also targeted and precise. Richard was similarly driven to daring pursuits, and enjoyed the lessons learnt in the process. Communitas is very important to both the Cranes; they typically did not travel on these big adventures alone but with at least one other person. They also thrive on riskiness. Richard describes his travels as 'a search for our physical and mental limits. By finding them, we could satisfy our wanderlust and settle down to normal lives. We came close to our limits but were never broken'.

A lot of the book is focused on the prosaic elements of travel – getting the right gear together, preparing to leave home, finding the way on the map, sorting out food and drink, and writing letters home. No matter how exotic the location, or extreme the hardships, we are reminded that the explorer, at heart, is no different from any other traveller, in their day-to-day needs and routines.

9   Re-enacting the Past

'As any schoolboy must be, I was thrilled by the elephants ... It was many years before there began to stir in me a desire to follow in Hannibal's footsteps, and of course my first thought was to do it on an elephant's back ... [before] finally settling for my own two feet'
From the Camargue to the Alps: A Walk Across France in Hannibal's Footsteps, Bernard Levin, 1985

There is a school of thought that all travellers essentially walk in the footsteps of others (Seaton, 2002). No journeys are ever unique, in the sense that others have either been to the places we seek out, or have embarked on the *process* of travel before us. The desire to be different leads us to adopt terms like 'traveller' and scorn the use of the epithet 'tourist'. We sometimes look for novel forms of tourism (swimming with sharks, travelling into space) or visiting out-of-the way or remote locations. Yet deep-down, we know we tread a well-worn path. Some travellers may actually derive a sense of comfort in the notion that they walk in the footsteps of others. This may lead them to search for avenues to recreate the past through their travel experiences. Seaton (2002) labels this 'ritual repetition' or 'emulative tourism'. He argues that we know very little about this process, despite its ubiquity across time and continued popularity.

Books are often a key element in this phenomenon. They can act as a kind of roadmap for these recreated journeys. Kieran Kelly took the journals of explorers, such as Gregory and Stuart with him, when he recreated their expeditions through the Australian Outback. In 1936, Jean Cocteau recreated Jules Verne's *Around the World in Eighty Days* to commemorate the centenary of Verne's birth. Sponsored by a Paris newspaper, he was surprised to find that:

> Those famous eighty days were a fantasy of Verne's imagination, a premonition of the future, like his photographs and aeroplanes, submarines and divers ... It turned out that in 1936, if we were to bring off Phileas

Fogg's wager following the route he selected as the best, screwing up boat and train connexions to the tightest, and eschewing airways, we would need exactly eighty days, neither more nor less. By now our project had assumed a different look. Ceasing to be an easy jaunt in the footsteps of the heroes ... of our school-days, it had turned into a record-breaking feat, a touch-and-go performance (1936: 5–6).

Books also provide us with a mechanism for living out these experiences vicariously, through reading about the recreated journeys of others. Thor Heyerdahl's *The Kon-Tiki Expedition* (1951) was a sensation when it was first published and remains an inspiration to current-day adventure travellers (Laing & Crouch, 2009a). Tim Severin wrote highly successful books about his recreated journeys, such as *Tracking Marco Polo* (1964), *The Sindbad Voyage* (1983), *In Search of Genghis Khan* (1991) and *Seeking Robinson Crusoe* (2002), accompanied by television documentaries. Another exponent of these recreated journeys is historian Michael Wood, who has written books, with a companion television series, such as *In the Footsteps of Alexander the Great* (1997).

There is a trend for these books to be either written by or about a celebrity travelling in the footsteps of their hero or heroine, which makes the accompanying documentary perhaps more commercially viable and likely to be picked up by the television broadcasters. Examples of this include Cocteau and the journalist Bernard Levin, with *Hannibal's Footsteps* (Levin, 1987), where he traced the journey the Carthaginian general made across the Alps, *sans* the famous elephants.

Comedians have taken up the reins in recent years. The comic actress Pamela Stephenson took a voyage through the South Pacific following the route of Robert Louis Stevenson, author of *Treasure Island*, and his sister Fanny. Her travel narrative ended up as a book *Treasure Islands: Sailing in the South Seas in the Wake of Fanny and Robert Louis Stevenson* (2005) and two-part documentary, featuring the reactions of her husband, Scottish comic Billy Connolly, to her journey. Python comedian Michael Palin went *Around the World in Eighty Days*, while Stephen Fry went to some of the remotest places on Earth in the 2009 television programme *Last Chance to See: Following in the Footsteps of Douglas Adams*. Host of *Grand Designs*, Kevin McCloud also took us, in 2009, on *Kevin McCloud's Grand Tour of Europe*. There are also travel products linked to recreations, such as the walking tour through Tuscany taking tourists 'in the footsteps of Sigeric', the Archbishop of Canterbury in the 1st century AD, and a travel company called *In the Footsteps* ('follow in the footsteps of heroes!'), that takes visitors on battlefield tours.

In this chapter, we look at why recreated travel is so popular, the role of books in this process, and what the recreationist is trying to achieve by these kinds of journeys.

Metempsychosis and the Recreated Journey

The concept of *metempsychosis* is relevant to an understanding of the recreated journey. It has a Platonic origin, referring to the idea of the 'transmigration of souls' (Long, 1948: 149) upon death to a new body. This concept has recently been applied in a tourism context to the taking on of 'the persona of a significant other or group, as a role model for a particular repeated journey' (Seaton, 2002: 155). Reijinders (2009: 174) sees this as a spiritual process, whereby the tourist aims 'to get into the skin of another, charismatic person, and ultimately become one with their soul'.

These fantasies often have their roots or source in travel narratives. Hennig (2002) argues that the tourist remains, at least partly, in an imaginary world, created by the books or brochures they have read or the films they have seen. Travel is, therefore, a ritual re-enactment of the myths embodied in these narratives, such as the explorer myth (Laing & Crouch, 2009c; Laing & Crouch, 2011). Sometimes the traveller literally goes on a recreated journey, which is what we focus on in this chapter.

Types of recreated journeys

The first type of recreation is the short walking tour. A number of these products are using the concept of a recreation inspired by a book or an author to brand or distinguish themselves from the competition (Plate, 2006; Reijinders, 2009). Edinburgh, for example, has its Rebus tours, where the visitor can walk to the places immortalised in Ian Rankin's *Rebus* crime series. These are not the picturesque sites traditionally associated with Edinburgh, such as the Castle, the Royal Mile and Princes Street. The Rebus tours take us to the underbelly of Edinburgh, the housing estates where social problems brew, the local police station and Salisbury Crags, where a character threw himself to his death in one of the novels. The first thing the guide asks the group is whether they have read a Rebus novel. Those who haven't are mercilessly lampooned for the rest of the tour. On the tour Jennifer took, she was the only person out of 13 visitors who hadn't yet read a Rebus book, which demonstrates the powerful link between the tour and the books. Walking tours of Bloomsbury (Figure 9.1) bring to life the bohemian life of the famous literary and artistic circle.

Figure 9.1 Plaque honouring the Bloomsbury Group in Gordon Square, London. Photo by J. Laing.

The second type of recreation is the longer guided tour, such as the *Lord of the Rings* tours analysed by Buchmann *et al.* (2010). These tours represent a kind of pilgrimage to the places depicted in the film but inspired by the books by J.R.R. Tolkien. It was noted that 'People were willing to "follow in the footsteps" to visit places that had attained an aura in their own eyes, authenticated by cast and crew comments' (Buchmann *et al.*, 2010: 245). The act of going to the places where things happened in the films and the books takes on a spiritual quality, inspiring a sense of awe among the tourists. Their visit to these sites makes them feel part of a wider community, composed of those who 'share their understanding and love of the stories' (Buchmann *et al.*, 2010: 241).

The third type of recreation is the recreated event, often commemorating the anniversary of some historical occurrence or significant time in history. The Battle of Hastings is recreated by English Heritage each October in the English town of Battle and depicts William the Conqueror's successful attempt to invade Britain (Figure 9.2). Some of these recreated events have a strong connection to books, such as the spate of Jane Austen fetes, assemblies and balls, and a recreation of Lord Capulet's Ball from Shakespeare's *Romeo and Juliet*.

Figure 9.2 Commentary by British Heritage at the Battle of Hastings re-enactment. Photo by W. Frost.

The fourth type of recreation is the individually recreated journey, which is the main focus of this chapter. These are the travel experiences that are often written about and inspire others. A popular form of recreated journey involves travelling in the footsteps of explorers (Seaton, 2002; Laing & Crouch, 2011). A book often acts as the catalyst for travel. Peter Treseder, who became a member of the first Australian team to ski across Antarctica to the South Pole, purchased a copy of *This Accursed Land*, the story of Sir Douglas Mawson's ill-fated 1911–1914 Antarctic expedition, while on his honeymoon, and found inspiration there for his future Polar travels (Brown, 1999).

These recreated journeys are, in turn, immortalised in another text, thus perpetuating the cycle. John and Julie Batchelor have retraced Henry Morton Stanley's expedition across Africa to find the source of the Nile and written their own book, *In Stanley's Footsteps* (Batchelor & Batchelor, 1990). Bergin (1981) has recreated the Burke and Wills fiasco, without the tragic dénouement. A modern-day traverse of the Sahara by John Hare in 2001 adopted the same route that Swiss-born British national Hanns Vischer took in 1906, when he journeyed for 1581 miles through the Sahara Desert from Tripoli to Lake Chad – the world's largest sand desert. Hare published a book about his re-enactment – *Shadows Across the Sahara* (2003) – and describes the inspiration he derived from Vischer's earlier book *Across the Sahara* (1910): '[It] caught my imagination. I loved his tales of stirring encounters in terrible desert wastes, where no water could be found for days and where oases were few and far between' (Hare, 2003: 62).

There are a number of reasons why these journeys might be undertaken. These include motivations such as escapism and nostalgia, a desire for authenticity and concerns about resurrecting reputations. A number can be conceptualised as a quest to find out 'the truth'; to understand what really happened in the past, as distinct from the myth, often handed down in the form of a book. These experiences might be characterised as an act of hero-worship or homage to legends of the past in some instances, or a form of role play or fantasy.

Escapism/Nostalgia

The re-enactments might provide an element of escapism, both for the writer/traveller and the reader. This is linked to nostalgia for the past, a time when things were simpler and travel more arduous. This makes these journeys more desirable in the eyes of the traveller. Thus, as Holland and Huggan (2000: xi) note, many travel writers 'hearken back to their precursors, seeking solace for a troubled present in nostalgic cultural myths'.

Bettina Selby is a pertinent example. She travels to Egypt to recreate the journey of explorer Amelia B. Edwards (Selby, 1988), and is influenced by the atlases and books she has read about African exploration, leading her to describe daydreams that 'began to be peopled by long trains of porters bearing Fortnum and Mason hampers. Armies of fanatical 'Fuzzy Wuzzies boiled out of the desert behind their Mahdi, hurling themselves against "thin red lines" of pith-helmeted soldiers with Kitchener moustaches' (1988: 7). This is a form of imperialist or colonial fantasy, in a post-colonial world. In this way, Selby has recreated a world that no longer exists, except in her imagination and the books that she reads:

> I realised that I had in a way been there before and that the same ghosts were lingering in this oasis [the Sudan] as stalked through the hill stations of northern India. It was the unmistakable aura of empire – tea and scones, croquet and chota pegs; and the sixty or seventy decaying railway engines I'd seen on the way in, all stamped 'Made in Darlington,' were part of that not yet forgotten world. (Selby, 1988: 120)

London Walks offers a popular stroll 'In the Footsteps of Sherlock Holmes', where one can 'go sleuthing [and] explore an area whose "everchanging kaleidoscope of life" intrigued Holmes and Watson'. This theme gives the walk its structure but also a sense of going back in time. Taking part in these walks might, therefore, represent a desire on the part of the traveller to remember or *commemorate* people or places from the past. Jennifer, however, felt disenchanted on a recent walk, that the images conjured up through her reading of the books were not matched by the reality of walking around modern London:

> The guide wore a baseball cap instead of a deerstalker hat, but had an encyclopaedic knowledge of the Sherlock books. The disorienting thing however was the weather. The London immortalised by Conan Doyle is one of hansom cabs, gloom, and pea-souper fogs. This adds to the atmosphere of the books, and heightens the tension and mystery. The day I took the walk, London was enjoying one of its rare summer days, where the sky was deep blue, showing the contrails of the planes arriving at and leaving Heathrow Airport. The population was either flopped on the grass, or sitting at pavement cafes, with as little clothing as they could get away with. A sign advertised 'Enjoy a Pimms' and the group dodged heavy traffic and cyclists on 'Boris Bikes'. This was as far from 221B Baker Street as I could imagine. Even the scheduled stops beside the few remaining gas lamps in London and sites frequented by Holmes such as Simpsons on the Strand, the Lyceum Theatre and Charing Cross Station could not evoke the London I had in my mind when I read the books. The final stop was a recreation of Holmes' study on the top floor of the Sherlock Holmes pub. It had been made for the Festival of Britain back in 1951, and epitomised the desire to make the imaginary come alive. There was a garbage bag at the front of the tableau. 'We're renovating it' said the bored-looking girl, staring at the group of tourists.

Authenticity

The vignette above illustrates the importance of authenticity in these re-enactments. This might reflect historical accuracy or simply a feeling that the re-enactment is in keeping with the spirit of the book or the original travel experience. Plate (2006: 107) examines a guided walking tour of Bloomsbury and its association with Virginia Woolf and notes that it provides an authentic experience for the tourist – these are the places referred to in the book or where the author lived or worked: 'To hear, sense and smell what she heard, sensed and smelled'. This works where the location has not changed drastically from that depicted in the book or books. Bloomsbury still retains the cream facades and iron railings of its pre-war glory, and one can almost picture Virginia out for a stroll or ensconced in one of the terraces.

A desire for authenticity might involve the traveller trying to ensure that the recreated journey uses similar equipment or is undertaken in a similar manner to the original. A book is often used as a guide or ultimate form of reference to make sure the recreation is accurate. Stress is placed on wearing the right clothes and doing things in-keeping with the 'spirit' of these past journeys.

For this reason, the use of technology is often limited or banned outright. Michael Asher, in his recreation of Thesiger's journeys in the Arabian Desert observes: 'We would take maps and compasses but nothing in the way of advanced technology, which would spoil the spirit of the adventure' (Asher, 1988: 9). Robert Swan saw walking across Antarctica without radios, in the footsteps of Scott, as 'an opportunity for truth' (Mear & Swan, 1987: 84). For Roger Mear, it was a way to demonstrate some of the extraordinary dedication shown by the explorers in Scott's day, 'to play the game by the old rules' (Mear & Swan, 1987: 234).

Tim Severin, in deciding to undertake the Brendan Voyage, in the footsteps of the Irish monk, refers to accounts written of the voyage, and stresses the importance of historical accuracy (Severin, 1978):

> Of course there would be an immense amount of work to do before the idea could be advanced. First, I had to satisfy myself that the scholarship behind the project was sound. I was determined at all costs not to let the Brendan Voyage, as I had already chosen to call it, become a mere survival test. I was under no illusion that it would require many months of painstaking preparations to prepare the voyage, followed by a fair amount of physical risk during the Atlantic passage itself. To warrant such risk and effort the endeavor had to produce worthwhile results. It had to strive toward a precise and serious purpose; at no time must that serious purpose be shaken.

Authenticity might also be a means to solve some of the great mysteries of the past. Why did some journeys fail? Did some journeys even take place at all? And were they recorded accurately?

Myth Made Real – Sorting Fact from Fiction

An example of a journey made to prove or disprove a historical conundrum was that of polar trekker Paul Landry. He was fascinated by the historical debate as to whether Cook or Peary reached the North Pole first. There was speculation that both had made up the claim. Landry 'spent years reading the various arguments and counter-arguments. One day, he put down his pen, returned the books to the library and went to see for himself' (Woodhead, 2003: 89). Landry arrived at the Pole 'only four days behind Peary' (Landry's expedition took 42 days in contrast to Peary's claim that he reached the Pole in 38 days) and his expedition appears to show that Peary's account might have been based on truth, although the jury is still out on this point (Conefrey & Jordan, 1998).

Both Thor Heyerdahl and Tim Severin appear to be chiefly motivated by the desire or curiosity to prove historical or mythical events were or could have been rooted in fact, rather than mere fiction. Severin (1978) saw his recreated sea voyage of Saint Brendan as 'a detective story'. This goes to the heart of explorer tales, which have often been a curious mix of hyperbole and exaggeration on the one hand, and scrupulous attention to detail on the other. The two books discussed below describe recreated journeys aimed at discovering what had, or was likely to have, happened in the past.

The Kon Tiki Expedition (Thor Heyerdahl, 1948)

Thor Heyerdahl is considered one of the pioneers of metempsychotic journeys. His most famous voyage was undertaken across the Pacific Ocean in a replica of a balsa raft, the Kon-Tiki (Figure 9.3). This was done to test his theories on the origins of the Polynesian race and culture and was later published as *The Kon-Tiki Expedition: By Raft Across the South Seas* (1951). The catalyst is an unnamed senior professor, who ridicules his ideas. By reaching his goal, he shows that this theory has some scientific merit.

This book also delves into the 'strange mystery of Easter Island' with its 'giants' heads cut in stone, with pointed beards and white men's features, brooding over the secret of centuries'. Heyerdahl wanted to know how they were carved and transported to their final resting place. He postulates that the answer lies with the craftsmen of Peru, and 'the same vanished civilisation erected similar giant statues in human shape on many of the other Pacific islands nearest to America'. Heyerdahl observes how they felt 'participators in the whole prehistoric adventure'. He subsequently returned to Easter Island on another voyage in an attempt to solve the mystery, which he published as *Aku-Aku, The Archaeology of Easter Island,* and *The Art of Easter Island*.

Heyerdahl is concerned that his journey will be misunderstood by others. He notes in his book the criticism his adventure initially received in academic circles, but how the public have supported and were intrigued by his work. His book is a means to set the record straight. Unlike those who merely sniped at home, Heyerdahl has actively sought to prove his theories and challenge accepted wisdom. It is reminiscent of the scenes in Conan Doyle's *The*

Figure 9.3 Mask at the Kon-Tiki Museum, Oslo. Photo by J. Laing.

Lost World (1912), when the travellers return home and have their tales of encountering dinosaurs scorned by scientists.

The voyage is described by Heyerdahl as akin to going back in time. By contrast, returning to America is described as 'on our way to the twentieth century which lay so far, far away' These journeys are a way of returning to the past and the books written about them help the reader to share in that fantasy.

The Brendan Voyage (Tim Severin, 1978)

In *The Brendan Voyage*, Tim Severin recreates the journey that formed the centrepiece of the legend of St Brendan's discovery of the New World in the

6th century. It meant travelling from Ireland across the Atlantic Ocean in a boat made of the hides of oxen. Both he and his wife had read *The Navigatio Sancti Brendani Abbatis* (the *Navigatio* or Voyage of Brendan) and felt it to be a curious piece of literature. The level of practical detail and absence of miraculous events intrigued them. It read like 'first-hand experience', albeit heavily embellished and perhaps exaggerated.

This was not the first metempsychotic journey that Severin had undertaken. This love of 'checking the truth', testing it out, is like a scientist testing out a theory. He uses this language, referring to his desire to 'discover the truth by practical experiment'. If he was able to show that this voyage was possible, then this might support the hypothesis that St Brendan discovered America 'almost a thousand years before Columbus and four hundred years before the Vikings'. Of course, it still would not confirm that St Brendan in fact made that voyage. Severin concedes this at the end of the book, noting that it would need an archaeological discovery or 'authentic relic' to do this. It did, however, contribute to 'serious historical debate' and at least encourage archaeological searches for an early Irish presence in the New World. It also changed the way we see the *Navigatio*, from being merely a 'splendid medieval romance', to one founded upon 'facts and observation which mingles geography and literature, and the challenge is how to separate one from the other'.

Severin refers to the 'scholarship' behind the voyage. He is not a mere adventurer; he identifies as an academic with a 'serious and precise purpose'. He stresses that this is not a race and risks need not be taken. The important thing is to remain true to the spirit of the original voyage. The crew thus decides to hold off sailing over winter, and continue when the weather warmed up: 'I consoled myself that this is what the Irish monks had done'.

The journey was as much about the preparation and anticipation as the actual travel phase. Severin describes the 'venture' as half-way over before the vessel even set sail across the Atlantic. The focus is the development of the boat. The crew does not wear medieval garb, not eat medieval food. They have a radio telephone, camera equipment and a paraffin stove. Their sole goal is to prove that the boat could theoretically make it across the Atlantic to America.

Severin has a deep love of history and compares his journey to historic voyages and explorers' feats ('the same coast had destroyed at least twenty galleons in the Spanish Armada'). The crew have sheepskins for warmth, as Severin read about their usefulness to polar explorers when sleeping on ice and notes that they would have been used in St Brendan's day. Sailing through the treacherous ice and prodding the boat away with hooks and their feet reminds Severin of the way 'Elizabethan sailors' used 'just the same simple technique'. He notes the satisfaction they felt at their success 'using the same basic materials which had been available to Saint Brendan and the Irish seagoing monks'.

These long voyages become a personal endurance test, despite the fact that they were undertaken by a crew. People retreated inside themselves and stopped talking as much: 'Each man reacted in his own way to events, and his experiences did not necessarily mix with the ideas of his companions'. Those on watch saw more than the others, and felt the personal responsibility of looking after the others. They suffered boredom at times, despite the dangers. Severin does not whitewash the narrative, but provides a detailed exposition of daily life on the boat, with its hazards and humour. A failed attempt to capture a harpooned pilot whale is treated as disappointing, even though it is unclear what they would have done with it and why this was necessary.

Severin distinguishes his voyage from those of the likes of Heyerdahl ('previous voyages in reconstructed historical vessels'), without naming him, noting that he was on a boat rather than a raft: 'Brendan was not simply a platform on which the winds and currents might carry us to our destination if we were lucky'. He also observes that the extreme cold and freezing water set his voyage apart ('this was not to be a sun-drenched cruise in bathing suits'). One gets the feeling that Severin regards his journey as more arduous and hence authentic, than the Heyerdahl version. He notes that they gained a greater appreciation of 'their medieval outlook', which was only possible by putting themselves in 'situations similar to the original'.

Resurrecting Reputations and Reviving Forgotten Heroes

Another strong motivation to recreate an explorer's journey is to seek to resurrect the reputation of fallen 'heroes' – the explorer who has been vilified by modern narratives, such as Robert Falcon Scott. He did not win the 'race' to the South Pole (dying in the attempt it must be added), and this doomed effort is often blamed on his failure to use dogs, unlike the winning team, headed by the Norwegian Roald Amundsen. Sir Ranulph Fiennes wanted to restore Scott's place in history by his unsupported traverse of Antarctica (Fiennes, 1993: 225):

In hauling our own loads across this area, greater in mass by far than the United States, we have shown that manpower can indeed be superior to dog-power and, in doing so, have partly exonerated Scott's much-abused theories on the matter.

Another famous recreated journey in the footsteps of Scott was made by Mear and Swan (1987). They also hoped to restore Scott's reputation as an adventurer, despite his failures (Mear & Swan, 1987: 27–28):

> We are a more cynical nation now and our heroes have been toppled from their pedestals. They have been denounced because they have been revealed as men with weaknesses and failings. Scott fell to the biased pen of Roland Huntford in his book *Scott and Amundsen*. Yet the truth lies somewhere between the two extremes. Robert's dream was not simply to walk to the South Pole but to rediscover Scott and bring alive the histories of those men that so inspired him.

Swan describes himself as 'obsessed' with history: 'What is the real story of Scott? I have a feeling that we may find it out there on the journey'. Both men wanted to recreate the expedition as it was done in 1911, and criticise the use of technology as despoiling modern day polar expeditions (Mear & Swan, 1987: 37):

> The mystery has gone. Helicopters whisk geologists to remote rocky nunataks and aircraft drop fresh milk and fruit to the South Pole station, even in the middle of winter. Those who seek adventure can no longer set out under the banner of science and close communion with the great forces of nature is no longer possible from within the restrictive protection of the modern Antarctic base.

Some journeys are aimed at shedding light on forgotten episodes of history, such as the explorer who has been written out of or overlooked in modern history-books. This is exemplified by the travel experiences of Kieran Kelly.

Tanami (Kieran Kelly, 2003)

Kieran Kelly is a middle-aged Sydney businessman with a passion for exploration. He has written two books of recreated journeys – one called *Hard Country, Hard Men* in the footsteps of the explorer Augustus Gregory and the second *Tanami*, traces his trek by foot across the Tanami desert, to complete a journey that defeated Gregory and the explorer John McDouall Stuart. Both are men he admires intensely, although he recognises their weaknesses.

Stuart was a brilliant explorer who travelled from South Australia to the Great Australian Bight in 1858, a distance of nearly 1700 kilometres, with only a compass for guidance and became the first white man to reach Central

Australia. His lack of planning however was acknowledged; a matter at which Kelly himself has excelled in his expeditions. Nevertheless, the man intrigued him: 'I was excited by the prospect of seeing central Australia, seeing what the little Scotsman had seen, walking where he had ridden and finding out what sort of person he had really been'. He later decides Stuart has been 'done a major disservice'. For example, he discovered what was later called the Lander River, while Mount Esther, named by Stuart, is not referred to on modern maps of the region. Kelly bemoans the errors on Australian maps, which he calls 'dangerously misleading to historians'. His expedition has exposed these errors, one of its contributions to posterity.

Similarly, he regards Gregory as an outstandingly successful explorer, who presided over scientific and artistic achievements, including those of fellow expeditioners, Ferdinand von Mueller, the botanist, and Thomas Baines, an artist, the latter of whose work is now part of the archives of the Royal Geographical Society. He describes the North Australian Expedition as making Gregory a 'household name', yet decries how quickly his reputation has been forgotten, unlike, say, the ill-fated Burke and Wills: '[Gregory] proves that winners, in Australia at least, don't always write history'. Kelly speculates that the success of Gregory's expeditions make him less likely to be used in the classroom. The spectacular failures are easier 'to teach', and he classes the Gallipoli carnage of innocents in this category. He hopes his recreated journey will redress the balance to a degree.

Kelly loves the logistics of an expedition, working out what to take and how to pack it. His methodical mind thrives on the planning stage, including plotting the routes the explorers took on to modern maps, with reference to their journals and sketchbooks. He is also a history buff and describes his home office 'crammed with reference books, navigational instruments and maps'. His intricately researched journeys are an attempt to resurrect forgotten heroes, but also a tribute to their skill and bravery at a time when men died trying to explore the Outback. Gregory and Stuart tried to cross the Tanami desert in central Australia in the 19th century, four years apart and from different sides – Gregory from the west and Stuart from the east. Both felt that the crossing would be a certain suicide mission, on the assumption that no water would be found there. Kelly wanted to understand why they had both turned back, and what might have happened had they instead chosen to go on. Was the crossing truly impossible by foot? His meeting with camel operator Andrew Harper results in their expedition to one of the most inhospitable and barren places on Earth. Kelly's sense of humour is a useful asset when things get tough. He observes: 'Australian deserts are more *Mad Max* than *Lawrence of Arabia*'. But he doesn't underestimate the size of his task, and the risks they are taking: 'Get lost out here and we could wander around in circles forever and no-one would find us'. In an emergency, despite the latest technology, including satellite phones, rescue might not arrive in time. They are dependent on their wits and skills as adventurers.

These kinds of expeditions give Kelly the trial or testing that he doesn't get sitting in an air-conditioned office. He refers to 'things of the male spirit', which are neglected in the modern era, and how he needs both physical and mental challenge. However, it is the recreation that is the vehicle for this. He seems to need that sense of walking in another's footsteps. Writing a journal, and later his books, is also linked to being an explorer. He tells his travelling companion Andrew Harper: 'I like to think we're keeping a journal that one day people might compare to the early explorers' journals'. His concern about his journal is so great that one night he dreams that it is eaten by a camel. Kelly also likes the idea that his great-grandson might discover his journals one day 'trawling through a dusty attic', and 'be fired up to come out here and retrace our steps or find the plaques we've left behind. I can only imagine what it would be like to know that this compass had been on one of my great-grandfather's expeditions'. Kelly achieves his goal, and observes: 'For a moment, for five brief weeks, I walked in the footsteps of giants'.

Hero-worship/Homage

Re-enacting a travel experience of the past might be a way to pay tribute to the courage and achievements of these explorers. Bettina Selby felt a kinship with explorers of the past and travelled to the source of the Nile, almost in homage to her explorer heroes or heroines: 'I went to pay my respects to Speke's memory at the place where the Nile really begins, where the waters of Lake Victoria start their exit through the Ripon Falls' (Selby, 1988: 231).

Occasionally these recreationists feel embarrassed at their own hubris in walking in their hero's footsteps. Jeffrey Tayler enacts the myths bound up in Thesiger's masterpiece *Arabian Sands* and is disappointed at not being able to match his literary hero's exacting standards during his expedition through the Sahara (Tayler, 2003: 174):

> I was falling short of Thesiger, who disparaged the amenities of civilization and 'learnt the satisfaction which comes from hardship and the pleasure which springs from abstinence' and who, among the Bedouin, found 'comradeship in a hostile world'.

Tayler notes however, at the end of his journey, that however much he would like to be like his hero: 'We were not Thesiger and his Bedouin, but lesser mortals who had walked a long way, suffered a lot, and exhausted them-selves. Still, we had done what we had set out to do'. This discomfiture at trying to emulate one's heroes might lead the traveller to adopt a form of self-parody (Holland & Huggan, 2000: 234). They sometimes adopt a mask of being an eccentric, perhaps to disguise the intensity of their feelings about the re-enactment and their seriousness of purpose.

Role Play/Fantasy

Some of these re-enactments can be understood as a type of role play or fantasy, such as that identified in a study of Arctic trekkers who used 'harsh environmental conditions and hard physical activities ... to inscribe them-selves into an idealized 'explorer' or 'pioneer' role' (Gyimóthy & Mykletun, 2004: 865). Polar trekker Patrick Woodhead (2003) went to a talk by Sir Ranulph Fiennes at the Royal Geographical Society. Woodhead is curious to experience being an explorer, even for a brief period. He wants 'a taste of this kind of life ... I just wanted to look into that window for the briefest of seconds. In doing so, I thought, perhaps I might understand what it actually is that they're all banging on about' (Woodhead, 2003: 18–19).

Virginia Morell, who journeyed to the source of the Blue Nile in Ethiopia, has a fantasy of the female Victorian traveller in whose footsteps she is walk-ing (Morell, 2001: 135):

> I walked along behind them with the umbrella open over my head, feel-ing like a modern version of the 19th century explorer Mary Kingsley, who traipsed across West Africa in full Victorian garb, carefully shaded by her black umbrella.

This interest in role play might also be present during the metempsychotic walking tour. Reijnders (2009) examines walking tours of sites associated with fictional detectives Inspector Morse (Oxford), Kurt Wallander (Ystad) and Baantjer (Amsterdam). He suggests that the tourist *becomes* the detec-tive, but also gets to relive the story, 'at the same time supplemented with new sensory impressions' (Reijinders, 2009: 174). The place itself gets imprinted with the narrative, and becomes, in effect, a 'guilty landscape', within which the traveller plays. The book is the script and the journey or travel experience becomes a performance or ritual drama. Writing books about these experiences, in turn, provides a new audience for these narra-tives. One that seemingly never tires of the path 'well travelled'.

10 Fantastic Journeys

'Tell me one last thing,' said Harry. 'Is this real?
Or has this been happening inside my head?'
'Of course it is happening inside your head, Harry, but
why on earth should that mean that it is not real?'
Harry Potter and the Deathly Hallows, J.K. Rowling, 2007

Fictional writers have full rein to invent characters, plots and situations. Some also invent fictional settings, which may range from the ordinary to the fantastic. These invented places may be the central appeal of a novel, utilising the imagination of both the author and reader. In this chapter, we are interested in examining fictional accounts of travel to unreal places. Such destinations may be categorised into two divisions. The first is lost or hidden worlds, places that might really exist, but need to be explored. The second division is of fantasy worlds, places that are clearly unreal. We are then interested in how travel to these places is represented and the meanings attached to this travel. Three main aspects are explored for each category:

(1) *The quest.* The purpose behind the travel.
(2) *The journey.* How the travel to these fantastic places is achieved.
(3) *The return.* What has been achieved and what has been brought back as proof of the journey.

Lost or Hidden Worlds

This first group of worlds are represented as real. They are part of the physical earth, but they are remote, just beyond the frontiers of our current geographical knowledge. The heroes are explorers, albeit fictional and they conform to the general characteristics and tropes of the exploration literature (see Chapters 8 and 9). The authors often reinforce this authenticity by giving detailed and seemingly accurate accounts of preparations, equipment and descriptions of their real embarkation points, exactly as we commonly find in real accounts by explorers. Even the imaginary worlds follow a semblance of reality, there may be lost civilisations, fountains of youth and prehistoric animals, but the general laws of physics are followed and there are no impossible creatures or aliens.

We consider these in chronological order. The majority come from the Age of Exploration and Imperial Expansion of the late 19th and 20th centuries. The Western powers were expanding rapidly and organising extensive exploring expeditions. The fiction of this period reflected these interests (see Chapter 5) and this led many novelists to speculate about the unknown territories that were about to be revealed. However, as explorers filled in the blanks in the world's maps, the scope for finding undiscovered worlds changed over time. While seemingly a dead genre, the popularity of the last two books considered indicates there is still a readership and possibilities in this type of fictional travel narrative.

Five Weeks in a Balloon (Jules Verne, 1862)

Explorer Dr Samuel Ferguson has perfected a new type of hot air balloon. He is joined by hunter Dick Kennedy on an expedition across the unmapped centre of Africa. They are particularly interested in finding the source of the Nile. Verne's first book, it was originally rejected as being too scientific and factual. On the advice of his new publisher, he rewrote it with a better balance of fictional drama.

While one of the lesser known of Verne's works, we have included it here as it is an excellent example of how fiction writers were only one step ahead of reality. The inspiration for this novel was the real life search for the source of the Nile. Verne (and his readership) were aware that this was topical and that there were a number of competing exploring parties in the field. Verne won this race, *Five Weeks* was published just before Speke's *Journal of the Discovery of the Source of the Nile* came out in 1863 (Martin, 1990).

Journey to the Centre of the Earth (Jules Verne, 1864)

Geologist, Professor Liedenbrock finds a coded message in an old book. Finally deciphering it, he discovers a message written hundreds of years before. It is from Arne Saknussemm, who claims to have discovered a passage to the centre of the earth. The professor mounts an expedition, with his nephew Axel and guide Hans. They start from a mountain crater in Iceland, then a hardly visited country. After months of travel they reach a massive ocean at the earth's core. There are giant mushrooms, dinosaurs and they even catch a glimpse of a prehistoric human. A volcanic eruption restores them to the earth's surface.

20,000 Leagues Under the Sea (Jules Verne, 1870)

Something is sinking ships. Is it a sea monster or a secret weapon? An expedition to investigate includes the oceanographer Professor Aronnax and a harpoonist Ned Land. Under attack, they fall overboard, but are rescued by the occupants of a giant submarine *The Nautilus*. It is under the command of the mysterious Captain Nemo, who is using his invention to destroy the navies of the major powers. They sail around the world, experiencing a series of underwater adventures.

King Solomon's Mines (Henry Rider Haggard, 1885)

Hunter Allen Quartermain is hired to guide Sir Henry Curtis and Captain John Good into the heart of Africa in a search for King Solomon's diamond mines. They discover Kukuanaland, a fertile plateau with a militaristic society. It is ruled by the bloodthirsty Twala. One of their party is Umbopa, who turns out to be the rightful king and has returned to claim his throne. They assist Umbopa and after a massive battle are successful. He then guides them to the fabulous mines.

She (Henry Rider Haggard, 1887)

Professor Holly is intrigued that his ward Leo has inherited an Egyptian pottery shard. It gives directions to the lost city of Kôr in the middle of Africa. They journey there and find it ruled by the tyrannical sorceress Ayesha ('She Who Must be Obeyed'). She is over 2000 years old, her immortality coming from the Pillar of Life, a fiery version of the Fountain of Youth.

The Lost World (Arthur Conan Doyle, 1912)

Professor Challenger delivers a public lecture on the existence of dinosaurs in an unexplored part of South America. Branded a liar and a crackpot, he proposes a scientific expedition to investigate. Along with Challenger, this comprises his chief critic Professor Summerlee, an explorer/hunter or 'sportsman' Lord John Roxton and a journalist Edward Malone. The Lost World is a near inaccessible plateau, on which are trapped dinosaurs, ape-men and modern Indians.

Lost Horizon (James Hilton, 1933)

Conway, the British Consul to Afghanistan, disappears. He is found in a Chinese hospital. He explains he was in an aeroplane that was hijacked and then crashed in Tibet. With him were his assistant Mallinson, an American Barnard and a British missionary Miss Brinklow. They are rescued and taken into a lamasery in the valley of Shangri-La. Cut off from the rest of the world, it is peaceful and idyllic, and the pure natural environment allows people to live for hundreds of years. The Head Lama explains that Shangri-La is a sort of life-boat or ark, preserving a portion of the world's culture from the coming Armageddon of a universal air war. The hijacking was an attempt to recruit new blood. Mallinson wants to leave. Conway, Barnard (a criminal on the run) and Brinklow decide to stay. In the end, Mallinson convinces Conway to help him return. Having told his story, Conway disappears again, searching for Shangri-La.

Jurassic Park (Michael Crichton, 1991)

Palaeontologists Alan Grant and Ellie Sattler journey to a mysterious island off the coast of Costa Rica. They are being paid by millionaire Richard Hammond who is building a theme park and wants their endorsement. They assume he will be using animatronics, but when they arrive they find he has created living dinosaurs. Hammond achieves this by cloning, using dinosaur DNA extracted from amber and fossils. Naturally, the dinosaurs escape and cause havoc.

Mutant Message Down Under (Marlo Morgan, 1995)

Initially released and marketed as non-fiction, protests from Aboriginal groups forced the publishers to admit this book was purely fictional. The American Morgan joins a mysterious tribe of Aboriginals as they trek across Australia. The tribe rejects Western materialism and are adept at hiding from the authorities. Their base is hidden underground in the Outback.

The quest

There is a strong common model in these works. The lost world is sought by an 'expedition' consisting of a diverse group of people. This diversity allows for dramatic and narrative interest. Indeed the party may be seen as a collection of archetypes. Foremost is a Professor, who is obsessed with exploring a particular field and functions to explain complex concepts and theories to the party and, of course, the reader. He is often juxtaposed with a Hunter or Military Man, who has practical skills, can defend them and functions as a co-leader. Then there may be a Younger Offsider – nephew, ward, assistant, journalist – who functions as a proxy for the reader in asking the older and wiser members of the party for explanations. Occasionally there is a Sceptic. A Servant (à la Passepartout in *Around the World in Eighty Days*) functions as an everyman. Each party contains an educated person, who understands the scientific and geographic significance of their discoveries and has the skills to be a reflective narrator. As discussed in Chapter 8, true explorers must carefully record their discoveries.

The journeys qualify as quests. They are a search. The main focus is geographic knowledge, the quest to discover an unknown part of the world. These are explorers on expeditions, albeit fictional. In *Five Weeks in a Balloon*, the search is for the source of the Nile. In *Journey to the Centre of the Earth*, it is the passageway to the earth's core. In *She*, it is a lost city in the African interior. *The Lost World* recounts an expedition to a mysterious plateau in South America. A slight variation comes in *King Solomon's Mines*, where the search is for a missing adventurer, who was himself seeking the lost world.

The other type of quest is for enlightenment. Rather than knowledge of a physical place, the heroes gain a different understanding of the world and perhaps themselves. In these stories, this knowledge is not the initial reason for the journey, but comes in a roundabout or accidental way. In *20,000 Leagues Under the Sea*, Aronnax and Ned Land have spent their whole lives 'studying' the ocean; their adventure gives them the opportunity to go beneath what they already know. Similarly, the scientists in *Jurassic Park* gain the opportunity to see and understand dinosaurs in a way they never imagined previously. In these two books, the knowledge gained is of a type that explorers and scientists are typically seeking. However, in the remaining two stories, a different type of knowledge is gained. In *Lost Horizon*, the troubled war veteran Conway gains an opportunity for healing his psychological wounds. Morgan, in *Mutant Message*, is initially an unwilling traveller, but quickly begins to understand that she is privileged in being allowed hidden insights.

The journey

Just as the imagined lost world is presented as possible, so the travel to it is plausibly represented. All the writers go to great lengths to describe the departure, equipment, routes and so on. In this, they are adapting the conventions of real explorer accounts and accordingly give their fiction a layer of authenticity.

Many of these works draw on knowledge gained from other media. Jules Verne was a meticulous researcher of the latest scientific knowledge and theories. Over a hundred years later, Michael Crichton took the same approach, blending what was in the scientific literature with fictional action stories. Rider Haggard and Conan Doyle drew on their personal experiences in Africa, while writers like Hilton, as well as Conan Doyle, were inspired by newspaper and magazine stories of isolated parts of the world. Such real knowledge provided the starting point, with the writers greatly embellishing what was possible. Morgan provides an interesting and controversial example of such embellishment. While writing of Australian Aborigines, the basis for her descriptions of their beliefs and customs was her knowledge of Native Americans.

The journeys start with a key, some sort of device that unlocks the adventure. This is either a machine or a message. A newly invented machine, allowing humans to go to places previously off limits, is a common motif in the works of Jules Verne. It is the new-fangled balloon that enables the crossing of Africa in a mere five weeks and the super-submarine *Nautilus* that provides access under the sea. The messages are variations on the treasure map in *Treasure Island*. They mysteriously fall into the possession of one of the heroes and their meaning is not clear until they are expertly decoded. In *Journey to the Centre of the Earth*, it is a medieval alchemist's book. In *She*, it is writing on an ancient pottery fragment that needs decoding. To make the journey to *King Solomon's Mines*, Quartermain uses a map he has copied from the one possessed by a dying explorer. Similarly, Challenger in *The Lost World*, while too late to save a dying adventurer, finds a sketch of a Stegosaurus among the dead man's possessions. Intrigued, he links this with native legends and this is the catalyst for his search. In both *Jurassic Park* and *Mutant Message*, the heroes receive a message to go to a certain place. They do not fully understand the message, but follow the directions anyway.

The journey is difficult. The conventions of the katabasis are followed. Danger and deprivation are necessary to highlight the importance of the quest. Death is a constant possibility, either from the harsh environment, dangerous animals or hostile locals. In all three Verne books, there are literal dangerous descents. Reaching *King Solomon's Mines* requires the dangerous crossing of deserts and mountains and the fighting of a battle. Two servants die and the heroes are all wounded in the battle. *She* involves a shipwreck and more African deserts and mountains, and again, a servant is killed and the heroes narrowly escape death. Similarly, the dangerous trip in *The Lost World* is first up the Amazon and then involves the scaling of the sheer cliff walls of the ancient plateau. In *Lost Horizon* the desert is the icy mountains of the Himalayas and one of the party – Mallinson – dies. The highest death toll is in *Jurassic Park*, where the katabasis is to traverse the island after the dinosaurs have escaped. In *Mutant Message* there is the ever-present threat of death through lack of water or snakebite, and a long and arduous journey through the desert. In all of them, the dangers are reflected in the enlightenment received through the hardship.

Gender and race are tricky issues in what is often a colonial genre. There are no women members of any of the expedition until Miss Brinklow in *Lost Horizon*. Rider Haggard presents his major female characters as archetypes – immortal sorceresses, intent on enslaving or killing the travellers. Native women are an incentive to remain and where that is seriously considered, the writers quickly kill off such romance by killing off the participants. The more recent *Jurassic Park* and *Mutant Message* feature women, but their characters are seriously under-written. The heroic travellers are all white. They have various native servants, who suffer a high mortality rate. *King Solomon's Mines* is distinguished by having a black hero in Umbopa. This might be explained by his being a king in exile, or it might just reflect Haggard's liberal views. As he has the narrator Quartermain explain right at the beginning of the book, many natives are gentlemen and many whites are not.

The return

Seemingly Lost Worlds must remain lost. The heroes may return and tell their stories, but they often have little tangible proof of their discoveries and the means of returning have disappeared or been removed. The convention is that the journey was so extraordinary, it cannot be easily repeated. These new discoveries are not going to be part of the beaten track of tourists.

Verne's beloved explosions prevent repeat visitation in *Journey to the Centre of the Earth* and *20,000 Leagues Under the Sea*. In the former, a volcanic explosion destroys the return path, in the latter, Nemo blows up the *Nautilus* rather than allow it to fall into the hands of the Great Powers. Though the heroes are saved, they are not able to salvage or souvenir anything. In *King Solomon's Mines*, the return is fruitful, they have diamonds and they find Curtis's lost brother. However, Umbopa warns them that he will fight to keep the white men out; he wants neither rum nor missionaries.

The catalyst for the expedition in *The Lost World* is the ridicule Professor Challenger suffers for his claims. The scientific community will not believe him without tangible proof (though he is able to convince journalist Malone). The book ends with another scientific meeting in which Challenger is once again ridiculed for poor quality photos. 'No picture would convince us of anything' shouts the chief sceptic (ironically, within a decade Conan Doyle would trash his reputation through his public belief in photos of fairies). Challenger then unveils his proof; they have brought back a live specimen of a pterodactyl. Frightened by the crowd it escapes (Merrian C. Cooper would borrow this idea for *King Kong*). They have also returned with diamonds and will use them to fund a new expedition. In *Jurassic Park*, the dinosaurs are destroyed by the Costa Rican military. Hammond is killed, his laboratory is in ruins and his technology is apparently lost. Even the scientific knowledge gained is questionable, for Grant and Sattler know that these were just genetically engineered replicas of dinosaurs.

Lost Horizon is unusual in that two of the explorers – Barnard and Brinklow – choose to stay. In both *King Solomon's Mines* and *The Lost World*, our heroes are offered women, power and wealth to stay, but they decide to return to their world. Implicit in those decisions is their preference for what they see as a better, more civilised, world. The opposite occurs in *Lost Horizon*. Barnard, Brinklow and Conway find the lost world far more civilised and preferable to the outside world on the brink of war. Only Mallinson hankers to return and he convinces Conway to aid him. Once rescued, Conway realises his mistake and slips out of hospital to search for Shangri-La again. A similar narrative occurs in *Mutant Message* (perhaps *Lost Horizon* is the inspiration). Morgan's journey leads her to realise how shallow and meaningless the modern Western lifestyle is. She returns because she is given the task of convincing us to see the errors of our ways. She is able to visit her lost world again, but she is not allowed to bring back any tangible artefacts, photos or any sort of evidence.

Fantasy Worlds

The second group of worlds are more fantastic and magical. They are presented as completely and utterly fictional, as they stretch or defy the laws of science. These fantasy worlds are populated with amazingly unreal creatures and beings. In some, there is a strong emphasis on anthropomorphism, a common staple of children's literature. Animals talk and dress in human clothing, and even some inanimate objects are alive with human personalities. Their impossibility is a major part of their attraction, as the best of this genre create detailed and charismatic environments that readers are drawn to and in which they become deeply and passionately immersed (Figure 10.1). In the modern world, the popular appetite for fantasy continues to grow, probably as it presents a comforting and welcome relief to the ills of modernity. It is not surprising that a number of the books we consider have inspired significant fan bases and sub-cultures.

Again, we are only concerned with stories of people from the real world and contemporary time travelling to these fantastic worlds. Accordingly, we do not consider works such as *Lord of the Rings* in this chapter, as it does not

Figure 10.1 Platform 9¾ at King's Cross Station, London – a portal for Harry Potter. Photo by J. Laing.

involve this type of journey. We consider six books (or book series) divided into two main groupings. These groupings are Impossible Worlds and Alternative Dimensions.

Impossible Worlds

Gulliver's Travels (Jonathan Swift, 1724)

Gulliver recounts his sea voyages to a series of bizarre worlds, which he reaches after mishaps, such as shipwrecks or being marooned. The first (and the most famous) is Lilliput, where the inhabitants are one twelfth the size of Gulliver. Following this is Brobdingnag, where they are twelve times larger than Gulliver. On the floating island of Laputa, the citizens are obsessed with science experiments. The Houyhnhnms are intelligent talking horses. They share their world with the Yahoos, degenerate humans.

Alice's Adventures in Wonderland (Lewis Carroll, 1865)

Bored, Alice sits by a riverbank in rural England. She sees a White Rabbit, dressed in human clothing, checking his pocket watch and muttering that he's late. Curious, Alice follows him, eventually down a rabbit hole. This leads her to Wonderland. The assorted entities she meets include the Caterpillar, the March Hare, the Mad Hatter, the Cheshire Cat and the Queen of Hearts. All can talk, though their conversation is often nonsensical and this frustrates Alice. Through consuming magic cakes and liquids, Alice can vary in size. Attacked by the Queen's soldiers (playing cards), Alice wakes up back on the riverbank.

The Lion, the Witch and the Wardrobe (C.S. Lewis, 1950)

During World War Two, the four Pevensie children – Peter, Susan, Edmund and Lucy – are sent to an old house in the country. Playing hide and seek, they discover an old wardrobe leads to the magical land of Narnia. Here there are mythical creatures (fauns, centaurs, dragons) and talking animals. However, Narnia is gripped by a perpetual winter, the work of a wicked witch. The arrival of the children is a sign that Aslan the Lion is coming. Like King Arthur, Aslan is destined to return and save the country. The Witch is defeated in battle, her spell is broken and spring returns. The children are crowned as the new rulers. They grow to adulthood, living like medieval princes and princesses. One day they find the entrance to the wardrobe. They re-enter the modern world. They are children again and have only been away a couple of hours.

Interpreting and imagining impossible worlds

There is no ambiguity with these three cases. These worlds cannot exist and they cannot be travelled to. The authors understand this; they attempt no rational explanation of the worlds or their creatures and entry is through simple means (a shipwreck, magic doors). However, this simplicity is part of their charm. The reader suspends disbelief and is immersed in these impossible worlds. Any attempt at explanation would wreck that illusion. They reinforce the concept that travel exposes us to extraordinary experiences.

These books operate at two levels. They may be enjoyed as simple imaginative fantasy tales, suitable for children and a guilty pleasure for adults. However, they all have deeper meanings, which the reader can engage with or not. Travel to these worlds allows the exploration of issues in our contemporary worlds. Swift's work is satirical of 18th century politics, human foibles and even the growing genre of explorers' tall tales. The surrealism of *Alice* suggests psychedelia and hallucination, an interpretation popular in the

1960s, as in Grace Slick's *White Rabbit*. Lewis's Narnia is built on ancient mythology and Aslan may be interpreted as a religious allegory; though in comparing notes, we found we had both read this as children and had enjoyed it as a pure children's fantasy, not picking up any of the symbolism.

The narrative structures of the quest, journey and return hold little importance in these books. The heroes are everymen, mainly functioning to mediate the experiences in the impossible world to the readers. Gulliver and Alice are passive observers, with Alice especially confused. They are not on quests, they have no objectives and they will not be transformed. The Pevensie children are drawn into a quest to defeat the Witch, but it is not about their personal development, except for Edmund. He has to live with the guilt of his betrayal of his family to the Witch, and learns the power of forgiveness and redemption. The journey and return are achieved through inexplicable means. The return brings the heroes back to where they started. Gulliver in England, Alice on the riverbank and the Pevensies in the wardrobe and returned to childhood. None have brought back any tangible evidence from the impossible worlds.

Alternative Dimensions

The Nomad of Time Trilogy (Michael Moorcock, 1971–1981)

Michael Moorcock finds a manuscript written by his grandfather (also Michael Moorcock). In 1903 Moorcock is suffering from nervous exhaustion and travels to an island in the Indian Ocean to recuperate. Bored, he falls in with the derelict Oswald Bastable, who tells him his story. Bastable was an army officer on the North-West Frontier of India. Trapped deep in an ancient temple, he finds himself transported to 1973. In this world there have been no world wars and the airship dominates. This vision of an alternate future where Victorian-era technology still holds sway has become known as Steampunk (Ashley, 2011) (Figure 10.2). Bastable becomes embroiled with revolutionaries who drop an atomic bomb on the airship yards at Hiroshima. The blast catapults him back to 1903. However, as he tells Moorcock, 'this is 1903 – or *a* 1903 – but it – it isn't *my* 1903'. There are small details that convince Bastable that he does not fit and some people do not recognise him. He will keep searching for a way back to his true world. Along the way he communicates his adventures in different worlds to the two Michael Moorcocks.

The playful Moorcock draws on the Edwardian children's classic *Five Children and It* by Edith Nesbit (see Chapter 3). His hero Bastable shares the same surname as the children in Nesbit's book, he comes from the same time

Figure 10.2 Steampunk exhibition at the Kew Bridge Steam Museum, London. Photo by J. Laing.

period, enjoys the impossible experience of flying and is exposed to political rhetoric in line with Nesbit's Fabian principles.

His Dark Materials trilogy (Philip Pullman, 1995–2000)

Lyra is a young girl living in an alternate world. It is Oxford, but there are airships and other different technologies. People's souls are visibly manifested as animals that always accompany them. These are known as *daemons*. With children, their daemons can change form at will, but once puberty is reached they become fixed as a specific animal. Young children are disappearing and it is somehow tied up with a shadowy and sinister religious organisation called the Magisterium. Lyra finds out that the children are being taken to an island in the Arctic. She joins an expedition to rescue them. Along the way they are helped by witches and a talking polar bear. In the second book, Lyra is joined by Will, a boy from our world. They find that there is an infinite variety of parallel universes. Various scientific experiments, including those with the lost children, are opening up passageways between these worlds. In turn, the Magisterium is working to preserve order by destroying these other worlds.

Harry Potter series (J.K. Rowling, 1997–2007)

In supernatural fiction, such as *Dracula* and *Twilight*, our world contains beings such as vampires and werewolves. They are adept at disguising themselves, posing as normal people. The plot of such fiction often consists of an outsider discovering their secret. *Harry Potter* is quite different. The unhappy, orphaned Harry lives with his horrid uncle and aunt in suburban England. On his 11th birthday, he discovers he is a wizard and is invited to Hogwart's School. Harry leaves the real world, where he is an outsider and journeys to a magical world where he finds the belonging and family he has always craved. The world of the wizards co-exists with the real, only ordinary people (Muggles) are not aware of it. It is a multi-faceted world that Harry explores, including Hogwarts, Platform 9¾ at King's Cross, Diagon Alley and Gringotts Bank. This parallel world has strict rules and a vast bureaucracy to keep its secrets. The wizards, for example, are forbidden to use magic on Muggles.

The quest

Unlike texts about impossible worlds, books of travel to alternative dimensions place greater stress on the reality of their worlds and follow the narrative structure of quest, journey and return. In all three book series, there is a single main character whose everyday life is disrupted by being thrust into these alternative worlds. They do not seek the journey, but are swept up by events. It is their destiny. Harry and Lyra are chosen by mysterious forces; both raised as orphans, they find they have been born with special powers. In contrast, Oswald is an everyman. Why he has been chosen is inexplicable.

Each has a quest that is gradually revealed. Initially, Lyra's mission is to rescue the kidnapped children. She then becomes focused on rescuing one particular friend. In saving Roger Parslow, she will defeat the Magisterium and restore the balance between the different worlds. Her journey is also a coming of age story. At the beginning, she is a wild and unruly child, constantly involved in pranks and trouble. As she progresses, she chooses to take on responsibilities, and her qualities of loyalty and good judgement become more pronounced.

Similarly, Harry Potter has two quests that parallel his heading towards adulthood. At first, his main concerns are common ones of fitting in at a new school, making friends, learning the customs and traditions of a close-knit society. As the series progresses, Harry finds he is involved in a singular quest to defeat Voldemort. As the series darkens, it switches from a coming of age story to a battle between good and evil. Harry voluntarily embarks on this quest, though he has doubts about his abilities and, in essence, he has no choice, for Voldemort has sworn to kill him.

Oswald Bastable's quest is purely personal. Finding himself in the future, he thoroughly enjoys this new world of airships, undertaking training to become an officer. However, his initial wonder begins to be tarnished. The peaceful future world is built on colonial inequities that he increasingly questions. He also realises that he is not in his world. He undertakes his personal quest to try and find a way back. As he proceeds on that mission, his values and beliefs are changing. If he ever did find a way back to his 1903, it is very likely he would no longer fit in there either. A twist is that the narrator – Moorcock's grandfather – is also a seeker. When first met, he is travelling the Indian Ocean, seeking to recover from nervous exhaustion. Finding out what happened to Bastable becomes an obsession, drawing him to travel further.

The journey

Reaching these alternative worlds requires journeys within the normal world. Bastable is an English soldier who discovers a portal underneath an Indian temple. To change worlds he must make that dangerous journey again and again. In the various Steampunk worlds he experiences, he is fascinated with new means of locomotion. These include airships and powerful submarines. On these he chooses to range all over the globe.

Lyra's journey starts in a wardrobe (a deliberate reference to *The Lion, the Witch and the Wardrobe*). As she becomes embroiled in the intrigue, her travel accelerates. Her first trip is from Oxford to London by airship. Then she sails to the Arctic, an important stage that allows for the introduction and assembly of her confederates. In the Arctic, she travels by polar bear, witch's broomstick and airship. Having reached the ends of the earth, her next stage takes her into the alternative dimensions. As with *The Nomad of Time*, the portal is situated in a hidden and remote place requiring courage and ingenuity to reach.

Harry Potter's travel is less exotic. Initially he needs the help of other wizards, who function as gatekeepers. They allow him to travel by a variety of magical conveyances. These include the Hogwart's Express (a steam train), a flying car and a flying double decker bus. As Harry becomes more immersed in his new world, he learns to use more complex means that he controls, including his flying broomstick, teleporting and the use of a cloak of invisibility.

In the early stages of their journeys, the heroes learn that they have special powers. Lyra has the rare power to use and accurately interpret the alethiometer, a type of magic compass. This allows her to divine the answer to questions, providing warnings of oncoming dangers and helping them to decide which path to take. Harry also has special magic powers and his physical connection with Voldemort makes him the only wizard able to defeat the evil lord. Bastable has no magic powers, but his training as a soldier gives him advantages in each world he encounters.

For all of them, their journey is a katabasis. We considered this for Harry Potter in Chapter 3. Lyra undertakes a quite literal descent into hell to retrieve her dead friend. In the course of her journey, her companions sacrifice themselves to protect her. To go through the portal, Bastable must go deep underneath the Indian temples. The various wars and massacres he experiences also function as a form of hell which he must endure.

The return

Bastable's quest is to return. He never achieves this. Nor can he ever produce any physical evidence of visiting alternative realities. Lyra is similarly frustrated. At the end of her adventure, the Magisterium is defeated and she realises she is in love with Will. Then she tragically finds that while it is possible to pass between the worlds, one cannot stay outside of their own world for an extended period. Lyra and Will are fated to live apart.

Harry Potter is happy to leave the real world behind once he discovers he is a wizard. He has been unhappy in it all his life. The early books each commence with Harry returning to the Dursleys for the holidays. The Dursleys try to prevent him returning to Hogwarts. They want him to be normal. The irony is that we learn Harry is safe at the Dursleys, thanks to a spell cast by Professor Dumbledore, but he never feels at ease there. In the later books, Harry holidays with the Weasleys; he has chosen the wizard world over the Muggles one and has no wish to return. Of course, Harry has always been a wizard, he just did not know it. In a sense, he is returning to the wizard's world that he really belongs to. It is his final defeat of Voldemort that allows him to return, to fully experience family life, to marry into the Weasleys and have children. His journey is now complete.

11 Transformations

'They were not railway children to begin with. I don't suppose they had ever thought about railways except as a means of getting to Maskelyne and Cook's, the Pantomime, Zoological Gardens, and Madame Tussaud's. They were just ordinary suburban children ...'
The Railway Children, E. Nesbit, 1906

The potential for travel to transform individuals is a powerful trope, which might be fostered or perpetuated by reading books. All narrative involves some form of transformation; if only the evolution of plot and character (Behr, 2005) and literature, in particular, 'has prepared us to expect the release of new aspects of ourselves in the presence of the fabled and the unfamiliar' (Hazzard, 2008: 18). This hope is particularly strong in those setting off on a pilgrimage, where the traveller seeks spiritual enlightenment and to overcome bad habits or weaknesses. Others cherish the ideal of understanding themselves better, creating a new identity or taking up a new path or direction in life. There may be a sense of destiny involved, where travel acts as the inexorable catalyst for becoming the person we were meant to be. In this chapter, we explore how books are perceived to change lives, how travel might prompt the writing of a book, and the books that promise that visiting a certain place will change a reader's life.

These transformations are generally held to be positive and affirming, although sometimes they result in the traveller losing something in the process; some form of sacrifice or exchange. Frodo in *The Lord of the Rings* carries the One Ring to Mount Doom, to destroy it and thereby annihilate the power of the evil Lord Sauron over Middle-earth. In doing so, he realises he can never return to a peaceful life in the Shire. The journey has changed him irrevocably. D'Artagnan in *The Three Musketeers* sheds his impetuosity and hot-headedness through the course of his journeys, but loses something of the dash and *brio* that make him such a beloved character.

Some transformations might not be immediately recognised or valued by the traveller. It is only upon the return home that the changes wrought by travel can be understood. Sometimes this process is helped through writing a book. Robyn Davidson in *Tracks* tells the story of her trek through the Australian Outback and explores what she has learnt about herself and her capabilities in extreme situations. In *A Year in Provence*, Peter Mayle traces his growing comfort with a less materialistic rural lifestyle. It sometimes takes contemplation at a distance to make sense of an experience.

Not all transformations are momentous and while small alterations wrought by travel can be important and meaningful to individuals, they are not the subject of this chapter. Instead, we are focusing on *life-changing experiences*. This is very much in the eye of the beholder, and what is judged to be an epiphany by one individual might be viewed very differently by an outsider. What interests us is not so much the size of the changes experienced in an objective sense, but what has occurred and the role that travel is perceived to play in this process.

We also acknowledge the argument that most tourists are not transformed through travel (Bruner, 1991). Each of the travellers in the books we discuss spends a considerable length of time in the places they visit, which Bruner (1991) notes might provide opportunities for transformations of the self. Ultimately, however, our focus is on the *discourse* of transformation through narrative, rather than exploring whether or not profound change actually occurs in tourists.

Spiritual Enlightenment

The tourist experience can be seen as 'a possible way to make meaning in a de-centred, secularised and increasingly alien world' (Digance & Cusack, 2002: 265). The pilgrimage is the archetype of this kind of travel, but some forms of adventure travel also involve a deep personal significance in accomplishment (Graburn, 1989; Smith, 1992; Zurick, 1995). While the spiritual is often most easily described in religious language (Underwood & Teresi, 2002), spiritual beliefs transcend the boundaries of particular religions and relate to a deep connection that is felt between human beings and the world around them (Sharpley & Jepson, 2011). The pilgrimage typically involves trials or dangers that 'transform' a person, and make them worthy of the challenges posed by the journey or quest (*liminal rites or rites of transition*), as well as preparing them for reincorporation back into their home community (Belk, 1992; Turner & Turner, 1978).

This spiritual or sacred travel incorporates an inner as well as an outer journey. The traveller explores the self, as well as the world around them. Particular landscapes or places encourage or are associated with these inner transformations. Well-known examples include the Australian Outback, the Kokoda Track in Papua New Guinea and the Camino Way in Spain. The Outback is remote, sparsely populated and potentially dangerous. In its extreme conditions, travellers can lose their way and die of thirst. Climbing Uluru, once quite popular, has claimed 35 lives since the 1960s, mainly to falls, heat exhaustion or heart attacks. The increasingly popular Kokoda Track is promoted as a test of endurance and spirit, but the steep climb in tropical conditions has also claimed the lives of a number of walkers. On the Camino Way, en route to Santiago de Compestela, pilgrims risk being hit by vehicles, falling along steep paths, or suffering from ailments related to the exertion of the walk. Films and books often reinforce these risky elements of the journey and perpetuate myths of the tourist in danger (Frost, 2010a). These hazards also provide the necessary preconditions for a spiritual experience to occur, as the pilgrim is tested and ultimately overcomes the hardships of the journey, as illustrated by the following three books – *Tracks*, *Lost Horizon* and *The Lord of the Rings* trilogy.

Tracks (Robyn Davidson, 1980)

Robyn Davidson decides to walk across the Australian Outback, from Alice Springs to the Indian Ocean, with camels and a dog. She describes it as a 'lunatic idea', but is clear about her motivations. In part it is a dream of freedom, but also a desire to 'change and control' her life – to escape 'the half-finished, half-hearted attempts at different jobs and various studies ... the self-indulgent negativity which was so much the malaise of my generation, my sex and my class'. On her trek, Davidson uses the metaphor of a snakeskin to describe the shedding or peeling away of conventions built up through exposure to Western society. Time spent in the Outback leads to a new 'self' emerging:

> This desocializing process – the sloughing off, like a snakeskin, of the useless preoccupations and standards of the society I had left, and the growing of new ones that were more tuned to my present environment – was beginning to show ...

Davidson learns to live without being ruled by deadlines. She contrasts the 'flow' she experiences when tuning into the rhythms of life out in the desert and in particular the lifestyle of Eddie, one of the indigenous men she meets, with her old routines of control and time management. She also experiences a type of 'cleansing' by nature during her Outback journey: 'My mind was rinsed clean and sparkling and light. Everything around me was bursting with life and vibrance ... I felt bigger somehow, expanded'. Travel for Davidson has become a type of *katharsis* – purifying her from the petty concerns and stultifying emotions of her old life (Campbell, 1949). This process of purification allows her to 'see much more clearly into my present relationships with people and with myself'. This is also a narrative about contact with the *sublime*; of nature as a conduit to spirituality, which has its roots in 18th-century romanticism (de Botton, 2002).

Davidson also learns about her own abilities and powers of fending for herself, as she handles obstreperous animals, and copes with the isolation of the Outback. The feeling of being in control is a new one, and exhilarating for Davidson. – 'I needed nothing and no one'. The journey represents the collapse of 'the last burning bridge back to my old self':

> If I could bumble my way across a desert, then anyone could do anything. And that was true especially for women, who have used cowardice for so long to protect themselves that it has become a habit.

The reality of what she sees and experiences in the Outback supersedes even her wildest imaginings. Davidson describes the enchantment of the desert, 'with writhing hills and crescents floating and shimmering in it and fire-coloured dunes lapping at their feet and off in the distance some magical, violet mountains ... Nothing as wildly beautiful as that had I ever seen, even in my dream landscapes'. This is the legacy of the journey – a stream of memories of overcoming adversity and understanding the priorities in her life ('I had pared down my possessions to nothing ... I felt free and untrammelled and light and I wanted to stay that way. If I could only just hold on to it').

Lost Horizon (James Hilton, 1933)

This book is a story within a story. A novelist, Rutherford, tells Woodford Green an odd tale about a mutual acquaintance, Hugh Conway, the former Consul for Baskul. Conway is missing, believed dead, after the hijacking of his plane. Rutherford has a chance encounter with Conway in a missionary hospital in China, and travels with him to Honolulu on a liner, before Conway disappears again, this time seemingly for good. Conway's account of his initial disappearance is startling and difficult for Rutherford to believe. He feels the need to confide the story to Green, and as it unfolds, we learn how Conway reached the community of Shangri-La, why he left it, and why he feels the need to return.

The term *Shangri-La* has entered the lexicon as a place of timeless beauty and mystical charms (Bishop, 1989). Modern travellers are entranced with the idea of visiting or finding their own version of Shangri-La. For example, the kayaker Peter Heller sought to paddle the Tsangpo Gorge in Asia, which he describes as having 'the inspiration for Shangri-La in James Hilton's novel *Lost Horizon*, and in Tibetan mythology, it cradles the most sacred landscape' (Heller, 2004: 2). The fictional Shangri-La is a lamasery 'in the wilds of Tibet', which oversees a small community living in the valley below. It is protected by a huge and impenetrable mountain range, and enjoys an idyllic climate. The lamasery is described as 'superb and exquisite'. Everything is restrained and refined. Shangri-La is a place for spiritual contemplation, encouraging its residents to be moderate in all things. The architecture and landscape encourage this, 'with the mystery that lies at the core of all loveliness'.

For Conway, this is a revelation, and one that accords with his own personality and inclinations. He finds himself with the luxury of time – in Shangri-La, the secret of long life has been discovered and practised, although death is still inevitable. Nothing need be rushed, including courtships, pursuit of interests, academic scholarship and self-knowledge. Conway has always been a person devoid of strong passions and ambitions. He is competent but cool, and desires a life of tranquillity. In Shangri-La, this can be given full rein, without the need to pretend to be anything he is not. Conway refers to Shangri-La as 'quite perfect. For years his passions had been like a nerve that the world jarred on; now at last that aching was soothed'. This is the *apotheosis* that Campbell (1949: 151) describes as an integral element of the hero's journey – where the individual goes 'beyond the last terrors of ignorance ... free of all fear'.

Conway's transformation is, in essence, becoming a more *authentic* version of himself – the person he always was, without artifice or defences. He observes: 'There were moments in life when one opened wide one's soul just as one might open wide one's purse if an evening's entertainment were proving unexpectedly costly but also unexpectedly novel'. Conway's dislike of leadership, however, will be tested – he is ultimately offered the position of High Lama upon the death of the incumbent. He gives this role up temporarily to help his subordinate Mallinson try to return home, but is eventually drawn back to Shangri-La and its lyrical delights. We are not told exactly why Conway decides, seemingly on the spur of the moment, to leave Shangri-La, except for a comment that his 'dream had dissolved, like all too lovely things, at the first touch of reality'. Perhaps he balks at the prospect of being in charge, after a taste of the joys of abdicating responsibility?

The concept of a utopia, an idyllic place or society without hardship, has its roots in Greek literature, but has been a constant motif in books, with examples such as Thomas More's *Utopia* (1516) and H.G. Wells' *A Modern Utopia* (1908). Many of these books explore the central paradox of a utopia – that it can be understood as a *dystopia* or disturbing place by some individuals, who balk at the idea of a place devoid of pain, challenge and adventure, and the emotions that these things bring to our lives, even if it protects people from extreme conditions, such as war or famine. John the Savage in Huxley's *Brave New World* (1932) hates the primitive reservation where he was brought up, but also cannot bear to live in the modern (futuristic) world where people opiate themselves to block out the vagaries of existence. For some people, Shangri-La is equally a 'prison', rather than a sanctuary.

The young Vice-Consul Mallinson describes Shangri-La as 'hellish', with its 'dark and evil' practice of abducting people to remain there forever, against their will, at least initially: 'A lot of wizened old men crouching here like spiders for anyone who comes near'. Life at Shangri-La is distasteful to him, with its icy restraint and self-discipline. He refers scornfully to Conway admiring a woman Lo-Tsen 'as if she is an exhibit in a museum'. Mallinson on the other hand loves her ardently, and wishes to take her away from a life where 'you're half-dead. Give me a short life and a gay one, for choice'. He is someone who lacks bravery and coolness under pressure, perhaps because he suffers from an excess of imagination and emotion. Mallinson does not change during his time in Shangri-La; it reinforces the good sides of his character as well as his flaws. His tragedy is that his escape attempt appears to lead to his own demise and that of Lo-Tsen, who has been kept artificially young at Shangri-La. Both, however, are willing to take these risks to taste freedom again. Their story is a form of katabasis, where they become the sacrificial victims on the journey home.

The Lord of the Rings trilogy (J.R.R. Tolkien, 1954–1955)

Zurick (1995) refers to the propensity of many travellers in the remote Himalayas to carry a copy of *The Lord of the Rings* in their backpack, perhaps in homage to one of the most loved and best-known of fictional journeys, but also perhaps in the hope that, like many of its characters, they too will undergo a form of transformation. All nine members of the Fellowship in *The Lord of the Rings* undergo 'immense moral and spiritual growth' (Wood, 2003: 84), particularly Frodo, Sam and Aragorn. It has been described as a *bildungsroman* (literally 'education novel' in German), which details 'the journey to maturation of its chief protagonists' (Morgan, 2010: 389).

Frodo's pilgrimage to destroy the Ring tests his resolve and courage. His first reaction to his task is one of fear. He wishes he had not found the Ring and that this burden had not been cast upon him ('I am not made for perilous quests'). Yet he accepts that it is his destiny, and desires to save the Shire;

a haven of peace and goodness. At the Council of Elrond, Frodo accepts his challenge. While he travels with some companions – the Fellowship – for a time, he must ultimately complete this journey alone, even with the solicitations of his fellow hobbit Sam. The Ring gets heavier as they approach Mount Doom, and Frodo is nearly killed by the spider Shelob. He is saved by Sam, his faithful friend.

Sam observes to Frodo that the old tales of adventure 'that really mattered' involve individuals who were landed in perilous situations through destiny, but refused to turn back. Frodo fulfils his task, on his hands and knees, crawling at times, sometimes carried by Sam; inch by terrible inch. He returns to the Shire, but not for long: 'I am wounded ... it will never really heal'. Once the final page of Frodo's story is written down in the Red Book, to 'keep alive the memory of the age that is gone' he takes his final journey to the Grey Havens, telling Sam:

> I tried to save the Shire, and it has been saved, but not for me. It must often be so, Sam, when things are in danger: some one has to give them up, lose them, so that others may keep them.

Sam the gardener is also transformed, overcoming his own fears to help his master destroy the Ring. As he makes his way towards Mordor, 'he felt through all his limbs a thrill, as if he was turning into some creature of stone and steel that neither despair nor weariness nor endless barren miles could subdue'. Sam's story is a triumph of love and indomitable will, qualities that his pilgrimage brings out and which help to secure the destruction of the Ring. He has the courage to propose to Rosie Cotton when he returns to the Shire – Sam is no longer the shy young hobbit of *The Fellowship of the Ring*. He eventually becomes the mayor of Hobbiton and accompanies Frodo to farewell him on his final journey to the Grey Havens. The story ends with Sam's return to hearth and home: 'Well, I'm back'.

When we first meet Aragorn, another member of the Fellowship, he is known as Strider, 'one of the wandering folk – Rangers'. While he is the heir to the throne of Gondor, his true identity has been kept hidden, to ensure he does not fall into the hands of the likes of Sauron. The kingdom is thus ruled by Stewards, until the true ruler can regain his throne. Aragorn steps forward at the Council of Elrond and pledges to help Frodo, declaring: 'I am Aragorn, son of Arathorn; and if by life or death I can save you, I will'. He is instrumental in the victories at the Battles of Helm's Deep and Pelennor Fields, where his courage and leadership inspire others. He is no longer in hiding. Aragorn accepts his destiny as ruler of Gondor, and even his appearance becomes more regal: 'the weatherworn Ranger was no longer there ... a light was in his eyes: a king returning from exile to his own land'. Upon Sauron's defeat and his crowning, he wins the hand of Arwen, the daughter of the Elvish king Elrond. His labours have been rewarded; the hero has triumphed over adversity.

Self-Discovery and Personal Identity

Spiritual development often goes hand in hand with self-actualisation. The pilgrimage, like the hero's journey, involves an initiation, where undergoing some form of testing brings with it greater self-awareness (Campbell, 1949). The traveller gains an insight into their own capabilities and sometimes about the boundaries they impose upon themselves. This self-discovery might be characterised as a *rite of passage*, or moving to the next stage of adulthood. Campbell (1949) sees the value of the mythic hero's journey in the way that it counteracts the modern trend towards delaying the process of growing up. Travel might, therefore, be seen as 'necessary to the psyche'; pointing the way towards spiritual and personal development. The traveller might also gain a renewed sense of personal identity, through interaction with other people and other places. We have chosen the following two books to explore some of these concepts.

I'm Off Then: Losing and Finding Myself on the Camino De Santiago (Hape Kerkeling, 2006)

Hape Kerkeling is a German comedian who decides to go on a pilgrimage to Santiago de Compostela. He records his thoughts and feelings each day in a diary, and notes that he has never before felt the urge to 'capture my life in words'. When we first encounter Hape, he is wryly humorous about his lack of fitness and medical conditions. His journey is motivated by reading Bert Teklenborg's *The Joy of the Camino de Santiago*, and he laughs at the title – 'Can a *route* bring you joy?' Kerkeling has spiritual questions that he hopes the journey will answer. He realises that before he can deal with the question 'Is there a God?' he needs to explore his own self-identity.

His first few days are inauspicious, as he deals with aching legs, and tiredness so great 'that I can barely hold my pen'. Kerkeling has brought a copy of Shirley MacLaine's *The Camino: A Journey of the Spirit* with him on the walk, while he, like others, finds it less than honest about the rigours of the journey, he notes the power of its inspiration: 'Whatever we may think of [these] books, it is incredible how many people they brought onto this trail. They paved the way'.

Day by day, Kerkeling gets fitter, mentally as well as physically, and learns how far he can push himself. He wryly comments on the pilgrims he meets, who seem so sure of themselves – 'I wonder why they're on a pilgrimage in the first place'. He is also aware that the walk might not lead to spiritual enlightenment, 'just as taking a vacation doesn't guarantee relaxation', and is honest about his doubts. Kerkeling therefore aims to let the journey unfold without preconceptions and 'see what new experiences each new day brings'. He does, however, observe: 'This journey ought to transform me in some way'. It does, but in ways he did not expect. He becomes more open to other people. At the start of his pilgrimage he avoids socialising with others, but as he continues towards Santiago, he begins to make close friends. This is an example of *communitas* within the pilgrimage; a bond formed with others who are undergoing the same experience (Turner & Turner, 1978).

Kerkeling provides several anecdotes about the prejudice he has encountered in his life over his sexuality, but also muses on opportunities he has had to act as a role model and break down barriers. The walk seems to put this in perspective, as does the writing of his book, where he airs some of his past grievances, including the struggles to build a career. He also learns to value having the time to think over things:

Since I've started my walk, I have the sense that my ingrained habits are loosening. Somewhat like my backpack, I am soaking things in. I used to push aside so many of my thoughts, figuring I had no time for them; now I let them take me where they will.

It also becomes an opportunity to dwell on spiritual matters – 'this trip seems to be turning into one long prayer for me'. By the final few days, he is dreading his arrival in Santiago, as 'when we reach our destination, it's all over'. Kerkeling now feels renewed and energised, and is less hard on himself than when he started the journey. He has survived 'the descent', and his katabasis concludes with a renewed sense of self-understanding and what he describes as a form of spiritual 'rebirth'.

The Three Musketeers (Alexandre Dumas, 1844)

The central thread of this tale is the journey of D'Artagnan to manhood. It is therefore a *bildingsroman*. We encounter D'Artagnan at the start of the book as a callow and innocent Gascon youth, who is described as a Don Quixote; a reference to his impetuosity and romantic nature, as well as his habit of 'tilting at windmills'. He is not used to the ways of the city, and provokes fights at every turn, keen to assert his masculinity and avenge his thwarted pride. Three musketeers, Athos, Aramis and Porthos, take him under their wing, and teach him the value of temperance and self-restraint. They also demonstrate the importance of fighting for a just cause and show him loyalty in difficult times. The sophistication of Paris is initially bewitching and bewildering to the young man, but his travels take him further, through France and even to London, on the Queen's behalf. He has left Gascony far behind.

D'Artagnan matures, in part the result of experiencing love and loss. He is betrayed by Milady, a temptress who has no hesitation in killing D'Artagnan's love interest, Constance, to achieve her own ends. He also ends up in the role he wanted – chief of the King's musketeers, but without his beloved friends by his side. D'Artagnan has learnt to negotiate with wily political figures, such as Buckingham and Cardinal Richelieu, makes his peace with his arch-enemy Rochefort, and is wiser and cooler under pressure, but has lost the exuberance of his early youth.

He has realised that life holds disappointments ('nothing henceforth, but bitter recollections') and is less straightforward than his younger self imagined. Like Campbell's hero, he travels along 'the necessary passages' of adulthood, through the vicissitudes of his life as a soldier and lover. Most cinematic versions of the book, however, overlook this ending, preferring to leave D'Artagnan as the eternally youthful and dashing swashbuckler; conquering ladies and foes alike with a smile and a flash of his sword.

A Fetish for Simplicity

Not all travel narratives deal with adventure or spiritual turmoil. One popular genre focuses on rustic utopias and bucolic lifestyles, often in European settings, and can be described as aspirational. The characters and writers are not necessarily transformed, but there is the promise that the reader might be if they travel to these places, and embrace a simpler lifestyle. There is an element of nostalgia in these books, which hark back to a time when life was less frenetic and impersonal. There is time to make meals from scratch, and watch the seasons unfold. The fantasy for the reader is that it would be possible for us to slow down, get rid of our encumbrances and spurn our materialistic goals, if only we could move to a Tuscan villa or a charming Provençal cottage.

Food is a big element of this fantasy. Elizabeth David's books were written at a time when Britain was either still in rationing or most people couldn't access the variety of produce available in parts of Europe. They contributed to the cult of the Mediterranean diet and the trend towards a sensual description of food, which has reached its culmination in the 'food porn' of Frances Mayes' *Under the Tuscan Sun* (1996) and Marlena de Blasi's *A Thousand Days in Venice* (2003).

A Book of Mediterranean Food (Elizabeth David, 1950)

Elizabeth David's cookbooks are read as much for their descriptions of lifestyle as they are for their recipes. Julian Barnes, in a preface to a reprint of *A Book of Mediterranean Food* refers to the 'aromatic memories' that David wrote down after leaving her war-time post in Egypt for a chilly Britain still under rationing. She poured into these books all she had learned of the pleasures of the table; the joy of colour, texture, taste and aroma. David extols 'those blessed lands of sun and sea and olive trees' and writes lovingly of the 'aromatic perfume of rosemary, wild marjoram and basil drying in the kitchens; the brilliance of the market stalls piled high with pimento, aubergines, tomatoes, olives, melons, figs and limes; the great heaps of shiny fish, silver, vermilion or tiger-striped . . .'. She is open about her rationale for writing these books, noting that she hoped they would be a form of 'escape from the deadly boredom of queuing and the frustration of buying the weekly rations; to read about real food cooked with wine and olive oil, eggs and butter and cream, and dishes richly flavoured with onions, garlic, herbs and brightly coloured Southern vegetables' (Figure 11.1). David sees this as making up for 'what is so often lacking in English cooking: variety of flavour and colour, and the warm, rich, stimulating smells of genuine food'.

A Book of Mediterranean Food is a wonderful melange of anecdotes, hints, recipes and quotations. David refers to Théophile Gautier's description of the Spanish soup gazpacho, and includes extracts from texts such as Henry James' *A Little Tour in France* and Gertrude Stein's *The Autobiography of Alice B. Toklas*. This is food that is inseparably linked to culture, particularly literature. David is quick to point out the hospitality that goes with these dishes, as well as how and when they are served, such as feast days or festivals. The fantasy world portrayed in her books has transformed the way we think about the Mediterranean, and lives on in the many books written about its produce, specialities and food culture, the proliferation of cooking tours and classes, and the image of the region as a 'foodie' paradise. Her work can also be seen as an influence on the next book we look at – *A Year in Provence*.

A Year in Provence (Peter Mayle, 1989)

Peter Mayle's book *A Year in Provence* is similarly centred on gastronomy. The first line reads 'The year began with lunch' and the final paragraph

Figure 11.1 Fresh produce in a shop window, Bologna, Italy. Photo by J. Laing.

describes his Christmas lunch in loving, unctuous detail. Peter and his wife have bought an 18th century Provençal farmhouse flanked by the Lubéron mountains. It is set within the bounds of a national park and affords them magnificent views of nature. While they are technically remote ('For most of the year, it is possible to walk for eight or nine hours without seeing a car or human being'), the book is full of anecdotes about the neighbours – those who work on the property, such as Faustin, those who assist in renovations, such as the electrician Menicucci and Didier the builder, and local identities, including the purveyors of home-made breads, pastries and cheeses, and the chefs and owners of the various restaurants. The couple learn to value these friendships and feel part of a community.

A comic touch is often used to highlight their Englishness and any failures of language or cultural barriers. Aldridge (1995) calls these books 'myths for the English', and there is a deliberate downplaying of their good fortune, but also the challenges they face, as if they wish to preserve these fantasies for their readers. Problems are made to seem ultimately trivial or just a necessary part of the process of shedding English reserve and uptightness. For example, Mayle finds it initially difficult to deal with the locals' relaxed notion of time-keeping and deadlines, but eventually learns to be less uptight and go with the flow: 'Little by little, we reverted to being philosophical, and came to terms with the Provençal clock. From now on, we told ourselves, we would assume nothing would be done when we expected it to be done; the fact that it happened at all would be enough'. Mayle also develops the French obsession with food, noting: 'Tell [the French] you are facing gastronomic hardship, and they will move heaven and earth and even restaurant tables to help you'. Sharp (1999: 204) argues that he is trying to maintain the fiction of being 'an informed outsider reporting his privileged information to other sophisticated urbanites'.

The book is divided into 12 chapters representing the months of the year and echoing the rhythm of the seasons. Although Mayle has been criticised for undervaluing the wonder of Provence (Sharp, 1999), we feel that some of the popularity of the book can be attributed to its visceral qualities. One can almost smell the lavender and the truffles, taste the wine and olive oil ('it was like eating sunshine'), and feel the baking heat of summer and the Mistral winds of winter. Perhaps the negativity is in part owing to the air of smugness that suffuses some of the text. Mayle and his wife luxuriate in their good fortune, gastronomically speaking. While olive oil was a luxury in England, 'in Provence it was an abundant daily treat ... we became fussy and no doubt insufferable about our oil, never buying it from shops or supermarkets, but always from a mill or producer, and I looked forward to oil-buying expeditions almost as much as trips to the vineyards'. Mayle's book perpetuates the ideal of France (and Italy) as a gourmet's delight and depicts the transformation of a traveller from bemused outsider to self-satisfied local.

Feminine Emancipation

Another form of narrative transformation focuses on the way that travel provides a mechanism for life-changing experiences in women. This narrative has been found in travel guidebooks (Wilson et al., 2009), but is also present in autobiographical texts. In the latter, it relates to escapist rather than spiritual journeys, often involving the fantasy of finding love and empowerment in a foreign land. These transformations are often associated with particular places – notably Italy, India and Africa – which seem to offer these women the opportunity to cast off their everyday responsibilities and adopt a new and freer lifestyle than they were able to enjoy at home. We explore two books – The White Masai and Eat, Pray, Love – from this transformative perspective.

The White Masai (Corinne Hofmann, 1999)

Corinne Hoffmann, a Swiss businesswoman, travels to Kenya for a holiday with her boyfriend. She sees Lketinga, a Masai warrior, on a boat and there is an instant attraction. She manufactures reasons to meet with him and later tells her boyfriend that she plans to come back to Kenya and pursue a relationship with Lketinga. Corinne has unrealistic expectations of what she will find living in Africa. Her view of the Masai is close to that of the 'noble savage' – she idealises her partner and overlooks his flaws in her entrancement at his beauty. Corinne is not an older woman looking for love, like the protagonist in *Shirley Valentine*, but when she finds it, she is transfixed. She rejects her old life for this obsession: 'I know that despite all the barriers between us, I have already become a captive of his world'. Others warn her that there are too many differences between them to make a relationship work.

Corinne moves to his village and they live in a traditional hut, a *manyatta*. She develops a business in the Masai village of Barsaloi, selling foodstuffs and basic necessities to the villagers. After much bureaucratic wrangling, Corinne marries Lketinga in a registry office, and later in a traditional Masai wedding. Life is basic and challenging, but she is initially happy. She calls the Masai 'my family, my people'. Her husband does not understand why she gets ill so often and so seriously. There are other cultural misunderstandings between them. He is jealous if she talks to another man and often leaves her for days at a time, to be with his warrior comrades. Corinne has a risky pregnancy, suffering from malnutrition, but eventually gives birth to a healthy baby girl. Her marriage goes downhill after this. She doesn't understand his way of thinking, and why he is so jealous, while he is uncomfortable with Western ideas of feminine freedom. There is a clash of values.

Corinne eventually leaves him and returns to Switzerland with their daughter. She has changed as a result of her experiences. She has learnt what she can cope with and realises that she does not need a lot materially, but cannot deal with the lack of freedom. The restrictions of the Masai culture are too great.

Eat, Pray, Love (Elizabeth Gilbert, 2006)

Elizabeth Gilbert is on the floor of her bathroom in the foetal position. Her marriage is over and she is in emotional turmoil. She is looking for salvation, and it turns up in the form of travel. Gilbert has the chance to spend a year in three places – Italy, India and Indonesia – and will write a book about her experiences. She sees Italy as a destination for pleasure, to rediscover the emotional side of her personality and give herself free rein for enjoyment. The second destination – India – is the place to seek out devotion; a state of spiritual discipline. The goal in Indonesia is to learn to achieve a balance between these two extremes in her life back home. Her plan is to explore herself, rather than the countries she visits, but travel is a necessary precondition to this goal. Her journey allows her to 'thoroughly explore one aspect of myself set against the backdrop of each country, in a place that has traditionally done that one thing very well'. Each of these travel experiences changes Gilbert, but the process is more torturous than she expected and she finds it hard to let go of old habits and the 'crutches' of self-pity and addictive behaviour.

Her time in Italy is focused on sensual pleasures, chiefly food and wine, and learning to speak the language, which she describes as 'more beautiful than roses'. None of these things has a 'practical application' – it is about embracing aspects of life that give her a blissful gratification. She admits that she has hardly visited any cultural attractions during her stay and even shuns love, preferring to heal in her own way. She is initially guilty over spending her time in a self-absorbed manner, but notes how important it was to her emotional health. She calls it 'mending my soul' and observes of her state when starting her Italian sojourn:

> When you sense a faint potentiality for happiness after such dark times you must grab onto the ankles of that happiness and not let go until it drags you face-first out of the dirt – this is not selfishness, but obligation.

India on the other hand is an emotional and spiritual roller-coaster:

> They want you to come here strong because Ashram life is rigorous. Not just physically, with days that begin at 3:00 AM and end at 9:00 PM, but also psychologically. You're going to be spending hours and hours a day in silent meditation and contemplation, with little distraction or relief from the apparatus of your own mind. You will be living at close quarters with strangers, in rural India. There are bugs and snakes and rodents. The weather can be extreme – sometimes torrents of rain for weeks on end, sometimes 100 degrees in the shade before breakfast. Things can get deeply real around here, very fast.

Gilbert discovers how far she can push herself, mentally and physically. She experiences an intensity of emotion and sensation that results from overcoming her need for control and letting go of her misery over her perceived failures in life.

Her third destination leads her to a state of peace and harmony with the world around her. She has 'never felt less burdened by myself or by the world' and achieves a 'state of happiness' she felt was beyond her reach. This is something she wishes to hold onto when she returns home and sees it as having benefits to others as much as herself: 'Clearing out all your misery *gets you out of the way*. You cease being an obstacle, not only to yourself but to anyone else. Only then are you free to serve and enjoy other people'. Gilbert meets a Brazilian man, Felipe, and feels able to build a relationship without giving her own self up in the process. The book ends with a simple Italian phrase uttered by Gilbert to her boyfriend as they jump off a boat onto the beach: '*Attraversiamo*' or 'Let's cross over'. She has made the leap to embrace change – and love.

Faking It: The Fictional Transformation

Occasionally transformations in travel narratives are faked, with the most notable example being *Mutant Message Down Under*. Concocted for a New-Age readership, it demonstrates that 'travel writers are often hoaxers (although few are mistaken for gurus); and in this sense, Morgan's sleight of hand might be seen in a less inquisitorial light' (Holland & Huggan, 2000: 190). Perhaps Morgan's book was merely an example of a post-modern simulacrum (Baudrillard, 1986; Eco, 1986), with some readers enjoying the joke once it has been exposed. For others it was appalling in its deception and cultural insensitivity. Either way, the controversy over the book (and the weakness of its prose) should not overshadow the power of its central theme – that travel can change our direction in life, through forcing us to see ourselves as we truly are.

Mutant Message Down Under (Marlo Morgan, 1991)

Marlo Morgan has a successful health practice in the United States and specialises in preventative healthcare. She is invited to Australia to provide training and develop materials for Australian health professionals. Morgan also assists programs for inner-city youth, including young Aboriginal people. On a visit to a tearoom, she is told by a fortune-teller that she has come to Australia because it is her 'destiny' to meet someone for 'your mutual benefit'. She subsequently receives a phone call inviting her to a meeting being held by a tribe of Aborigines. Morgan assumes she is to attend an award luncheon. Instead she is driven to a shed in the Outback and her belongings, including clothes burnt. She is to accompany the tribe on a 'walkabout' lasting three months, and is told: 'This is what you were born to do ... it is your message'. She steps out 'into the unknown'. Her journey can be characterised as a katabasis, which involves testing, in the form of physical and mental challenges, self-discovery and personal growth.

The story ends with her re-entry into 'Mutant' society. She now understands the shallowness of her previous existence: 'For the first time, it seemed my life was totally honest … There was no pretense – no ego fighting for attention. In the group there was no gossip or anyone trying to out-maneuver someone else … I was learning how it felt to be in a state of unconditional acceptance'. She also learns not to question things and to have patience, even with suffering, as it teaches valuable lessons. Morgan later notes: 'For my own soul growth I had gently closed a door and entered a new place, a new life that was equal to a step up a spiritual rung on a ladder'. She makes the choice to become a messenger – 'to touch the lives of those I was destined to touch'.

This is fiction presented as real. Originally it was marketed as non-fiction. After a public outcry, the back cover of the book was changed to acknowledge that this is a 'fictional account', though the introduction still claims it to be entirely true. Apart from the lack of any evidence that Morgan had worked professionally in Australia, her accounts of Australian Aboriginal customs are clearly based on North American Indigenous practices.

The question remains whether her desired ends justify her dubious means. Holland and Huggan (2000) characterise this as an example of a 'narrative of disappearance' or 'allegory of salvage' with respect to a vanishing world, species or culture. The question remains whether writers like Morgan fake a transformation because it's what readers expect from a travel narrative – that life on the road can lead to unexpected paths and insights.

12 They All Lived Happily Ever After

> 'And Aragorn the King Elessar married Arwen Undómiel in the
> City of the Kings upon the day of Midsummer, and the tale of
> their long waiting and labours was come to fulfilment'.
>
> The Return of the King, J.R.R. Tolkien, 1955

Alain de Botton in *The Art of Travel* writes of his gloomy return from a trip to Barbados: 'I felt despair to be home' (2002: 239). Not all travellers have this mindset, but it is important to remember that coming home after a journey can lead to mixed emotions. The return is a fundamental part of the travel narrative and represents the denouement of the hero's journey, the katabasis and the rite of passage. The traveller has survived the hardships of the road and has returned to the familiarity of everyday life and, in many cases, family and friends. This is normally, but not inevitably, a happy event. A strong trope in many travel narratives, not just fairytales, is that the traveller will 'live happily ever after'. Some individuals embrace a whole new life, made possible through the empowerment of their journey and what they have endured, or the people they have met upon the way. However, others, having been transformed, cannot return home and pick up the threads of their lives. They have seen or experienced too much.

This chapter deals with the return home, as exemplified in books. We explore several themes, including the refusal to return (Campbell, 1949), difficulties of 'aggregation' back into society (Turner & Turner, 1978), the return as an element in a *rite of passage* (Turner & Turner, 1978; van Gennep, 1909), the power of the traveller to bestow boons, and personal benefits accruing from the quest, including marriage or power (Campbell, 1949).

Of course, some travellers never return home. The katabasis often involves a sacrificial victim, such as the elf Dobby in *Harry Potter*, who dies on a beach helping to save Harry from the evil witch Bellatrix. Others do not make it back across the threshold. Captain Ahab in *Moby Dick* drowns in his ill-fated attempt to kill the Great Whale, and Captain James Cook is killed by natives in Tahiti before he can return home from his third voyage of discovery. In some children's books such as *The Magic Faraway Tree, Peter Pan* or *The Amulet*, there is the fear of being trapped in an enchanted world or the past or future forever. The return is not assured, nor is a happy ending.

The Refusal of the Return

Campbell (1949) refers to the phenomenon where the hero/traveller does not wish to return, or refuses the responsibility of returning with a boon or trophy. Conway in *Lost Horizon* tries to return to Shangri-La, as nowhere else fulfils the role of home for him anymore or gives him the 'deep calm' he seeks. His work in the Consular Service no longer engages him, he has no prospects of advancement, there are no family or relatives 'who'll worry over me acutely', and the prospect of having to repeat his story *ad nauseum* at dinner parties bores and appals him.

Amos in *The Searchers* is the 'quintessential Western loner' (Clauss, 1999: 12) and must wander in an endless journey that will never reach fulfilment. He does not belong in civilised society. While he lives like a Commanche, speaking their language fluently, he neither fits into their society, nor wants to.

Peter Pan refuses to stay in the Darling children's nursery with the other Lost Boys, as he does not want to grow up. He can merely look through the window at family life, but has 'ecstasies innumerable that other children can never know'. One question often posed with regard to *Peter Pan* is whether it is a hero's tale (Hunt, 2001). Gilead (1991) calls it 'The Return as Tragic Ambiguity', in that a sense of loss or tragedy accompanies the return home. Wendy realises that she wants to grow up and become a woman, but at the same time mourns her inability to accompany Peter on more adventures ('O Peter, don't waste the fairy dust on me').

The refusal to return or move on is well illustrated in *The Sun Also Rises* by Ernest Hemingway, where the central characters appear doomed to be perpetual expatriates.

The Sun Also Rises (Ernest Hemingway, 1926)

This first novel by Hemingway chronicles members of the *Lost Generation*, the term given by Gertrude Stein to those who came of age during the Great War and found it difficult thereafter to settle down. Many of these disaffected young people came to Paris, particularly Americans, with 15,000 US expatriates recorded in 1927 (Field, 2006). The novel is partly autobiographical, and sows the seeds of the mythic personality of Hemingway as a drinking, smoking, brawling man without roots, searching for a purpose through his writing, as well as contributing to the mythology of 1920s Paris (Field, 2006; Robinson & Andersen, 2002). The reader becomes an insider (Field, 2006), and gains a glimpse of a life where people are either 'one of us', as the character Lady Brett Ashley says, or not. Hemingway's Paris was also frequented by writers and artists such as T.S. Eliot, Ezra Pound, Ford Madox Ford and F. Scott Fitzgerald (Atherton, 1986; Field, 2006) and has been lovingly recreated in Woody Allen's 2011 film *Midnight in Paris*.

The Sun Also Rises (also known as *Fiesta*) provides a snapshot of the lives of a coterie of young people who travel to Spain from Paris to see the Running of the Bulls (San Fermin) festival at Pamplona. The association between Hemingway and Spain is also strong (Robinson & Andersen, 2002), through this and novels such as *For Whom the Bell Tolls*. The group consists of the Americans Jake, Bill and (Robert) Cohn, Mike from Scotland, and his English fiancée Brett. Jake fought in the First World War, and met Brett when he was sent to England for recuperation. Bill was in Paris 'right after the armistice', which suggests he was also a soldier. Several of the men are writers (Bill & Cohn), while Jake works as a journalist for an agency. Mike is an 'undischarged bankrupt'. All are world-weary (Atherton, 1986), especially Jake, and appear to drift through life.

The novel functions as a form of travelogue (Field, 2006), with such detailed exposition of the places frequented by the group, such as the restaurant La Closerie des Lilas on the Left Bank, that one could almost follow it on a map. The excessive and arguably obsessive drinking is precisely detailed and so regimented in terms of timeframes and frequency that it almost becomes a form of discipline that the group must adhere to; much like their wartime responsibilities. The bullfights and Running with the Bulls in Spain are also documented in microscopic detail. This bestows upon the novel a sense of authenticity (Field, 2006). Interestingly, Jake criticises Cohn for taking books literally and getting his opinions through books.

While Field (2006) refers to the *rite of passage* undergone by Jake, it is more accurate to say that he is still coming to terms with the effects of the war, both physically and mentally. Jake has been wounded, and while Hemingway is coy about spelling this out ('what happened to me is supposed to be funny'), it results in an inability to consummate his love for Brett Ashley ('she only wanted what she couldn't have'). Despite the endless movement here and there, Jake is essentially passive, being driven rather than taking the controls, although he does act as a guide for the others (Atherton, 1986). He is also cynical. Life is a matter of 'paying' for what you need and

Figure 12.1 Cafe scene near Notre Dame, part of Hemingway's Paris. Photo by J. Laing.

getting 'your money's worth'. Hemingway, however, is more optimistic for this generation, with his title (*The Sun Also Rises*) taken from the Bible and representing hope. Jake restlessly moves from bar to cafe (Figure 12.1) within Paris, with a brief excursion to Spain each summer for the San Fermin fiesta, fishing or watching the bullfights. Paris always calls him back like a siren ('this is a good town') and one gets the feeling that he will never be able to leave and return to the United States. As his friend Bill tells him: 'You're an expatriate. You've lost touch with the soil'.

Difficulties of Aggregation – Settling Down and Fitting In

While some travellers return home safely, the sacrifices and burdens they have endured make it impossible for them to take up the threads of their old life, or fit in with their contemporaries. At the most extreme is the explorer Merriwether Lewis. Weighed down by debt and the inability to complete his journal, he commits suicide. Another explorer Speke was rumoured to have shot himself, after doubt was cast on his claims about finding the source of the Nile, notably by Richard Burton (Murray, 2008).

At the end of *The Prisoner of Zenda*, Rudolf has become a sacrificial victim in a form of katabasis. He has saved the throne for his look-alike relative, the real king, and relinquished the love of his life, the beautiful Flavia, for the sake of duty. Rudolf is now a recluse, rather than the carefree *bon-vivant* we meet at the start of the book, and pines for his lost love. He is no longer content to waste his days in pleasure and self-indulgence, but cannot find a purpose in life. Rudolf hints at the possibility of further travel, noting that he has unfinished business with Rupert, his 'alter-ego' who killed the king's brother Michael. He cannot resist the lure of travel and the hope that a future journey will cure his *ennui* and provide a sense of meaning that is lacking back home.

Other travellers experience disappointment with their life in their home town or community, compared with the excitement and beauty of the places they have visited. They are discontented with their lot and long for escape. In *Ivanhoe*, King Richard remains reckless and impulsive, unable to settle down to be a responsible monarch. Sherlock Holmes craves the thrill of solving crime and lives for 'dramatic moments', while Charles Ryder in *Brideshead Revisited* dreams of returning to Brideshead, but cannot recreate the magic that he once found there. The Pevensie children in the *Chronicles of Narnia* series miss their lives as monarchs and the grandeur of the Narnian landscape. Three of the four children eventually return to Narnia, and remain there forever at the end of *The Last Battle*. Home for them is no longer wartorn Britain and there are hints in this Christian allegory that they have made the final journey – 'on the day the world ended'.

An example of the painful wrench of returning home from travel is *My Family and Other Animals*; Gerald Durrell's humorous tale of his family's Greek idyll.

My Family and Other Animals (Gerald Durrell, 1956)

The Durrell family have moved from colonial India to Bournemouth and are experiencing 'the type of weather calculated to try anyone's endurance'. Dissatisfied with England, they exchange the wet, wintery drizzle for the whitewashed and sun-kissed brilliance of the island of Corfu. In an allusion to Carroll's Alice, they enter the 'bright looking-glass world of Greece'. The island is portrayed as Edenic and unspoilt – a contrast to the gloom and unhealthy atmosphere of England, where the whole family have colds and ailments. It is a fantasy along the lines of *The Swiss Family Robinson* (1812), as the family returns to nature and escapes the restrictions of English society. Gerald, the youngest child, is particularly fortunate, living a life that many children could only dream of. His interest in animals is heightened through the people he meets (particularly his various tutors), and his freedom to roam and explore the island with his dog is described in wonderful prose, which makes one ache for the carefree existence of a childhood summer. Durrell notes his delight at 'this profusion of life on our very doorstep' and 'the island waiting, morning cool, bright as a star, to be explored'. The family moves to a villa that is picturesquely perfect: 'The moment we saw it, we wanted to live there – it was as though the villa had been standing there waiting for our arrival. We felt we had come home'.

The eventual return to England is a blow after the pastoral delights and warmth of Greece. Mrs Durrell, 'in order to quell the angry mutterings of rebellion', tells her children that it is only temporary – 'We should look on it merely as a holiday, a pleasant trip. We should soon be back again in Corfu'. They say 'tearful goodbyes' and experience a terrible depression that 'lasted all the way back to England'. The family, with its menagerie of animals, is described by the Swiss rail staff as 'One Travelling Circus and Staff', much to Mrs Durrell's annoyance. Lawrence, Gerald's brother and author of *The Alexandria Quartet*, calls this comment a 'penalty' for the family leaving Corfu; where the Durrells felt appreciated and understood, in spite of, but perhaps because of, their eccentricities. As the train heads towards England, their gloom deepens. For the rest of his life, Gerald Durrell will be a restless wanderer (Botting, 1998).

The Hero's Return

The hero's return often involves some form of 'magic flight', a form of rescue, and the crossing of the return threshold (Campbell, 1949). After the Ring is destroyed in *The Lord of the Rings*, Frodo and Sam are rescued from the slopes of Mount Doom by Gwaihir the eagle, who takes them to the land of Ithilien. Campbell (1949) labels this 'rescue from without', which enables the return to society. After Frodo and Sam recover, they ride towards the Shire with some of the Fellowship as their companions. The Shire boundaries mark the 'return threshold', but there are gates that have never been there before. Their homecoming is marred by the destruction wrought by Saruman the wizard and his followers in their occupation of the Shire. The hobbits have one final battle, to stop the 'scouring' of the Shire and restore peace to their homeland.

Ernest Shackleton's successful voyage from Elephant Island in the *James Caird* and trek across the then unexplored South Georgia Island, with its treacherous peaks and crevasses, as depicted in *South*, is another example of the hero's return. It is often referred to by other adventure travellers as inspirational in its jaw-dropping audacity and the grim determination and courage displayed by the team of three in order to get help and rescue their fellow crew members, trapped back on Elephant Island (Laing & Crouch, 2009a, 2009c, 2011). Peter Hillary recalls Shackleton being one of his father Edmund's heroes: 'I remember hearing the stories, how Shackleton lost his ship in the ice but not a single man … so in that way Shackleton was part of my life education, the part handed down' (Hillary & Elder, 2003: 303). The trek is ultimately one of self-discovery, of seeing how much the human spirit can endure, and the return allows the explorer to reflect on the meaning of the journey. Shackleton notes: 'We had pierced the veneer of outside things … We had seen God in his splendours, heard the text that Nature renders. We had reached the naked soul of men'. He is by his own admission, not prone to false modesty, and realises the extraordinary nature of what he has achieved through his expedition. His story is also unusual for an explorer's tale, in that the most famous often involve those who do not return. We tend, as a society, to lionise the failed explorers like Scott or Burke and Wills, perhaps because they remind us of the failed hero of mythology – those who overreached themselves, like Icarus flying too close to the sun.

In *Journey to the Centre of the Earth*, Axel, the hero, is ejected from a volcano on Stromboli, which enables him to escape from the earth's bowels with his uncle and their guide. Axel even uses mythological references to describe his return, referring to the Aeolian archipelago 'where Aeolus kept the winds and the storms chained up, to be let loose at his will'. While there is a scientific explanation given for this 'miracle', it would appear to be a form of 'magic flight', which catapulted the protagonists back to the world 'above'. It is also a literal version of the katabasis, with the return from the underworld. The final chapter is called 'All's Well That Ends Well', where the hero records the celebrations at his return, including a grand fête staged by the city of Hamburg and a public audience for the Professor at the Johannaeum. The story ends with Axel's marriage to his fiancée and in his words 'I was the happiest of men'.

A New Way of Life

The final stage of the katabasis involves 'a figurative death of the old self and rebirth into a new role' (Clauss, 1999: 4), as the hero re-emerges from the underworld. Many travel narratives feature this myth of rebirth, couched in terms of embracing a new way of life. This might involve a career change or transforming in some way, as discussed in the previous chapter.

In the beginning of *Around the World in Eighty Days*, Phileas Fogg is described as an uptight, rule-bound bachelor, whose eccentricities can be laughed at by a reader, but which would make him excruciating to live with. His life revolves around his club, gambling and the inviolate nature of his routines. Everything is pre-planned and orderly. Travel changes Fogg – for the better, we feel. He learns that the best-laid plans don't always go smoothly, and that the fate of other people matter more to him than winning his bet. Fogg becomes less stiff and more human through his adventures. He engages with the world around him, including getting into fights and going shopping, instead of passively observing events from afar. Fogg is prepared to delay his trip to save the Indian widow Aouda from death through suttee, and then searches for his valet Passepartout when he is lost. Upon arriving in London, Fogg thinks he has lost the bet to travel around the world in less than 80 days. When he is at his lowest ebb, Aouda proposes to him. Fogg has won the hand of the woman he loves and the bet is no longer important.

Some changes in lifestyle are not voluntary, but forced upon the traveller as the result of changes that occur back home while they are gone. In *The Lost World*, the young journalist Malone departs on his expedition in the hope that his efforts will impress Gladys, a woman he has fallen in love with. Gladys opines that she would 'love to be envied for my man' and reveals what to the reader seems to be the most ghastly egotism: 'It is never a man that I should love, but always the glories he has won, for they would be reflected on me'. Malone, blinded by his infatuation, seizes upon the opportunity to make Gladys proud of him, and dashes off to South America. Upon his return from the successful expedition, with evidence of their findings laid before a meeting of the Zoological Institute, Malone makes his move. Alas, Gladys has married someone else in the interim, a mild-mannered solicitor's clerk. Outraged, Malone rescinds his earlier decision to name one of the lakes he found after Gladys. He heads off 'like all disconsolate and broken-hearted heroes, into the darkness'. Unlike Odysseus, his Penelope has not waited for him. Malone learns that life goes on for those at home while the traveller is away and that the homecoming, as a result, can be bitter.

Rites of Passage: The End of Childhood/Innocence

A rite of passage relates to a category of rituals that accompany 'changes of place, state, social position and age in a culture' (Turner & Turner, 1978: 249). Van Gennep (1909) has identified three phases of these periods of transition in life: separation, the liminar or marginal phase and aggregation.

These may occur during a travel experience. The separation marks the retreat from home or a community, to embark on the journey. At the margins or *limen*, the traveller enters a realm of mid-transition. The liminal state has been compared with being in the womb, death, or experiencing a state of darkness (Turner & Turner, 1978). The traveller finally returns home, and must take up a new place in their community or society, having been transformed through their experiences. We focus on this final stage of the rite of passage in this chapter.

In *The Adventures of Tom Sawyer*, Tom and Huck have survived their trip down the river and struggle in the caves, which nearly costs them their lives. They find hidden treasure that makes them rich. Through all these picaresque adventures, they develop as young men. Initially they are tearaways and love to play practical jokes and get into scrapes. Their biggest joke – to turn up at their own 'funeral' – upsets Tom's Aunt, and they learn how much they are loved by others. They feel ashamed at their behaviour. Huck, however, cannot bear living with the Widow Douglas. He feels 'tied up' and heads back to the woods and freedom. Growing up, for him, is about realising his priorities and what he can and cannot stand. Tom is still a boy, as Mark Twain observes at the end of the book: 'The story could not go much further without becoming a history of a man'. However, he is no longer the same boy. He is taken seriously by the villagers of St Petersburg and ends up in Judge Thatcher's good books. He can now court the Judge's daughter Becky.

For others, the loss of childhood innocence is a dark episode or restricting. Travel adventures are not to be repeated. The carefree young hero settles for domesticity, even shunning further opportunities to leave home. Mattie Ross in *True Grit* is both physically and emotionally scarred. She will neither marry nor travel again. Jack Hawkins in *Treasure Island* has also had his fill of exotic journeys.

Graburn (1983) refers to 'rite of passage' tourism, where a traveller is typically going through a major life transition, which makes this person look to the long-term and take an interest in their own self-development. Examples include a divorce or ending of a relationship, illness, or attempting to solve or change problematic personal or work situations (Ross, 1994). Hape Kerkeling in *I'm Off Then* is motivated to go on a pilgrimage owing to ill-health, as well as the need to explore questions of spirituality. His journey could also be characterised as a rite of passage, where the liminal space of the road to Santiago de Compostela allows him to be his authentic self and to understand himself better. On his return, he is more comfortable in his own skin and is enriched through his journey. Kerkeling is now able to reintegrate back into his life as a comedian. Other examples of rites of passage include

H.V. Morton in *In Search of England*, Elizabeth Gilbert in *Eat, Pray, Love* and explorers' tales, such as those by Isabella Bird and Edith Durham. Ill-health plagued Morton, Bird, and Durham before they took the plunge to explore, while Gilbert travels to recover from a hostile marriage breakdown.

Many backpackers are undergoing a rite of passage as young adults, often travelling during a gap year between school and university and using this time for self-discovery, socialisation and a taste of independence (Loker-Murphy & Pearce, 1995; Ooi & Laing, 2010; O'Reilly, 2006). There are 'societal expectations [on the backpacker] to return to a role of responsible adulthood upon their return home' (Ooi & Laing, 2010: 194). The ultimate backpacker fantasy novel (or perhaps nightmare might be more apt) is *The Beach*.

The Beach (Alex Garland, 1996)

This is an allegory of paradise lost and like *Lord of the Flies*, depicts the gradual moral decline of an isolated group of individuals who start to turn on each other. Keeping 'the Beach' secret from outsiders becomes so important to some of them that they would kill their fellow travellers to ensure the secret does not leak out.

Richard, a young backpacker, is given a map by a man he meets in a Bangkok fleapit. Thailand is described as 'backpacker central, land of the beaten track'. A beach is marked on the map. The man (known as Mr Duck or Daffy) is later found dead in his room, with his wrists slashed. A fellow traveller Zeph tells Richard about an urban myth doing the rounds about a hidden beach, pristine and secret:

> Think about a lagoon, hidden from the sea and passing boats by a high, curving wall of rock. Then imagine white sands and coral gardens never damaged by dynamite fishing or trawling nets. Freshwater falls scatter the island, surrounded by jungle – not the forests of inland Thailand, but jungle. Canopies three levels deep, plants untouched for a thousand years, strangely coloured birds and monkeys in the trees.

Zeph's friend Sammy calls it 'paradise ... it's Eden'. This vision 'consumes' Richard, but he does not realise the truth – one can never leave the Beach alive. The comparison of the beach with Eden is also interesting; Law *et al.* (2007: 142) note that this is 'an ill-fated Garden of Eden', alluding to the evil that comes to pervert its ideals.

Richard eventually finds his way there and the beach life assimilates him: 'You look around, take on board, adjust, accept'. He forgets about his old life. The people living at the Beach are paranoid about being discovered by tourists: 'Set up in Bali, Ko Pha-Ngan, Ko Tao, Borocay, and the hordes are bound to follow. There's no way you can keep it out of Lonely Planet, and once that happens it's countdown to doomsday'. Eventually, however, he sees the downside of the Beach, the way that people develop a group-think mentality and start to lose the ability to think for themselves. They also become selfish, wanting to keep their beach hidden from outsiders, no matter what it takes or who it hurts. The irony is of course that the tourist thus destroys what it most wants (Law *et al.,* 2007).

Zeph and Sammy are killed when they try to find the beach, and Richard does not try to help his old friends. Several backpackers become sick or injured, and no attempt is made to take them to medical aid on the mainland. This contributes to the death of an injured young man. Richard is appalled and frightened by what others have become, and what he sees in himself. He starts to hallucinate and dreams he sees Daffy again.

Richard eventually escapes from the beach with two others and manages to return home. He is no longer the innocent he was when he first travelled to Bangkok. He has seen the dark side of travel – and travellers – and is changed forever. His book is a testimony to his rite of passage through a brush with savagery.

The Power to Bestow Boons

Part of the myth of the happy return involves the hero bringing back something valuable to society – a 'trophy [such as] the runes of wisdom, the Golden Fleece, or his sleeping princess' (Campbell, 1949: 193). This boon is the preserve of the hero and often involves great sacrifices or hardship. It may be a special person. Martin in *The Searchers* rescues Debbie after she is abducted by Indians and restores her to the society of her childhood. It might be a valuable object or treasure, as in *Treasure Island*, *The Adventures of Tom Sawyer* or *King Solomon's Mines*.

The boon may also be intangible. Detectives like Sherlock Holmes, Miss Marple and Kurt Wallander solve crimes, which restores order in society. Some take the law into their own hands to put matters right, as they see it. Mattie Ross in *True Grit*, with the help of Rooster Cogburn, tracks down Tom Chaney, who killed her father, and shoots him. Many explorers travel to solve mysteries, such as finding the source of the Nile, the mythical El Dorado or the North-West Passage. Modern explorer journeys may restore forgotten reputations, such as Kieran Kelly's trek in the footsteps of Gregory to highlight the latter's achievements. In *Beau Geste*, John's return from a posting with the French Foreign Legion clears his brother Michael's name.

Michael's written confession reveals that he stole a jewel to protect his aunt. In *Harry Potter*, the reward is the destruction of Voldemort and the freedom from tyranny; both for the 'Muggle' and magic worlds.

A boon can also involve the removal or annihilation of someone or something. Harry Potter returns the Elder Wand 'back where it came from (presumably in Dumbledore's final resting place)', as he fears its corruptive power, much like Frodo's destruction of the One Ring in *The Lord of the Rings* was necessary to eliminate a source of evil. Milady is killed in *The Three Musketeers*. Both D'Artagnan's lover and enemy, literary conventions require vengeance for her killing of the innocent Constance.

In other cases, the hero is able to distribute largesse at the end of their journey to someone who deserves it. Allan Quartermain in *King Solomon's Mines* divides the diamonds he took from the mines of Kukuanaland with his travel companions and George Curtis, whose disappearance was the original reason for setting out on the expedition. Quartermain was unable to take all the spoils; just a few gems that he could carry in his pocket. Rather than being a greedy pillage of the wealth of another society or community, this boon represents just compensation for their labours in freeing the people of Kukuanaland from the despotic rule of King Twala and restoring the rightful heir Umbopa to his throne.

Benefits of the Journey: The Happy Ending

We now turn to the happy ending; the one that we all crave. The hero's journey or katabasis may both lead to various benefits for the traveller. A classic one is marriage. All good fairytales end with the nuptials of the hero and heroine, and as Mark Twain notes at the conclusion of *The Adventures of Tom Sawyer*: 'When one writes a novel about grown people, he knows exactly where to stop – that is, with a marriage'. *The Lord of the Rings* finishes with the marriage of Aragorn to Arwen, which is permitted by her father now that her suitor is the King of Gondor. Arwen, however, makes a sacrifice; she gives up her immortality for love. Jane Austen's novels usually end with the marriage of the heroine after she has learnt some important moral lesson – Elizabeth weds Darcy in *Pride and Prejudice* after she learns to appreciate his finer qualities, while Anne Elliot in *Persuasion* finally ends up betrothed to the man she rejected in her youth on the advice of a family friend. Anne is no longer at the mercy of other's opinions and learns to trust her own judgement of human nature and character.

Some travellers gain power or influence as a result of their journey. Professor Challenger's tale of dinosaurs living in a remote part of South

America is finally treated as scientifically credible at the end of *The Lost World*. D'Artagnan becomes the head of the musketeers in *The Three Musketeers*. Their travels have equipped them for these new responsibilities.

Others gain new insights or self-awareness. Charles in *Brideshead Revisited* puts his experiences at Brideshead as a young adult into perspective when he returns there during the Second World War. As Hape Kerkeling in *I'm Off Then* says, with reference to his pilgrimage: 'Maybe I'm drawing nearer not only to Santiago but also to myself'. The journey to the self is the ultimate form of travel and potentially never ends. Perhaps this is the salient message behind most travel narratives, and a reason for the enduring compulsion and drive to see beyond the next horizon.

13 Conclusion

*'The recounting of a journey and its ensuing mysteries and hardships
is the oldest form of storytelling, and yet it never feels worn'*
Whybrow, 2003: 15

The texts referred to in this book were selected for the truths we felt they revealed about travel. They cover many different genres and span as far back as the 18th century. We felt, however, it was important to begin our analysis with an overview of the 'conventional' view of literary tourism, as a departure point for the rest of the book. While this is acknowledged as a tourist niche attracting wide and growing academic interest, it is not the focus of our study.

Our analysis of the different genres of literature, including Westerns, historical novels, crime and children's books, suggests that travel is conceptualised in a remarkably similar way throughout different eras and cultural contexts. We attribute this, in part, to the fact that these works are almost all based on a mythological structure, either the hero's journey (Campbell, 1949) or the katabasis derived from Greek mythology. It is these mythic dimensions that give many of these books their significance, power and long lasting appeal. They acknowledge the darker side of travel – its testing and often hellish qualities. They also illustrate the ability of travel to change an individual's life and enable them to understand themselves more deeply, as a result of their experiences.

This book engages with current debates in tourism research. For example, the notion of whether travel is truly transformative has been contested by Bruner (1991), and there is research underway into the role of long distance walking trips in the transformation of tourists (Saunders *et al.*, 2010). We provide another facet to this debate by noting that travel is generally depicted as transformative in literature, and arguing that this may raise expectations for the traveller that might not be met in reality.

This book also supports the view that forms of tourism are motivated by a 'dramatic world-view' in Western society, which has its roots in classical

Greek theatre (Celsi *et al.*, 1993). It is described as a 'fundamental cultural lens through which individuals frame their perceptions, seek their self-identities, and engage in vicarious or actual behaviors' (Celsi *et al.*, 1993: 2). Our work suggests that this world-view is encouraged by books, which often adopt particular dramatic structures like the katabasis.

Postmodern society is obsessed with connectivity and collective behaviour, chiefly exhibited through new media, such as social networking sites (Gretzel & Jamal, 2009; Månsson, 2009). Our study reveals, however, that while reading is a solitary activity, it also leads to a 'collective gaze' (Urry, 2002), in the sense of a common understanding of travel. We argue that the book is a powerful agent for cultural change, in this case through its influence on ideas of travel, the way we experience travel and potentially on travel behaviour, including motivations. This is despite the fact that more recent forms of media, such as television and film, are often argued to be more influential than books in a social sense (Butler, 1990).

We contend, therefore, that the power of books and their link with travel is an important social and cultural phenomenon, which warrants further research. Future studies might usefully examine a number of themes developed in this book. The mythic dimension of many books may help to explain why we gravitate towards certain stories and their enduring popularity across the generations. In a tourism context, it can be argued that all books involve some kind of journey or movement (Vogel, 1974) and thus these mythic elements also tell us something about the complexity of travel, and how we feel about it and approach it, both as children and adults. Future research might also extend our analysis to books of other genres and from different cultural contexts, particularly those from a non-Western canon. The undervalued role of children's books as rich sources of our understanding of the phenomenon of tourism (Laing & Crouch, 2009a) could also be a fruitful area of further study. Far from being lightweight fare, these books often contain deeper themes drawn from mythology, which make their narratives resonate with readers, young or old. They start us on an imaginative pathway (Zurick, 1995), where travel is mysterious, magical and often life-changing.

Books

Allende, I. (2005) *Zorro*. New York: Harper Collins.

Asher, M. (1988) *Two Against the Sahara: On Camelback from Nouakchott to the Nile*. New York: William Morrow.

Austen, J. (1813) *Pride and Prejudice*. 1981 reprint. Harmondsworth, Middlesex: Penguin.

Barrie, J.M. (1911) *Peter Pan*. 2008 reprint. London: Puffin.

Berger, T. (1964) *Little Big Man*. 1965 reprint. London: Eyre & Spottiswoode.

Bird, I. (1879) *A Lady's Life in the Rocky Mountains*. Oxford: John Beaufoy Publishing.

Blyton, E. (1943) *The Magic Faraway Tree*. 1990 reprint. Melbourne: Reed.

Burnaby, F. (1876) *A Ride to Khiva: Travels and Adventures in Central Asia*. 1972 reprint. London: Charles Knight & Co.

Burton, R.F. (1855) *Personal Narrative of a Pilgrimage to El-Medinah and Meccah*. 1964 reprint of the 1893 memorial edition. New York: Dover.

Carroll, L. (1865) *Alice's Adventures in Wonderland*. 2010 reprint. London: Penguin.

Chandler, R. (1953) *The Long Good-Bye*. 1977 reprint. London: Penguin.

Christie, A. (1950) *A Murder is Announced*. 2002 reprint. London: Harper.

Cocteau, J. (1936) *Round the World Again in 80 Days*. 2000 reprint. London and New York: Taurus Parke.

Conan Doyle, A. (1887) *A Study in Scarlet*. 2003 reprint. New York: Bantam.

Conan Doyle, A. (1912) *The Lost World & Other Stories*. 1995 reprint. Ware: Wordsworth Classics.

Crane, R. and Crane, N. (1987) *Journey to the Centre of the Earth*. 1988 reprint. London: Corgi.

Crichton, M. (1991) *Jurassic Park*. 1993 reprint. London: Arrow.

Custer, G.A. (1874) *My Life on the Plains*. 1963 reprint. London: The Folio Society.

David, E. (1950) *A Book of Mediterranean Food*. 2005 reprint. London: The Folio Society.

Davidson, R. (1980) *Tracks*. 1998 reprint. London; Basingstoke; Oxford: Pan Macmillan.

Dumas, A. (1844) *The Three Musketeers*. 2001 reprint. London: Wordsworth.

Durham, E. (1909) *High Albania*. 1985 reprint. London: Virago.

Durrell, G. (1956) *My Family and Other Animals*. 2006 reprint. London: The Folio Society.

Fiennes, R. (1993) *Mind Over Matter: The Epic Crossing of the Antarctic Continent*. Great Britain: Sinclair-Stevenson.

Garland, A. (1996) *The Beach*. 2008 reprint. London: Penguin.

Gilbert, E. (2006) *Eat, Pray, Love: One Woman's Search for Everything across Italy, India and Indonesia*. 2007 reprint. London: Bloomsbury.

Hemingway, E. (1927) *The Sun Also Rises*. 2004 reprint. London: Arrow.

Heyerdahl, T. (1948) *The Kon-Tiki Expedition. By Raft across the South Seas* (F. H. Lyon, trans.). 1996 reprint. London: Flamingo.

Hillary, E. (1955) *High Adventure*. 1956 reprint. London: The Companion Book Club.

Hilton, J. (1933) *Lost Horizon*. New York: William Morrow.

Hofmann, C. (1999) *The White Masai*. 2011 reprint. London: Nassau.

Hope, A. (1894) *The Prisoner of Zenda*. 2007 reprint. London: Penguin.

Ingalls Wilder, L. (1935) *Little House on the Prairie*. 1971 reprint. New York: Harper Trophy.

Kelly, K. (2003) *Tanami: On Foot across Australia's Desert Heart*. Sydney: Pan Macmillan.

Kerkeling, H. (2006) *I'm Off Then: Losing and Finding Myself on the Camino de Santiago*. 2009 translation. New York: Free Press.

Larsson, S. (2005) *The Girl with the Dragon Tattoo*. 2009 reprint. London: Quercus.

Leigh Fermor, P. (1977) *A Time of Gifts*. 2004 reprint. London: John Murray.

LeMay, A. (1954) *The Searchers*. 1978 reprint. Boston: Gregg.

Lewis, C.S. (1950) *The Lion, the Witch and the Wardrobe*. 2000 reprint. London: HarperCollins.

Lewis, C.S. (1951) *Prince Caspian*. 2000 reprint. London: HarperCollins.

Lewis, C.S. (1952) *The Voyage of the Dawn Treader*. 2000 reprint. London: HarperCollins.

Lewis, C.S. (1953) *The Silver Chair*. 2000 reprint. London: HarperCollins.

Lewis, C.S. (1954) *The Horse and his Boy*. 2000 reprint. London: HarperCollins.

Lewis, C.S. (1955) *The Magician's Nephew*. 2000 reprint. London: HarperCollins.

Lewis, C.S. (1959) *The Last Battle*. 2000 reprint. London: HarperCollins.

Mankell, H. (1991) *Faceless Killers*. 2009 reprint. London: Vintage.

Mayle, P. (1989) *A Year in Provence*. 2000 reprint. London: Penguin.

Mear, R. and Swan, R. (1987) *In the Footsteps of Scott*. London: Grafton Books.

McCulley, J. (1924) *The Mark of Zorro*. 2005 reprint. London: Penguin.

Moorcock, M. (1971) *The Warlord of the Air*. 1984 omnibus. London: Panther.

Moorcock, M. (1974) *The Land Leviathan*. 1984 omnibus. London: Panther.

Moorcock, M. (1981) *The Steel Tsar*. 1984 omnibus. London: Panther.

Morgan, M. (1991) *Mutant Message Down Under: A Woman's Journey into Dreamtime Australia*. 1995 reprint. London: Thorsons.

Morell, V. (2001) *Blue Nile: Ethiopia's River of Magic and Mystery*. Washington, D.C.: Adventure Press.

Morton, H.V. (1927) *In Search of England*. 2006 reprint. London: Methuen.

Murphy, D. (1965) *Full Tilt: Ireland to India on a Bicycle*. 2010 reprint. London: Eland.

Nesbit, E. (1902) *Five Children and It*. 1959 reprint. Harmondsworth: Penguin.

Nesbit, E. (1906) *The Railway Children*. 2010 reprint. London: Puffin.

Portis, C. (1968) *True Grit*. London: Jonathon Cape.

Pullman, P. (1995) *Northern Lights*. 2007 reprint. London: Scholastic.

Pullman, P. (1997) *The Subtle Knife*. 2007 reprint. London: Scholastic.

Pullman, P. (2000) *The Amber Spyglass*. 2007 reprint. London: Scholastic.

Rider Haggard, H. (1885) *King Solomon's Mines*. 1991 reprint. Oxford; New York: Oxford University Press.

Rider Haggard, H. (1887) *She: A History of Adventure*. 1991 reprint. Bloomington; Indianapolis: Indiana University Press.

Rowling, J.K. (1997) *Harry Potter and the Philosopher's Stone*. London: Bloomsbury Publishing.

Rowling, J.K. (1998) *Harry Potter and the Chamber of Secrets*. London: Bloomsbury Publishing.

Rowling, J.K. (1999) *Harry Potter and the Prisoner of Azkaban*. London: Bloomsbury Publishing.

Rowling, J.K. (2000) *Harry Potter and the Goblet of Fire*. London: Bloomsbury Publishing.
Rowling, J.K. (2003) *Harry Potter and the Order of the Phoenix*. London: Bloomsbury Publishing.
Rowling, J.K. (2005) *Harry Potter and the Half-Blood Prince*. London: Bloomsbury Publishing.
Rowling, J.K. (2007) *Harry Potter and the Deathly Hallows*. London: Bloomsbury Publishing.
Scott, W. (1819) *Ivanhoe*. 1965 reprint. London: Dent.
Selby, B. (1988) *Riding the Desert Trail*. London: Sphere Books.
Severin, T. (1978) *The Brendan Voyage*. 1983 reprint. London: Arrow Books.
Shackleton, E. (1919) *South: The Story of Shackleton's Last Expedition, 1914–1917*. 1983 reprint. London: Century.
Stanley, H.M. (1872) *How I Found Livingstone: Travels, Adventures and Discoveries in Central Africa: Including an Account of Four Months' Residence with Dr. Livingstone*. 1890 reprint. London: Sampson, Low, Marston, Searle & Rivington.
Stephenson, P. (2005) *Treasure Islands: Sailing in the South Seas in the Wake of Fanny and Robert Louis Stevenson*. London: Headline Books.
Stevenson, R.L. (1883) *Treasure Island*. 2010 reprint. London: Penguin.
Swift, J. (1724) *Gulliver's Travels into Several Remote Nations of the World*. 2010 reprint. London: Penguin.
Tayler, J. (2003) *Glory in a Camel's Eye: Trekking through the Moroccan Sahara*. New York: Houghton Mifflin.
Tolkien, J.R.R. (1954) *The Fellowship of the Ring*. 2001 reprint. London: HarperCollins.
Tolkien, J.R.R. (1954) *The Two Towers*. 2001 reprint. London: HarperCollins.
Tolkien, J.R.R. (1955) *The Return of the King*. 2001 reprint. London: HarperCollins.
Travers, P.L. (1934) *Mary Poppins*. 1964 reprint. London: Collins.
Twain, M. (1876) *The Adventures of Tom Sawyer*. 2010 reprint. Camberwell: Penguin.
Verne, J. (1873) *Around the World in Eighty Days*. 1994 reprint. Ware: Wordsworth.
Verne, J. (1862) *Five Weeks in a Balloon*. 1994 reprint. Ware: Wordsworth.
Verne, J. (1864) *Journey to the Centre of the Earth*. 1996 reprint. Ware: Wordsworth.
Verne, J. (1870) *Twenty Thousand Leagues Under the Sea*. 1993 reprint. London: Everyman.
Waugh, E. (1945) *Brideshead Revisited: The Sacred and Profane Memories of Captain Charles Ryder*. 2008 reprint. London: Penguin.
Wren, P.C. (1924) *Beau Geste*. London: John Murray.

Secondary References

Adams, P.G. (1983) *Travel Literature and the Evolution of the Novel*. Lexington: The University Press of Kentucky.

Adler, J. (1989) Travel as performed art. *American Journal of Sociology* 94 (6), 1366–1391.

Aldridge, A. (1995) The English as they see others: England revealed in Provence. *The Sociological Review* 43 (3), 415–434.

Allen, B. (2002) *The Faber Book of Exploration: An Anthology of Worlds Revealed by Explorers Through the Ages*. London: Faber and Faber.

Alter, A. (2011) Exit music. *The Weekend Australian Review*, 30–31 July 2011.

Ambrose, S.E. (1997) *Undaunted Courage: Meriwether Lewis, Thomas Jefferson and the Opening of the American West*. New York: Simon & Schuster.

Anderson, C.C. (1992) The golden West: Enduring myths, persistent facts. *Children's Literature Association Quarterly* 17 (1), 3–4.

Ashley, M. (2011) *Out of This World: Science Fiction But Not As You Know It*. London: The British Library.

Atherton, J. (1986) The itinerary and the postcard: Minimal strategies in *The Sun Also Rises*. *ELH* 53 (1), 199–218.

Barnard, R. (2002) Tourism comes to Haworth. In M. Robinson and H-C. Andersen (eds) *Literature and Tourism: Essays in the Reading and Writing of Tourism* (pp. 143–154). London: Thomson.

Batchelor, J. and Batchelor, J. (1990) *In Stanley's Footsteps: Across Africa from West to East*. London: Blandford.

Batey, M. (1996) *Jane Austen and the English Landscape*. London: Barn Elms.

Baudrillard, J. (1986) *America*. New York: Verso.

Beeton, S. (2005) *Film-induced Tourism*. Clevedon: Channel View Publications.

Behr, K.E. (2005) 'Same-as-difference': Narrative transformations and intersecting cultures in Harry Potter. *Journal of Narrative Theory* 35 (1), 112–132.

Belk, R.W. (1992) Moving possessions: An analysis based on personal documents from the 1847–1869 Mormon migration. *Journal of Consumer Research* 19, 339–361.

Belk, R.W. and Costa, J.A. (1998) The mountain man myth: A contemporary consuming fantasy. *Journal of Consumer Research* 25, 218–240.

Bergin, T (1981) *In the Steps of Burke and Wills*. Sydney: Australian Broadcasting Commission.

Bergsten, S. (1978) *Mary Poppins and Myth*. Stockholm: Almqvist & Wiksell International.

Billone, A.C. (2004) The boy who lived: From Carroll's Alice and Barrie's Peter Pan to Rowling's Harry Potter. *Children's Literature* 32, 178–202.

Bishop P. (1989) *The Myth Of Shangri-La: Tibet, Travel Writing and the Western Creation of a Sacred Landscape*. London: Athlone.

Blake, K.S. (1995) Zane Grey and images of the American West. *Geographical Review* 85 (2), 202–216.

Bosmajian, H. (1983) Vastness and contraction of space in Little House on the Prairie. *Children's Literature* 11, 49–63.

Botting, D. (1998) *Gerald Durrell: The Authorised Biography*. London: HarperCollins.

Bridges, R. (2002) Exploration and travel outside Europe (1720–1914). In P. Hulme and T. Youngs (eds) *The Cambridge Companion to Travel Writing* (pp. 53–69). Cambridge: Cambridge University Press.

Brown, I. (1999) *Extreme South: Struggles and Triumph of the First Australian Team to the Pole*. Terrey Hills, NSW: Australian Geographic.

Bruner, E. (1991) Transformation of self in tourism. *Annals of Tourism Research* 18, 238–250.

Buchmann, A., Moore, K. and Fisher, D. (2010) Experiencing film tourism: Authenticity and fellowship. *Annals of Tourism Research* 37 (1), 229–248.

Butcher, W. (1990) *Verne's Journey to the Centre of the Self: Space and Time in the Voyages Extraordinaires*. Basingstoke: MacMillan.

Butler, R.W. (1990) The influence of the media in shaping international tourist patterns. *Tourism Recreation Research*, 15 (2), 46–53.

Calder, H. (1974) *There Must be a Lone Ranger: The Myth and Reality of the American Wild West*. London: Hamish Hamilton.

Campbell, J. (1949) *The Hero with a Thousand Faces*. 1993 reprint. Princeton, NJ: Princeton University Press.

Campbell, M.B. (1988) *The Witness and the Other World: Exotic European Travel Writing, 400–1600*. Ithaca, London: Cornell University Press.

Carter, R.A. (2000) *Buffalo Bill Cody: The Man behind the Legend*. New York: Wiley.

Caton, K. and Santos, C.A. (2007) Heritage tourism on Route 66: Deconstructing nostalgia. *Journal of Travel Research* 45 (4), 371–386.

Celsi, R.L., Rose, R.L. and Leigh, T.W. (1993) An exploration of high-risk leisure consumption through skydiving. *Journal of Consumer Research*, 20 (1), 1–23.

Clauss, J.J. (1999) Descent into Hell: Mythic paradigms in *The Searchers*. *Journal of Popular Film and Television* 27 (3), 2–17.

Clausson, N. (2005) Degeneration, *fin-de-siècle* gothic, and the science of detection: Arthur Conan Doyle's *The Hound of the Baskervilles* and the emergence of the modern detective story. *Journal of Narrative Theory* 35 (1), 60–87.

Conefrey, M. (2007) *The Adventurer's Handbook: Life Lessons from History's Great Explorers*. London: Collins.

Conefrey, M. and Jordan, T. (1998) *Icemen: A History of the Arctic and its Explorers*. London: Boxtree.

Connell, J. and Gibson, C. (2005) *Music and Tourism: On the Road Again*. Clevedon: Channel View Publications.

Conrad, J. (1926) *Last Essays*. 2011 reprint, In H.R. Stevens and J.H. Stape (eds). Cambridge: Cambridge University Press.

Coyne, M. (1997) *The Crowded Prairie: American National Identity in the Hollywood Western*. New York; London: Taurus.

Crompton, J. (1979) Motivations for pleasure vacation. *Annals of Tourism Research* 6 (4), 408–424.

Cunningham, V. (1994) *In the Reading Gaol: Postmodernity, Texts and History*. Oxford: Blackwell.

Dann, G.M.S. (2002) Dreams, love and death in Venice. In M. Robinson and H-C. Andersen (eds) *Literature and Tourism: Essays in the Reading and Writing of Tourism* (pp. 239–278). London: Thomson.

Davis, W.C. (1999) *Three Roads to the Alamo: The Lives and Fortunes of David Crockett, James Bowie and William Barrett Travis*. New York: Harper.

De Botton, A. (2002) *The Art of Travel*. 2003 reprint. London: Penguin.

Devonshire, D., Leigh Fermor, P. and Mosley, C. (2010) *In Tearing Haste: Letters between Deborah Devonshire and Patrick Leigh Fermor*. New York: New York Review of Books.

Digance, J. and Cusack, C. (2002) Glastonbury: A tourist town for all seasons. In G. Dann (ed.) *The Tourist as a Metaphor of the Social World* (pp. 263–280). Wallingford, UK: CABI.

Dippie, B.W. (1992) Jack Crabb and the sole survivors of Custer's Last Stand. In P.A. Hutton (ed.) *The Custer Reader* (pp. 473–487). Lincoln; London: University of Nebraska Press.

Dunn, J. (2000) *Virginia Woolf and Vanessa Bell: A Very Close Conspiracy*. 2008 reprint. London: Virago.

Eco, U. (1986) *Travels in Hyper Reality*. San Diego: Harcourt Brace Jovanovich.

Edwards, M. (2001) The adventures of Marco Polo, Part III. *National Geographic* 200 (1), 26–47.

Egan, M. (1982) The Neverland of Id: Barrie, Peter Pan, and Freud. *Children's Literature* 10, 37–55.

Elliott, M. (2007) *Custerology: The Enduring Legacy of the Indian Wars and George Armstrong Custer*. Chicago; London: Chicago University Press.

Ewert, A. (1989) *Outdoor Adventure Pursuits: Foundations, Models and Theories*. Columbus, OH: Publishing Horizons.

Falconer, R. (2005) *Hell in Contemporary Literature: Western Descent Narratives since 1945*. Edinburgh: Edinburgh University Press.

Fawcett, C. and Cormack, P. (2001) Guarding authenticity at literary tourism sites. *Annals of Tourism Research* 28 (3), 686–704.

Fellman, A.C. (1996) 'Don't expect to depend on anyone else': The frontier as portrayed in the Little House. *Children's Literature* 24, 101–116.

Field, A.N. (2006) Expatriate lifestyle as tourist destination: *The Sun Also Rises* and experiential travelogues of the Twenties. *The Hemingway Review* 25 (2), 29–43.

Frey, C. (1987) Laura and Pa: Family and landscape in Little House on the Prairie. *Children's Literature Association Quarterly* 12 (3), 125–128.

Frost, W. (2006) Braveheart-ed Ned Kelly: Historic films, heritage tourism and destination image. *Tourism Management* 27, 247–254.

Frost, W. (2008) Projecting an image: Film-induced festivals in the American West. *Event Management* 12 (2), 95–103.

Frost, W. (2010a) Life changing experiences: Films and tourists in the Australian Outback. *Annals of Tourism Research* 37 (3), 707–726.

Frost, W. (2010b) *Jurassic Park* and visitor interpretation for museum dinosaur exhibitions. In A. Filippoupoliti (ed.) *Science Exhibitions: Communication and Evaluation* (pp. 193–217). Edinburgh: Museumsetc.

Frost, W. (2011) From *Winnie-the-Pooh* to *Madagascar*: Fictional media images of the zoo experience. In W. Frost (ed.) *Zoos and Tourism: Conservation, Education, Entertainment?* (pp. 217–226). Bristol: Channel View Publications.

Frost, W. and Hall, C.M. (2009) Reinterpreting the creation myth: Yellowstone National Park. In W. Frost and C.M. Hall (eds) *National Parks and Tourism: International Perspectives on Development, Histories And Change* (pp. 16–29). London; New York: Routledge.

Frost, W. and Laing, J. (2011) *Strategic Management of Festivals and Events*. Melbourne: Cengage.

Gilead, S. (1991) Magic abjured: Closure in children's fantasy fiction. *PMLA* 106 (2), 277–293.

Goetzmann W. (1979) Paradigm lost. In N. Reingold (ed.) *The Sciences in the American Context: New Perspectives* (pp. 21–34). Washington DC: Smithsonian Press.

Graburn, N. (1983) The anthropology of tourism. *Annals of Tourism Research* 10, 9–33.

Graburn, N.H.H. (1989) Tourism: The sacred journey. In V.L. Smith (ed.) *Hosts and Guests: The Anthropology of Tourism* (2nd edition) (pp. 21–36). Philadelphia: University of Pennsylvania Press.

Green, M. (1980) *Dreams of Adventure, Deeds of Empire*. London: Routledge.

Gregory, D. (1999) Scripting Egypt: Orientalism and the cultures of travel. In J. Duncan and D. Gregory (eds) *Writes of Passage: Reading Travel Writing* (pp. 114–150). London: Routledge.

Gretzel, U. and Jamal, T. (2009) Conceptualizing the Creative Tourist Class: Technology, mobility and tourism experiences. *Tourism Analysis* 14 (1), 471–481.

Grilli, G. (2007) *Myth, Symbol and Meaning in Mary Poppins: The Governess as Provocateur*. London: Routledge.

Griswold, J. (1992) *Audacious Kids: Coming of Age in America's Classic Children's Books*. New York: Oxford University Press.

Gyimóthy, S. and Mykletun, R.J. (2004) Play in adventure tourism: The case of Arctic trekking. *Annals of Tourism Research* 31 (4), 855–878.

Hains, B. (2002) *The Ice and the Island: Mawson, Flynn and the Myth of the Frontier*. Carlton South: Melbourne University Publishing.

Handley, W.R. (2009) The popular Western. In J.T. Matthews (ed.) *A Companion to the Modern American Novel 1900–1950* (pp. 437–453). Chichester: Wiley.

Hardyment, C. (2000) *Literary Trails: Writers in their Landscapes*. London: The National Trust.

Hare, J. (2003) *Shadows Across the Sahara*. London: Constable and Richardson.

Hazzard, S. (2008) Italian hours. In S. Hazzard and F. Steegmuller (eds) *The Ancient Shore: Dispatches from Naples* (pp. 1–5). Chicago, London: University of Chicago Press.

Heller, P. (2004) *Hell or High Water: Surviving Tibet's Tsangpo River*. Crows Nest, Australia: Allen & Unwin.

Hennig, C. (2002) Tourism: Enacting modern myths. In G. Dann (ed.) *The Tourist as a Metaphor of the Social World* (pp. 169–187). Wallingford, UK: CABI.

Herbert, D. (2001) Literary places, tourism and the heritage experience. *Annals of Tourism Research* 28 (2), 312–333.

Hewison, R. (1987) *The Heritage Industry: Britain in a Climate of Decline*. London: Methuen.

Higson, A. (1993) Re-presenting the national past: Nostalgia and pastiche in the heritage film. In L. Friedman (ed.) *Fires Were Started: British Cinema and Thatcherism* (pp. 109–129). London: UCL Press.

Hillary, P. and Elder, J.E. (2003) *In the Ghost Country: A Lifetime Spent on the Edge*. Milsons Point, NSW: Random House Australia.

Hitt, J. (1990) *The American West from Fiction (1823-1976) into Film (1909-1986)*. Jefferson NC: McFarland.

Hodgson, J. (1985) Introduction. In E. Durham, *High Albania*. London: Virago.

Holland, P. and Huggan, G. (2000) *Tourists with Typewriters: Critical Reflections on Contemporary Travel Writing*. Michigan: University of Michigan Press.

Hollindale, P. (1993) Peter Pan: The text and the myth. *Children's Literature in Education* 24 (1), 19–30.

Hollindale, P. (1997) *Signs of Childness in Children's Books*. Stroud: Thimble.

Hollindale, P. (2005) A hundred years of Peter Pan. *Children's Literature in Education* 36 (3), 197–215.

Holtsmark, E.B. (2001) The *katabasis* theme in modern cinema. In M.M. Winkler (ed.) *Classical Myth and Culture in the Cinema* (pp. 23–50). Oxford, New York: Oxford University Press.

Hulme, P. (2002) Travelling to write (1940–2000). In P. Hulme and T. Youngs (eds) *The Cambridge Companion to Travel Writing* (pp. 87–101). Cambridge: Cambridge University Press.

Hulme, P. and Youngs, T. (2002) Introduction. In P. Hulme and T. Youngs (eds) *The Cambridge Companion to Travel Writing* (pp. 1–13). Cambridge: Cambridge University Press.

Hume, K. (1974) Romance: A perdurable pattern. *College English* 36 (2), 129–146.

Hunt, P. (2001) Introduction. In P. Hunt and M. Lenz (eds) *Alternative Worlds in Fantasy Fiction*. London, New York: Continuum.

Hussey, A. (2006) *Paris: The Secret History*. London: Viking.

Hutton, P.A. (1992) From Little Bighorn to Little Big Man: The changing image of a western hero in popular culture. In P.A. Hutton (ed.) *The Custer Reader* (pp. 395–423). Lincoln, London: University of Nebraska Press.

Huxley, J. (1954) *From an Antique Land; Ancient and Modern in the Middle East*. New York: Crown.

Iwashita, C. (2006) Media representation of the UK as a destination for Japanese tourists. *Tourist Studies* 6 (1), 59–77.

Jeal, T. (2007) *Stanley: The Impossible Life of Africa's Greatest Explorer*. London: Faber.

Jenkins, H. (2001) The cultural logic of media convergence. *International Journal of Cultural Studies* 7 (1), 33–43.

Joyce, J. (1939) *Finnegans Wake*. New York: Viking Press.

Jung, C.G. (1938) *Psychology and Religion*. New York: Yale University Press.

Kelly, K. (2000) *Hard Country, Hard Men. In the Footsteps of Gregory*. Sydney: Hale & Iremonger.

Kincaid, J. (1992) *Child-Loving: The Erotic Child and Victorian Culture*. New York: Routledge.

Kitses, J. (2004) *Horizons West: Directing the Western from John Ford to Clint Eastwood*. London: British Film Institute.

Knight, S. (2003) *Robin Hood: A Mythic Biography*. Ithaca, London: Cornell University Press.

Knight, S. (2004) *Crime Fiction, 1800–2000: Detection, Death, Diversity*. Basingstoke, New York: Houndmills.

Knights, B. (2006) In search of England: Travelogue and nation between the wars. In R. Burden and S. Kohl (eds) *Landscape and Englishness* (pp. 165–184). Amsterdam, New York: Rodopi B.V.

Kooistra, P. (1989) *Criminals as Heroes: Structure, Power & Identity*. Bowling Green: Bowling Green State University Press.

Laing, J.H. and Crouch, G.I. (2005) Extraordinary journeys: An exploratory cross-cultural study of tourists on the frontier. *Journal of Vacation Marketing* 11 (3), 209–223.

Laing, J.H. and Crouch, G.I. (2009a) Exploring the role of the media in shaping motivations behind frontier travel experiences. *Tourism Analysis* 14, 187–198.

Laing, J.H. and Crouch, G.I. (2009b) Lone wolves? Isolation and solitude within the frontier travel experience. *Human Geography/Geografiska Annaler B* 91 (4), 325–342.

Laing, J.H. and Crouch, G.I. (2009c) Myth, adventure and fantasy at the frontier: Metaphors and imagery behind an extraordinary travel experience. *International Journal of Tourism Research* 11, 127–141.

Laing, J.H. and Crouch, G.I. (2011) Frontier tourism: Retracing mythic journeys. *Annals of Tourism Research* 38 (4), 1516–1534.

Langford, N.P. (1905) *The Discovery of Yellowstone Park (1870)*. 1972 reprint. Lincoln: Bison Books.

Lansing Smith, E. (1990) *Rape and Revelation: The Descent to the Underworld in Modernism*. Lanham, London: University Press of America.

Law, L., Bunnell, L. and Ong, C-E. (2007) The Beach, the gaze and film tourism. *Tourist Studies* 7, 141–164.

Lawson, V. (2004) Poppins Memorial Lands in Park. *Sydney Morning Herald*, 13 March 2004.

Levin, B. (1987) *Hannibal's Footsteps*. London: Hodder & Stoughton.

Light, D. (2007) Dracula tourism in Romania: Cultural identity and the state. *Annals of Tourism Research* 34 (3), 746–765.

Lindenfeld, D. (2009) Jungian archetypes and the discourse of history. *Rethinking History* 13 (2), 217–234.

Loker-Murphy, P. and Pearce, P.L. (1995) Young budget travellers: Backpackers in Australia. *Annals of Tourism Research* 22 (4), 819–843.

Long, H.S. (1948) Plato's doctrine of metempsychosis and its source. *The Classical Weekly* 41 (10), 149–155.

Lowe, V. (2007) *Stories, Pictures and Reality: Two Children Tell*. London, New York: Routledge.

Lowenthal, D. (1985) *The Past is a Foreign Country*. Cambridge: Cambridge University Press.

Lowenthal, D. (1998) *The Heritage Crusade and the Spoils of History*. Cambridge: Cambridge University Press.

Loy, R.P. (2004) *Westerns in a Changing America 1955–2000*. Jefferson NC: McFarland.

Lundberg, C. and Lexhagen, M. (2012) Bitten by the Twilight saga: From pop culture consumer to pop culture tourist. In R. Sharpley and P.R. Stone (eds) *The Contemporary Tourist Experience: Concepts and Consequences*. Abingdon: Routledge.

MacCannell, D. (1999) *The Tourist: A New Theory of the Leisure Class*. Berkeley and Los Angeles, CA: University of California Press.

Malmgren, C.D. (2001) *Anatomy of a Murder: Mystery, Detection and Crime Fiction*. Bowling Green, OH: Popular Press.

Månsson, M. (2009) The role of media products on consumer behaviour in tourism. In M. Kozak and A.Decrop (eds) *Handbook of Tourist Behaviour: Theory and Practice* (pp. 226–236). New York, Abingdon, Oxford: Routledge.

Månsson, M. (2010) Negotiating authenticity at Rosslyn Chapel. In B.T. Knudsen and A.M. Waade (eds) *Reinvesting Authenticity: Tourism, Place and Emotions* (pp. 169–180). Bristol: Channel View Publications.

Månsson, M. (2011) Mediatized tourism. *Annals of Tourism Research* 38 (4), 1634–1652.

Månsson, M. (2012) Media convergence: Tourist attractions in the making. *Tourism Review International* 15 (3), 227–241.

Maoz, D. (2004) The conquerers and the settlers. In G. Richards and J. Wilson (eds) *The Global Nomad: Backpacker Travel in Theory and Practice* (pp. 109–122). Clevedon: Channel View Publications.

Martin, A. (1990) *The Mask of the Prophet: The Extraordinary Fictions of Jules Verne*. Oxford: Clarendon.

Mawson. D. (1915) *The Home of the Blizzard: The Story of the Australasian Antarctic Expedition 1911–1914*. 1996 reprint. Kent Town: Wakefield Press.

McCloud, K. (2009) *Kevin McCloud's Grand Tour of Europe*. London: Phoenix.

McKercher, B. and du Cros, H. (2002) *Cultural Tourism: The Partnership between Tourism and Cultural Heritage Management*. New York: Haworth.

McManis, D.R. (1978) Places for mysteries. *Geographical Review* 68 (3), 319–334.

McNelly, W.E. (1973) Archetypal patterns in science fiction. *The CEA Critic* 35 (4), 15–19.

Melton, J.A. (2002) *Mark Twain, Travel Books and Tourism: The Tide of a Great Popular Movement*. Tuscaloosa: The University of Alabama Press.

Mordue, T. (2001) Performing and directing resident/tourist cultures in Heartbeat country. *Tourist Studies* 1 (3), 233–252.

Morgan, A. (2010) *The Lord of the Rings*: A *mythos* applicable in unsustainable times? *Environmental Education Research* 16 (3/4), 383–399.

Morsberger, R.E. and Morsberger, K.M. (2005) Introduction. In J. McCulley, *The Mark of Zorro* (pp. vii–xii). London: Penguin.

Mowder, L. (1992) Domestication of desire: Gender, language and landscape in the Little House books. *Children's Literature Association Quarterly* 17 (1), 15–19.

Muresan, A. and Smith K.A. (1998) Dracula's Castle in Transylvania: Conflicting heritage marketing strategies. *International Journal of Heritage Studies* 4 (2), 86–102.

Murray, N. (2008) *A Corkscrew is Most Useful: The Travellers of Empire*. 2009 reprint. London: Abacus.

Nicholson, V. (2002) *Among the Bohemians: Experiments in Living 1900–1939*. 2003 reprint. London: Penguin.

Nikolajeva, M. (2000) Tamed imagination: A re-reading of Heidi. *Children's Literature Association Quarterly* 25 (2), 68–75.

O'Guinn, T.C. and Belk, R.W. (1989) Heaven on earth: Consumption at Heritage Village, USA. *Journal of Consumer Research* 16 (2), 227–238.

O'Neill, P. (2009) Destination as destiny: Amelia B. Edwards's travel writing. *Frontiers: A Journal of Women Studies* 30 (2), 43–71.

Ooi, N. and Laing, J.H. (2010) Backpacker tourism: Sustainable and purposeful? Investigating the overlap between backpacker tourism and volunteer tourism motivations. *Journal of Sustainable Tourism* 18 (2), 191–206.

O' Reilly, C.C. (2006) From drifter to gap year tourist. *Annals of Tourism Research* 35 (4), 998–1017.

Osborn, M. (2001) Deeper realms: C.S. Lewis' re-visions of Joseph O'Neill's *Land Under England*. *Journal of Modern Literature* 25 (1), 115–120.

Palin, M. (1989) *Around the World in Eighty Days*. 1990 reprint. London: BBC Books.

Parkes, C. (2009) *Treasure Island* and the romance of the British Civil Service. In H. Montgomery and N.J. Watson (eds) *Children's Literature: Classic Texts and Contemporary Trends* (pp. 69–80). Basingstoke: Palgrave Macmillan.

Pearce, P.L. and Lee, U. (2005) Developing the travel career approach to tourist motivation. *Journal of Travel Research* 43 (3), 226–237.

Phillips, R. (1999) Writing travel and mapping sexuality: Richard Burton's sotadic zone. In J. Duncan and D. Gregory (eds) *Writes of Passage: Reading Travel Writing* (pp. 70–91). London: Routledge.

Phipps, A. (2003) Languages, identities, agencies: Intercultural lessons from Harry Potter. *Language and Intercultural Communication* 3 (1), 6–19.

Pilkington, W.T. and Graham, D. (1979) Introduction: A fistful of Westerns. In W.T. Pilkington and D. Graham (eds) *Western Movies* (pp. 1–13). Albuquerque: University of New Mexico Press.

Pitchford, S. (2008) *Identity Tourism: Imaging and Imagining the Nation*. Bingle UK: Emerald.

Plate, L. (2006) Walking in Virginia Woolf's footsteps: Performing cultural memory. *European Journal of Cultural Studies* 9 (1), 101–120.

Pratt, M-L. (2008) *Imperial Eyes: Travel Writing and Transculturation* (2nd edn). New York, Abingdon, Oxford: Routledge.

Rayner, G. (2010) Sherlock Homes fans stage last-ditch attempt to save Conan Doyle's home. *The Telegraph*, 16 December 2010.

Reijnders, S. (2009) Watching the detectives: Inside the guilty landscapes of Inspector Morse, Baantjer and Wallander. *European Journal of Communication* 24 (2), 165–181.

Reijnders, S. (2010) Places of the imagination: An ethnography of the TV detective tour. *Cultural Geographies* 17 (1), 37–52.

Reijnders, S. (2011) *Places of the Imagination: Media, Tourism, Culture*. Farnham, UK; Burlington, USA: Ashgate.

Richards, G. and Wilson, J. (2006) Youth and adventure tourism. In D. Buhalis and C. Costa (eds) *Tourism Business Frontiers: Consumers, Products and Industry* (pp. 40–47). Oxford; Burlington: Elsevier.

Richards, J. (1997) *Films and British National Identity: From Dickens to Dad's Army*. Manchester: Manchester University Press.

Robertson, J.P. (2001) What happens to our wishes: Magical thinking in Harry Potter. *Children's Literature Association Quarterly* 26 (1), 198–211.

Robinson, M. (2002) Between and beyond the pages: Literature-tourism relationships. In M. Robinson and H-C. Andersen (eds) *Literature and Tourism: Essays in the Reading and Writing of Tourism* (pp. 39–79). London: Thomson.

Robinson, M. and Andersen, H-C. (2002) Reading between the lines: Literature and the creation of touristic spaces. In M. Robinson and H-C. Andersen (eds) *Literature and Tourism: Essays in the Reading and Writing of Tourism* (pp. 1–38). London: Thomson.

Robinson, M. and Smith, M. (2006) Power, politics and play: The shifting contexts of cultural tourism. In M. Smith and M. Robinson (eds) *Cultural Tourism in a Changing World: Politics, Participation and (Re)p. esentation* (pp. 1–17). Clevedon: Channel View Publications.

Rosa, J.G. (1974) *They Called him Wild Bill: The Life and Adventures of James Butler Hickok*. Norman: University of Oklahoma Press.

Rosaldo, R. (1989) *Culture and Truth: The Remaking of Social Analysis*. London: Routledge.

Rose, J. (1994) *The Case of Peter Pan, or the Impossibility of Children's Fiction*. Basingstoke: Macmillan.

Rosenstone, R.A. (1995) *Visions of the Past: The Challenge of Film to Our Idea of History*. Cambridge USA: Harvard University Press.

Ross, G.F. (1994) *The Psychology of Tourism*. Melbourne: Hospitality Press.

Runte, A. (1979) *National Parks: The American Experience*. Lincoln; London: University of Nebraska Press.

Ryan, C. (2003) Risk acceptance in adventure tourism – paradox and context. In J. Wilks and S.J. Page (eds) *Managing Tourist Health and Safety in the New Millennium* (pp. 55–65). Oxford: Elsevier.

Said, E. (1978) *Orientalism*. New York: Pantheon Books.

Sampaio, M. (2011) Millennium Trilogy: Eye for eye and the utopia of order in modern waste lands. *Cross-Cultural Communication* 7 (2), 73–81.

Sargent, A. (1998) The Darcy effect: Regional tourism and costume drama. *International Journal of Heritage Studies* 4 (3/4), 177–186.

Saunders, R., Weiler, B. and Laing, J. (2010) Long distance walks: Where are they going? Proceedings of the *Council for Australian Tourism and Hospitality Education (CAUTHE) Conference*, Hobart, Tasmania, 8–11 February 2010.

Schmid, D. (1995) Imagining safe urban space: The contribution of detective fiction to radical geography. *Antipode* 27 (3), 242–269.

Seaton, A.V. (2002) Tourism as metempsychosis and metensomatosis: The personae of eternal recurrence. In G. Dann (ed.) *The Tourist as a Metaphor of the Social World* (pp. 135–168). Wallingford, UK: CABI Publishing.

Selänniemi, T. (2003) On holiday in the liminoid playground: Place, time and self in tourism. In T.G. Bauer and B. McKercher (eds) *Sex and Tourism: Journeys of Romance, Love and Lust* (pp. 19–31). Binghamton, NY: Haworth Hospitality Press.

Seymour, M. (1992) *Ottoline Morrell: Life on the Grand Scale*. 1993 reprint. Sevenoaks, Kent, UK: Sceptre.

Sharp, J.P. (1999) Writing over the map of Provence: The touristic therapy of *A Year in Provence*. In J.S. Duncan and D. Gregory (eds) *Writes of Passage: Reading Travel Writing* (pp. 200–218). London: Routledge.

Sharpley, R. and Jepson, D. (2011) Rural tourism: A spiritual experience? *Annals of Tourism Research* 38 (1), 52–71.

Sherman, W.H. (2002) Stirrings and searchings (1500-1720). In P. Hulme and T. Youngs (eds) *The Cambridge Companion to Travel Writing* (pp. 17–36). Cambridge: Cambridge University Press.

Sides, H. (2006) *Blood and Thunder: The Epic Story of Kit Carson and the Conquest of the American West*. New York: Anchor.

Sjöholm, C. (2010) Murder walks in Ystad. In B.T. Knudsen and A.M. Waade (eds) *Re-investing Authenticity: Tourism, Place and Emotions* (pp. 154–168). Bristol: Channel View Publications.

Slotkin, R. (1990) The continuity of forms: Myth and genre in Warner Brothers' *The Charge of the Light Brigade*. *Representations* 29, 1–23.

Smith, K.A. (2003) Literary enthusiasts as visitors and volunteers. *International Journal of Tourism Research* 5 (2), 83–95.

Smith, V.L. (1992) Introduction: The quest in guest. *Annals of Tourism Research* 19 (1), 1–17.

Smulders, S. (2003) 'The only good Indian': History, race and representation in Laura Ingalls Wilder's Little House on the Prairie. *Children's Literature Association Quarterly* 27 (4), 191–202.

Squire, S.J. (1994) The cultural values of literary tourism. *Annals of Tourism Research* 21 (1), 103–120.

Stanford Friedman, S. (2011) Towards a transnational turn in narrative theory: Literary narratives, traveling tropes, and the case of Virginia Woolf and the Tagores. *Narrative* 19 (1), 1–32.

Stewig, J.W. (1980) *Children and Literature*. Boston: Houghton Mifflin.

Su, J.J. (2002) Refiguring national character: The remains of the British estate novel. *Modern Fiction Studies* 48 (3), 552–580.

Sutherland, Z. and Arbuthnot, M.H. with chapters contributed by Monson, D.L. (1991) *Children and Books* (8th edition). New York: HarperCollins.

Swarbrooke, J., Beard, C., Leckie, S. and Pomfret, G. (2003) *Adventure Tourism: The New Frontier*. Oxford: Butterworth Heinemann.

Taylor, J. (1994) *A Dream of England: Landscape Photography and the Tourist's Imagination*. Manchester: Manchester University Press.

Tetley, S. and Bramwell, B. (2002) Tourists and the cultural construction of Haworth's literary landscape. In M. Robinson and H-C. Andersen (eds) *Literature and Tourism: Essays in the Reading and Writing of Tourism* (pp. 155–170). London: Thomson.

Thompson, C. (2011) *Travel Writing*. London, New York: Routledge.

Timothy, D.J. and Boyd, S.W. (2003) *Heritage Tourism*. Harlow, UK: Pearson.

Tolkien, J.R.R. (1964) *Tree and Leaf*. 2001 reprint. London: HarperCollins.

Travers, P.L. (1975) On not writing for children. *Children's Literature* 4, 15–22.

Tunbridge, J.E. and Ashworth, G. (1996) *Dissonant Heritage: The Management of the Past as a Resource in Conflict*. Chichester, UK: Wiley.

Turner, F.J. (1893) *The Frontier in American History*. 1962 reprint. New York: Holt, Rinehart, and Winston.

Turner, V. and Turner, E. (1978) *Image and Pilgrimage in Christian Culture: Anthropological Perspectives*. Oxford: Basil Blackwell.

Underwood, L.G. and Teresi, J.A. (2002) The daily spiritual experience scale: Development, theoretical description, reliability, exploratory factor analysis, and preliminary construct validity using health-related data. *Annals of Behavioral Medicine* 24 (1), 22–33.

Urry, J. (2002) *The Tourist Gaze* (2nd edn). London; New York: Routledge.

van Gennep, A. (1909) *The Rites of Passage*. 1960 reprint. Chicago: University of Chicago Press.

Van Nortwick T. (1992) *Somewhere I Have Never Travelled: The Second Self and the Hero's Journey in Ancient Epic*. New York: Oxford University Press.

Vogel, D. (1974) A lexicon rhetoricae for 'journey' literature. *College English* 36 (2), 185–189.

Waetjen, J. and Gibson, T.A. (2007) Harry Potter and the commodity fetish: Activating corporate readings in the journey from text to commercial intertext. *Communication and Critical/Cultural Studies* 4 (1), 3–26.

Walle, A.H. (1997) Pursuing risk or insight: Marketing adventures. *Annals of Tourism Research* 24 (2), 265–282.

Wang, N. (2000) *Tourism and Modernity: A Sociological Analysis*. Kidlington, Oxford: Pergamon.

Waterfield, G. (2007) Realms of memory · Changing perceptions of the country house. In M. Forsyth (ed.) *Understanding Histor c Building Conservation* (pp. 88–95). Oxford, UK; Maldon, USA: Blackwell.

Watkins, T. (1992) Cultural studies, new historicism and children's literature. In P. Hunt (ed.) *Literature for Children: Contemporary Criticism* (pp. 173–209). London, New York: Routledge.

Watson, C. (1971) *Snobbery with Violence: English Crime Stories and their Audience*. 1987 reprint. London: Methuen.

Watson, N. (2006) *The Literary Tourist*. Basingstoke, New York: Palgrave Macmillan.

Watson, N.J. (2009) Introduction. In N.J. Watson (ed.) *Literary Tourism and Nineteenth-Century Culture* (pp. 1–12). Basingstoke, New York: Palgrave Macmillan.

Watts, S. (2003) *Rough Rider in the White House: Theodore Roosevelt and the Politics of Desire.* Chicago: University of Chicago Press.

Wearing, S. (2002) Re-centring the self in volunteer tourism. In G. Dann (ed.) *The Tourist as a Metaphor of the Social World* (pp. 237–262). Wallingford, UK: CABI.

Weber, K. (2001) Outdoor adventure tourism: A review of research approaches. *Annals of Tourism Research* 28 (2), 360–377.

West, B. (2001) Crime, suicide and the anti-hero: 'Waltzing Matilda' in Australia. *The Journal of Popular Culture* 35 (3), 127–141.

Wheeler, F., Laing, J., Frost, L., Reeves, K. and Frost, W. (2011) Outlaw nations: Tourism, the frontier and national identities. In E. Frew and L. White (eds) *Tourism and National Identities: An International Perspective* (pp. 151–163). London and New York: Routledge.

Whybrow, H. (2003) Introduction. In H. Whybrow (ed.) *Tales of the Great Explorers 1800–1900* (pp. 15–21). New York, London: Norton.

Willard, P., Lade, C. and Frost, W. (forthcoming) Darkness beyond memory: The battle-fields at Culloden and Little Big Horn. In L. White and E. Frew (eds) *Popularising and Politicising Place: Dark Tourism and Place Identity Around the World.* London: Routledge.

Wilson, E., Holdsworth, L. and Witsel, M. (2009) Gutsy Women? Conflicting discourses in women's travel guidebooks. *Tourism Recreation Research* 34 (1), 3–11.

Winkler, M.M. (2001) Tragic features in John Ford's *The Searchers.* In M.M. Winkler (ed.) *Classical Myth and Culture in the Cinema* (pp. 118–147). Oxford, New York: Oxford University Press.

Wood, M. (1997) *In the Footsteps of Alexander the Great: A Journey from Greece to Asia.* Los Angeles, Berkeley: University of California Press.

Wood, R.C. (2003) *The Gospel According to Tolkien: Visions of the Kingdom in Middle-Earth.* Louisville, US: Westminister John Knox Press.

Woodhead, P. (2003) *Misadventures in a White Desert.* London: Hodder & Stoughton.

Woodside, A.G. and Megehee, C.M. (2009) Advancing consumer behaviour theory in tourism via visual narrative art. *International Journal of Tourism Research* 12 (5), 418–431.

Youngs, T. (2002) Africa/The Congo: The politics of darkness. In P. Hulme and T. Youngs (eds) *The Cambridge Companion to Travel Writing* (pp. 156–173). Cambridge: Cambridge University Press.

Zezima, K. (2010) J.D. Salinger a recluse? Well, not to his neighbours. *The New York Times,* 31 January 2010.

Zipes, J. (2001) *Sticks and Stones: The Troublesome Success of Children's Literature from Slovenly Peter to Harry Potter.* New York, London: Routledge.

Zurick, D. (1995) *Errant Journeys.* Austin: University of Texas Press.

Index